THE
GENTLEMEN'S
CLUB

GARY M. DOUGLAS

WITH CONTRIBUTIONS BY DR. DAIN HEER

ACCESS
CONSCIOUSNESS®
PUBLISHING

The Gentlemen's Club
Copyright © 2014 Gary M. Douglas
ISBN: 978-1-939261-99-1

Published by
Access Consciousness Publishing, LLC
www.accessconsciousnesspublishing.com

Printed in the United States of America

There were three men in the original Gentlemen's Club class who were married. Not long after the classes were complete, I received phone calls from the women who were married to these guys. Each one of them said, "Thank you so much for doing these classes. I've got back the man that I fell in love with."

CONTENTS

Foreword...vii

Chapter 1: Stepping Up to Something Different........................9

Chapter 2: Creating Sex and Relationship from an
Awareness of What Is 43

Chapter 3: You Are the Valuable Product.............................71

Chapter 4: Become the King of Possibilities.........................103

Chapter 5: The Phenomenal Sex, Copulation, and
Relationship You Could Be Choosing...................139

Chapter 6: What Do You Really Desire? 173

Chapter 7: Being Good in Bed..195

Chapter 8: What Is a Gentleman? 217

Chapter 9: What Do You Actually Want in a
Relationship?..259

Chapter 10: The Aggressive Presence of Sexualness....................291

Chapter 11: Choosing Commitment 311

Chapter 12: Decoding Women's Subtext................................335

The Access Consciousness Clearing Statement® 359

Glossary 363

What Is Access Consciousness?...369

Index of Chapter Titles and Headings 371

Other Access Consciousness® Books..379

About the Author...381

FOREWORD

The Gentlemen's Club is based on a series of twelve teleclasses I facilitated with a group of awesome and courageous men. My intention with The Gentlemen's Club classes was to create a males-only environment where participants could speak freely about being a man in this reality. There is a lot of energy in these conversations. Female readers may flinch at some of our "men's club" language, but I am hoping they'll come away from the book with a deeper appreciation for the men in their lives and a greater recognition of what it takes to create a relationship from a totally different reality.

In the discussions that follow, there may be some words, concepts, and tools you have never encountered before. There may also be some common words like be, human, or receiving that we use in ways that seem unfamiliar. We have tried to define them all in a glossary at the end of the book.

You will also find the clearing statement we use in Access Consciousness®. It's short-speak that addresses the energies that are creating the limitations and contractions in your life. When you first read it, it may twist your head around a little bit. That's our intention. It's designed to get your mind out of the picture so you can get to the energy of a situation.

With the clearing statement, we're addressing the energy of the limitations and barriers that keep us from moving forward and expanding into all of the spaces that we would like to go.

The Access Consciousness Clearing Statement is "Right and Wrong, Good and Bad, POD and POC, All 9, Shorts, Boys and Beyonds"®. There is a brief explanation of what the words mean at the end of the book.

You can choose to use the clearing statement or not; I don't have a point of view about that, but I do want to invite you to try it and see what happens.

1

STEPPING UP TO SOMETHING DIFFERENT

*Do you want to function from trying to change things
so they look different?
Or do you want to do something different that will work for you?*

Gary:

Welcome to The Gentlemen's Club. Let's start with a question.

Trusting Yourself as a Man / Trusting Other Men

Class Participant:

I'm starting a men's empowerment group, but the take-up by men is very slow. Do you have any suggestions for me?

Gary:

Don't call it "men's empowerment." Men supposedly have all the power. In truth, they are totally disempowered—but they don't know that. If you call it "empowerment," nobody's going to come because they don't even know they need or want empowerment. Call it "Making Your Life with Women Easier."

Dain:

Men want their life with women to be easier more than they want to be empowered and more than they want to be connected with other men. Most of the things most men do are about trying to get a woman or get laid. For most men, the idea of meeting together with other men is a place of too much potency. It scares them off.

A few years ago, we did an Access Consciousness Level Two and Three class in Santa Barbara. Some of the Access Consciousness ladies went out that night and they saw two guys get in a fight. The ladies said, "You know what? It was obvious that what those guys really wanted was to have sex with each other, but they couldn't have that in their worlds, so they got into a fight instead. The fight was their way of expressing it."

When you talk to men about getting men together as men, it brings up all the stuff they're not supposed to be, not supposed to do, and especially not supposed to be and do together.

It's been very interesting to hear the feedback from the ladies on The Salon des Femmes calls. After two calls, they were saying things like, "I thought listening to a bunch of women and not having any men to play with or flirt with was going to suck, but now I feel like I've got all these sisters, and it's amazing how much more of me I have and how much more connected I feel with women and myself."

I realized, in hearing that feedback, that we as men have the same thing. We create a separation from each other rather than coming together. If we could change that, we could truly change the word. And we'd also have better sex, we'd be the potency of us, and we'd have a lot more fun.

Gary:

I've got a process:

What stupidity are you using to create the separation of men and women, women and women, and men and men are you choosing? Everything that is times a godzillion, will you destroy and uncreate it all? Right and Wrong, Good and Bad, POD and POC, All Nine, Shorts, Boys, and Beyonds.

Class Participant:

In that process, you asked, "are you choosing?" I tend to say, "that you *are* choosing." I realize you don't say that. Can you tell me why?

Gary:

"That you are choosing" justifies your reason for choosing. It's a fixed point of view. It is saying, "I am choosing this because _____." You would prefer to believe you are choosing for a *reason* rather than *just choosing*. I am trying to get you to see that there is no reason for what you choose—you just choose. That's why I ask, "Are you choosing?"

Class Participant:

Thank you.

Creating Partnership with Men

Class Participant:

Can you talk about the separation I create with other men?

Gary:

The one thing you're *not* supposed to do is have sexual energy with other men. That's like a big no-no. So you do whatever you have to do in order to not have sexual energy with other men. Yet just about everything in sexual energy is about receiving. Without sexual energy, you have no receiving. So when we cut ourselves off from receiving sexual energy with other men, we also cut off our receiving from women, from relationship, and from sex. We cut ourselves off from receiving with money and business and everything else.

If you can have men with men, then you have a place where you can create a partnership, which can create money, or you can create a partnership, which creates fun or all kinds of things. For example, Dain and I spend the majority of our time together. We are willing to be there as men for our friends. I encourage Dain to go out and have sex with different women, I encourage him to do whatever he wants, but he is my friend and he has my back. If you create a separation of men from men, you can't ever assume that a man will have your back.

Dain:

You assume that men will stab you in the back. But most of the time, it's not going be the man in your life who stabs you in the back.

Class Participants:

(Laughter)

Gary:

Women don't stab you in the back. They just cut off your testicles!

Dain:

When men buy the idea that sexual energy isn't supposed to be there between them, they cut themselves off from the nurturing and the caring, the expansive, generative, creative, and healing energy they have with other men.

Gary:

The "I've got your back" energy.

Dain:

You also cut off yourself off from having that energy for yourself and with yourself.

Gary:

You are a man and you have to separate from you. So you can't have your own back. And that's why so many of you give yourselves away, especially to women.

Dain:

So many of you are thinking, "Oh, maybe I can find the woman who will finally complete me, who will fill this void I'm not filling for myself." You, separating from yourself, is part of the separation of men from men.

We tend to look at it as though the men we're separating from are outside of us, but you have to separate from you in order to make the separation from other men real.

Gary:

The question I have is: Do you trust you as a man?

Dain:

And the answer is "Hell no!"

Class Participant:

The answer is "No."

Gary:

If you can't have your own back, where do you find someone who will have your back? You can't let a man have your back, so who can have your back?

Dain:

You think that if a man has your back, you won't know what he might do when he's back there; you won't let him have your back because he could get you in the balls.

Gary:

It's insanity.

Dain:

It's total insanity. When you allow yourself those rare moments of closeness with a man without having a point a view about it, it opens up your world so dynamically.

Gary:

It's an amazing gift and an amazing possibility.

Dain:

What stupidity are you using to create the separation of men and women, women and women, and men and men you are choosing? Everything that is times a godzillion, will you destroy and uncreate it all? Right and Wrong, Good and Bad, POD and POC, All Nine, Shorts, Boys, and Beyonds.

Gary:

What stupidity are you using to create the separation of men and women, women and women, and men and men you are choosing? Everything that is times a godzillion, will you destroy and uncreate it all? Right and Wrong, Good and Bad, POD and POC, All Nine, Shorts, Boys, and Beyonds.

Hey Dain, do you know how they separate the men from the boys in Greece?

Dain:

With a crowbar!

Gary:

Just thought we should interject a sick joke to keep you guys on your toes. Okay, let's run that again.

What stupidity are you using to create the separation of men and women, women and women, and men and men you are choosing? Everything that is times a godzillion, will you destroy and uncreate it all? Right and Wrong, Good and Bad, POD and POC, All Nine, Shorts, Boys, and Beyonds.

Hold on. We have to add "men and boys" to that process. Some weird energy came up after we told that joke, and I realized we try to create separation between men and boys. Men are being mentors to boys without ever having the boy's back.

Dain:

We grow up with the idea that we're alone. We believe that not only are we bad and wrong; we're not even worthy of someone having our back.

Gary:

We don't even think we're worthy of having our own back, which is why I think men don't trust themselves.

Dain:

What stupidity are you using to create the separation of men and women, women and women, and men and men, and men and boys you are choosing? Everything that is times a godzillion, will you destroy and uncreate it all? Right and Wrong, Good and Bad, POD and POC, All Nine, Shorts, Boys, and Beyonds.

Cutting Off Your Sense of Beauty

Gary:

You know, we might as well add "men and girls" to that process, as well. I've noticed that if an adult male sees a young girl and he has an ounce of sexual energy, he has to go into judgment of himself for being some kind of pervert or a terrible person or someone who wants to have sex with children, none of which is necessarily true.

If I see a beautiful horse, for me it's a horse. I see a beautiful horse and it's a turn-on! Seeing the beautiful horse move is all I care about. I don't have to do anything with it. I don't have to own it. I don't have to have a place where I can control it. I just recognize that the horse is beautiful.

Men cut off their sense of beauty because they are afraid that it's a sexual energy and that "means" something.

Dain:

When you, as a "straight" man, have this sense of beauty, you think it means you're somehow gay or soft.

Gary:

It's called "metrosexual."

Dain:

Exactly. Metrosexual is where you can have all of the good stuff of gay men and all of the good stuff of straight men combined: metro-sexual.

Gary:

Yeah.

Class Participants:

(Laughter)

Dain:

What was that?

Gary:

Somebody was laughing because we're funny.

Dain:

Oh, I haven't heard that sound in a while. That's why I didn't know what it was.

Class Participants:

(Laughter)

Gary:

You've been talking to women too much!

Dain:

What stupidity are you using to create the separation of men and women, women and women, men and men, men and boys, and men and girls you are choosing? Everything that is times a godzillion, will you destroy and uncreate it all? Right and Wrong, Good and Bad, POD and POC, All Nine, Shorts, Boys, and Beyonds.

Gary:

Good lord. The amount of charge on that is just unbelievable!

"We've Got Each Other's Back"

Dain:

I was having dinner with our friend Ricky the other night. It was the first time he and I had ever had any one-on-one time together. I was telling him about the friendship I have with Gary. I said, "We've got each other's back, but that wasn't apparent at day one. Our friendship has developed over time. We have created a level of trust by being us, choosing that which would support the other, and having the other's back."

I said, "When I first got to know Gary, I gave him all kinds of information he could have used to skewer me and stab me in the back, but he didn't take it that way. And he gave me all kinds of stuff I could have used against him too, but I didn't do that. It was 'How can we contribute to each other and support each other?' We'd been hanging out, having an amazing friendship for about a year, and one day he came over and said, 'Our friendship is done.'"

I asked, "What are you talking about?"

Gary said, "You've been judging me. You've been judging me really harshly. The rest of the world can judge me. That's fine, but I don't give my friends permission to judge me, so our friendship is over. You can keep working for Access Consciousness, but our friendship is finished as of now. I don't want to be your friend anymore. It does not work for me."

I was like "Whoa!" When he said, "You're judging me," in my mind I literally went to "Well yeah, of course! Isn't that what friends do?" This was my point of view.

Gary:

That's what lovers do, not friends.

Dain:

He left and I felt a void in my life and my world. I said, "Wait a minute. There has never been a time when Gary hasn't had my back, and I'm judging him? This is fucked. Even if he goes away, I need to change this for myself."

I called him and I said, "Gary, you are absolutely right, and I'm really sorry. I want to change this, but I don't know how. I don't know what to do about it, so I'm asking for your help. I will pay for a session if I have to, but will you please help me get through this?"

Gary said, "Okay, I'll give you an hour, and we'll see where we go from there." It took forty-five minutes for me to realize that I was choosing to judge him. It felt like shoving my head through a brick wall to realize that I was choosing to do this, because it felt so automatic.

When I finally got that, it changed my whole world and my whole reality. I saw that my judgment was that if he cared about me as much as he did, it was because he was interested in having sex with me. He was gay and just wanted sex. He just wanted to get me in bed. That was the underlying thing holding in place the mountains of judgment I had erected against my friend.

Is it possible that you won't allow yourself to have a friendship with a man, because somewhere in your universe, you have concluded and judged that only a man who wanted to have sex with you would be kind and caring and look out for you? Everything that brought up times a godzillion, will you destroy and uncreate it all? Right and Wrong, Good and Bad, POD and POC, All Nine, Shorts, Boys, and Beyonds.

Gary:

I was working with somebody the other day. I always had the sense that he had been molested, but he would never say it. In the session, I asked him something, and it came up that there had been a soccer coach he felt had molested him.

I asked him, "What do you mean? What did the coach do?"

He said, "Well, he used to rub my shoulders. He said he was trying to take the knots out."

I asked, "Did your coach have any sexual energy when he did that?"

He said, "Yeah!"

I asked, "Did he have sexual energy toward you?"

He said, "Yeah."

This guy didn't have a sexual experience with his coach. The coach was trying to help him. He had a sense of loving and caring for the kid, and the kid interpreted it as sexual desire, so he cut off his awareness of a man who gave off that kind of energy. He concluded it was about sex, and as a result, he felt violated.

Every place you have felt violated when some man actually saw you as a really cute kid or as somebody who was so adorable he could hardly stand it, or who didn't feel that he had to shut down his sexual energy around you and you rejected him and rejected yourself and went into the wrongness of it and it created some kind of separation of you from you, or of you from him, or of you from men, or of you from men and boys, will you destroy and uncreate all of that? Right and Wrong, Good and Bad, POD and POC, All Nine, Shorts, Boys, and Beyonds.

Apparently some of you have had similar experiences. Did any of you have an experience like that, where somebody who was a "male" actually felt sexual to you, and you felt like you were being violated or that he wanted something from you that you couldn't or wouldn't deliver?

Everything that brings up times a godzillion, will you destroy and uncreate it, please? Right and Wrong, Good and Bad, POD and POC, All Nine, Shorts, Boys, and Beyonds.

The Kindness Men Have

Class Participant:

As I was growing up, I couldn't find the kindness men have. When I met you and Dain and a lot of the guys in Access Consciousness, it was like "Oh! This is it. This is what I was looking for!" I wouldn't let myself see it when I was younger.

Gary:

What happened when you were younger that you didn't want to know about that created a place where you had to separate from you and other men in order to have a sense you could find the kindness you knew ought to exist?

Class Participant:

I saw how the men around me were acting. I saw what my grandfather did with my sisters and what my dad did with my mother, and I decided, "If that's what being a man is, I don't want to be it."

Gary:

Everything you decided you didn't want to be, because you didn't see kindness there and because what you saw was pain and suffering and hurt and wrongness and meanness, will you destroy and uncreate all of that and claim you? Right and Wrong, Good and Bad, POD and POC, All Nine, Shorts, Boys, and Beyonds.

Dain:

Another part of that was coming up while you were talking. How much were you aware of your mom's dislike or hatred of men, your sister's dislike or hatred of men, and your grandmother's dislike or hatred of men?

Gary:

Well, it wouldn't even be hatred. It would be total distrust.

Dain:

Okay, cool. Total distrust, which is exactly what we walk around with for ourselves.

Gary:

Yeah, that's what you end up doing. You can't trust that women are going to trust men. You don't see any terms of trust from women to men, you don't see any terms of trust from men to men, so the end result is—you can't trust you, because you're a man.

Dain:

The thing that's so twisted about this is that you're picking it up out of a woman's world, and you never spot that. It's there underneath everything else, eating at you all the time. It didn't come from a man and it didn't come from you. It was something you were supposed to uphold as a point of view. You were not supposed to be like the men the women didn't trust. Does that make sense?

Class Participant:

Yeah.

Gary:

Women don't trust themselves either. They are seldom good at doing hate, but they are good at doing distrust, and they will do hateful and mean things in the name of empowerment and in the name of gaining power, because they feel powerless in the face of a total lack of honoring and a total lack of trust.

Everything that brought up or let down, can we destroy and uncreate all of that, please? Right and Wrong, Good and Bad, POD and POC, All Nine, Shorts, Boys, and Beyonds.

Dain:

There's a lot of stuff on not trusting yourself as a man, and not trusting other men, either. You get the projected lack of trust from mothers, sisters, aunts, and all females because they see what they have come to define as true: they can't trust men. The reality is, they don't trust themselves and they don't trust men. You don't trust yourself and you don't trust men either, so how much caring for you can you actually have?

None. And what little caring there may be is eroded away by mistrust, so you can't have any caring for you. You can't have your own back. You have to separate from you at all times. And you don't see other men who are caring.

As you grow up and you'd really like to have sex, you see that the guys women are attracted to are the assholes of the world and you say, "Wait a minute. This is so frigging confusing." You have no way of perceiving the energy of the caring and the potency you are. You don't even have a clue that it's a good thing to head toward what's true for you.

Gary:

So many women have a distrust of themselves and their choice of men. All they can do is choose a man who is equally distrustful. Some of you have chosen mates who have that kind of distrust because it fits your own vibration and your own entrainment to the lack of trust you feel for yourself.

Dain:

You pick women who see you a certain way and you think you are that way. You think you're unworthy of being trusted, and you buy the lie that that's who you are. But you're not. Not one of you is like that.

What stupidity are you using to create the separation of men and women, women and women, men and men, men and boys, and men and girls you are choosing? Everything that is times a godzillion, will you destroy and uncreate it all? Right and Wrong, Good and Bad, POD and POC, All Nine, Shorts, Boys, and Beyonds.

Creating Separation

Class Participant:

I don't sense that I have a problem receiving sexual energy from a man, but I do sense that I'm creating separation in general. I'm creating the separation as if I have a problem with a man's sexual energy.

Gary:

Do you actually receive the energy from a man? Or do you receive the point of view about yourself that you have an open mind?

Class Participant:

Yeah, that.

Gary:

Everything you've done to create an open point of view that eliminates you, will you destroy and uncreate all of that? Right and Wrong, Good and Bad, POD and POC, All Nine, Shorts, Boys, and Beyonds.

Class Participant:

Is that creating separation?

Gary:

Your reason and justification for creating separation is "Yes, but I have an open mind." A lot of people say, "Yes, but I have an open mind."

"But I have an open mind" is the lie you tell yourself to keep you functioning in the separation you have created. You buy the idea that an open mind is all it takes to overcome the separation rather than an awareness of what could truly be different.

Class Participant:

Yeah. Wow.

Gary:

How much have you used your open mind as a justification for creating separation while pretending you are not doing that? A lot? A little? Or megatons? Everything that is times a godzillion, will you destroy and uncreate it all? Right and Wrong, Good and Bad, POD and POC, All Nine, Shorts, Boys, and Beyonds.

Dain:

What stupidity are you using to create the separation of men and women, women and women, men and men, men and boys, and men and girls you are choosing? Everything that is times a godzillion, will you destroy and uncreate it all? Right and Wrong, Good and Bad, POD and POC, All Nine, Shorts, Boys, and Beyonds.

Class Participant:

I'd like to change that. I'd like to create something else, be something else, and do something else—and I'm totally lost in how to do that.

Gary:

Well, you've not seen an example of how to be present as you and enjoy you, have you?

Class Participant:

No.

Gary:

Have you thought that judging you was enjoying you?

Class Participant:

Yes, that may be the only way I can enjoy me.

Gary:

The only way to enjoy you is to judge you out of the wrongness of you so you can enjoy how you're right. That doesn't expand your universe in any way, so there's something wrong with that point of view.

Dain:

What stupidity are you using to create the separation of men and women, women and women, men and men, men and boys, and men and girls you are choosing? Everything that is times a godzillion, will you destroy and uncreate it all? Right and Wrong, Good and Bad, POD and POC, All Nine, Shorts, Boys, and Beyonds.

Sexual Energy and Receiving

Gary:

Let's add another one to that: "And you from you."

What creates the sense of sexualness? It's the sense of receiving. If you have a man like Dain who can receive you totally and who has no judgment of you, you are being received. This is the same sexual energy you'd like to get from a woman, but I would be willing to bet money that you reject Dain's sexual energy the same way you reject women's sexual energy. It's about how you're not willing to receive everything you're capable of receiving for, to, with, and by you.

Everything that brought up, and everything that is times a godzillion, will you destroy and uncreate it all? Right and Wrong, Good and Bad, POD and POC, All Nine, Shorts, Boys, and Beyonds.

Do you have any idea what I said?

Class Participant:

I'm a little lost here.

Gary:

That's the problem. Do you realize how often you've been lost about relationships with men?

Class Participant:

Yeah, and women.

Gary:

Yeah. You get lost with women, but it's okay to get lost with a woman because you are still sexually excited by her.

Class Participant:

Yeah, absolutely.

Gary:

But if you get lost with a man, it's because the man is x, y, or z, which isn't anything except a judgment.

Class Participant:

Yeah, I can sense that I'm keeping a comfortable distance, so I guess I'm cutting off receiving. I don't know why, but I do that.

Gary:

You're cutting off anything that doesn't fit the prescribed pattern of willingness to receive.

Class Participant:

I could easily say that I have never had a role model in my life who has done anything different, so I can claim, "Oh, I didn't know blah, blah, blah," but I don't want it to be like this. I want to choose something else. I just feel lost.

Gary:

That's the reason we're doing this call. That's the reason that we're doing this process. Let's do it again, Dr. Dain.

Dain:

What stupidity are you using to create the separation of men and women, women and women, men and men, men and boys, men and girls, and you from you are you choosing? Everything that is times a godzillion, will you destroy and uncreate it all? Right and Wrong, Good and Bad, POD and POC, All Nine, Shorts, Boys, and Beyonds.

Choosing Something Different

Class Participant:

When I see myself creating that separation, is it appropriate to ask what to do, how to be, and how to create something different? When I end up in the energy of separation, I step away and withdraw my energy. I withdraw myself, actually.

Gary:

You have to ask: An infinite being would choose this for what reason? You have to get that you choose to withdraw. It's always a choice, and if you're going to change it, you've got to say, "Okay I'm choosing this, and I would choose this for what reason?" Then you say, "I'm going to choose different no matter what it looks like."

Class Participant:

I've been trying to do something different, but I don't end up with any change, and then I feel even more stupid...

Gary:

What would it be like if you were willing to recognize that doing something different only requires you to look at what you would choose? You don't even have to choose it.

Class Participant:

Look at what you would choose and not choose it?

Gary:

Yeah. Let's say you got mad at your girlfriend, and you said, "You know what? I want to do something different. What would be different from getting mad?"

You might say, "Let's see, getting even would be a choice, yelling at her would be a choice, loving her would be a choice," and as you did that, you'd begin to see you have multiple choices, not just one.

Class Participant:

Yeah.

Gary:

You're looking for what will solve the problem you've defined as the fact that you withdraw. That's too complicated. The simple fact is you withdraw. That's the sum total of it. There's nothing else. So you say, "I'd like to do something different. What would not withdrawing look like? Wow, that would be like staying here, being here, and doing whatever it takes."

Class Participant:

Yeah.

Gary:

Do you get what I'm talking about?

Class Participant:

Yeah, this helps a lot.

Gary:

Cool. Choosing not to withdraw opens doors to other choices. Ask: What other choice do I have here? If I'm not going to choose this, what other choices do I have? If you start functioning from what other choices you have, other possibilities can occur.

Class Participant:

Yeah, absolutely.

Gary:

Everybody's always trying to get me to show them how to create a solution and I keep saying, "All you have to do is choose."

They say, "Yes, but I can't."

Why not? Because you keep looking at what's wrong or how you have to fix what's wrong in order to choose something different. No. Just recognize, "This isn't working." And then ask: "What can I do different?"

Class Participant:

I get that. I see that I was asking for some sort of solution. This helps a lot.

Gary:

If I don't choose that, what other choices do I have?

Class Participant:

Yeah, that is awesome.

Gary:

That's how you get out of doing the same thing over again, thinking you're going to get a different result.

Change vs. Different

Class Participant:

I've been totally lost there, and I had no clue how to change it.

Gary:

"I've had no clue how to change it" is one of the places where you've been trained and entrained to. It's a woman's point of view. "I have to have a problem. Now I have to change it" not "I have to do something different."

Class Participant:

That's exactly what I've been doing.

Gary:

The question is not, "How can I change this?" or "What can I do different in order to change this?" That's asking about *change*. It's: What can I do *different* here?

You have to be willing to do and be *different*, not *differently*. Doing something *differently* is still trying to change it. You have to be willing to be or do whatever it takes to be different enough to get what you're asking for.

Class Participant:

Thanks a lot.

Class Participant:

I'm not getting the difference between *change* and *different*.

Gary:

Right now, change your position in the chair.

Class Participant:

Okay.

Gary:

Now do something different. Would you still stay in the chair or would you do something different?

Class Participant:

Oh, I see!

Gary:

Change is about sticking with what you've got and adding something to it or subtracting something from it or moving it a different way—but staying where you are.

Class Participant:

That's not actually doing something different then, is it? You're just having the same old, same old.

Gary:

Exactly. That's the reason, when you go to change something, you lose choice. But if you do something different, you have more choice. Women often say to the men they're in relationship with, "We need to change this." What that means is not "You need to do something different" but "You need to adjust you to fit where I want you to be."

Class Participant:

That's what I've been doing with my relationship. I've been asking her to change rather than for the relationship to be different. And it's not changing, and it's not different.

Gary:

Well, it is changing; it just isn't working better.

Class Participant:

Yeah.

Gary:

If you're trying to change the relationship, you're trying to sit on the chair facing in a different direction. You're not trying to do something different that allows a different choice. Does that help?

Class Participant:

Yeah, that helps immensely. I was talking to a friend yesterday about the way women are more complicated than men. I seem to have bought the point of view from women that I have to change things, and that feels really complicated.

Gary:

Yeah, that's what every man learns from the women around him. A woman's point of view is always going to be "What do you need to change? How can I change you?" It is complicated, because you can't see what they want you to change—and they won't tell you.

Class Participant:

Yeah.

Gary:

When you're willing to *change* the relationship, you're not willing to leave the relationship.

Different means "Okay, so what would I like to do different here?" *Different* can mean leaving the relationship. You have more choices.

Class Participant:

Thank you.

Dain:

You've been picking this up since the time you had a mother. *Different* opens up all possibilities because you're no longer tied to what was an integral part of what has to go forward into the future, which is what *change* is about.

You've got to function from: What can I be or do different today that would make this what I would like it to be? If you're only changing things, you're trying to *change the way they look,* not *do something different that creates a different result.* Do you get that?

Class Participant:

Yeah, got it!

Gary:

What stupidity are you using to create the need of change as more real than the possibility of difference are you choosing? Everything that is times a godzillion, will you destroy and uncreate it all? Right and Wrong, Good and Bad, POD and POC, All Nine, Shorts, Boys, and Beyonds.

When you have a need of change, you're operating from a conclusion. You're not asking, "What other possibilities are available here?" This is the difference between choosing to be a man and trying to function like a woman.

A woman will wear a dress and she'll use different accessories to change its appearance. Most women have been taught to change appearance, not to do something different. Does that mean anything? No. It's just the way they function. You have to be willing to look at how they function and see how you want to function. Do you want to function from trying to change things so they look different? Or do you want to do something different that will work for you?

What Can I Do Different?

Class Participant:

I'm sure you guys have talked about this before but I've never heard it. I've been looking at all the things that haven't been working for me lately and all the ways I've been trying to change them without asking, "What can I do different here?" It's always "How can I make this a little bit better?" or "How can I make this work a little bit better?" rather than "What can I do different?"

Gary:

When you get into relationship, you tend to do *change*, not *different*, because the underlying foundation you're creating from is "I have this relationship."

Dain:

The relationship becomes a center point around which everything else revolves. It's like taking a string and nailing one end of it into the ground and telling yourself you can only go out as far as the string goes. This is one of the reasons a lot of guys start to get tired once they're in a relationship. You go home to your girlfriend or your partner and it's "I just want to sit here and drink beer" or "I just want to watch television" or "I just want to go smoke" or "I just want to do something." You're in change; you're not continuously being *different;* and there's not enough vibrancy in change. It's not enough living; it's not enough difference for you.

Gary:

If you started functioning from *different,* you would create the vitality that created your relationship in the first place.

Dain:

And you would have the woman begging for more! You'd have her respecting you, you'd have her desiring you, you'd have her turned on by you all the time. But you try to play their game, so to speak. You go into change, which makes them not want to respect you. They think they can run over you, they can own you, they can control you, and they believe you have no value.

Gary:

Which is not what they truly want to have.

Dain:

Right, and unfortunately who's the one imposing that on you?

Gary:

You are.

Dain:

We've seen men who seem to be the biggest assholes on the planet, and women are all over them. The thing that will make you more attractive than those unkind, uncaring, asshole men will ever be is the willingness to create something different.

Gary:

The important part of this is creating. When you're trying to change, you're not trying to create. You're trying to take what has been instituted and alter it sufficiently so it's no longer uncomfortable. Is that enough for you?

Dain:

You think you're supposed to live from *change* rather than *difference*. That idea is so frigging intensely underneath everything.

Gary:

It's what we've been entrained to.

Dain:

When you begin to think about choosing something different, your cellular structure starts to vibrate. You think you're freaked out by *different*, you think you don't like *different*, you think you just want to be able to change enough to make it better, but that's what kills you. You have to get out of that entrained mode, and the way to do that is to ask: What can I be or do different here that will allow a completely different possibility to show up now?

Everything that doesn't allow that, times a godzillion, will you destroy and uncreate it please? Right and Wrong, Good and Bad, POD and POC, All Nine, Shorts, Boys, and Beyonds.

What stupidity are you using to create the need of change as more real and more necessary than the possibility of difference you are choosing?

Gary:

Women go to "It's necessary for you to change," and when any-thing becomes a necessity, you have to resist.

What if you chose to do something different with the men in your life? Would that mean you'd have to have sex with them? No, because right now you're maintaining your relationships with them, you're try-ing to change your relationship with men while not doing something different than what you've done in the past. It's all about change.

Women learn early on that you have a paper doll and you put new paper dresses on it to make it appear changed and different. But it's not actually different; its appearance has been changed by what they've put on it. Is that enough?

My ex-wife once said, "Gary and I have such a different relation-ship now that I have changed the way he dresses."

Dain:

Wow. "Look, I've made a male doll out of him."

Gary:

I was her male doll.

Dain:

How many of you have become the male doll in most of the relationships you've been in? Everything that is times a godzillion, will you destroy and uncreate it please? Right and Wrong, Good and Bad, POD and POC, All Nine, Shorts, Boys, and Beyonds.

The thing that gets you there is the separation of you from you.

What stupidity are you using to create the need of change as more real and more necessary than the possibilities, choices, and questions of difference you are choosing? Everything that is times a godzillion, will you destroy and uncreate it please? Right and

Wrong, Good and Bad, POD and POC, All Nine, Shorts, Boys, and Beyonds.

Gary:

You've been asking, "How can I change this?" rather than "What other choices, what other possibilities, and what other questions can I have here?" which means you cannot be contributed to. You can only try to give to someone else. Does that make sense?

Class Participant:

Totally.

Class Participant:

This is so good. It's spot-on for my whole life. I see how I have stopped the choices to do something different.

Gary:

Unfortunately, we have not been given an awareness of difference. Part of this information came up in Costa Rica when I was talking with Dain about a situation in his life. He asked, "How do I fix this?" I asked, "Why would you fix it? You can do something different."

Dain:

I said, "That's not what people do. Nobody in the world does something different. You fix it so it works better." Gary just about fell over.

Gary:

I had to lie down. It so startled me, because I had spent all my time creating Access Consciousness from the point of view that if you knew you could choose different, you would.

It was startling and stunning to me that my reality was so different from everybody else's.

Dain:

What stupidity are you using to create the need of change as more real and more necessary than the possibilities, choices, and questions of difference you are choosing? Everything that is times a godzillion, will you destroy and uncreate it please? Right and Wrong, Good and Bad, POD and POC, All Nine, Shorts, Boys, and Beyonds.

When you function from possibilities, choice, and question, it is a contribution that goes in both directions. It is about the contribution you are to others and the contribution you are to yourself. If you stop trying to change you to fit in the relationship and start looking at "What would have to occur different here for me?" you will get a different set of questions, a different set of possibilities, and a different set of choices you can start to function from. I can pretty much guarantee most men never look at what would have to happen different for their relationship to work for them.

You go to "How can I change me?" rather than "How can we do something totally different, whatever it is?" or "What can we be or do different?" or "What can I be or do different that will allow a different possibility, choice, and question to show up in order to be a different contribution and to be contributed to differently?"

Possibility, Choice, Question, and Contribution

Gary:

Do you get that you would really like to be a contribution?

Class Participant:

Yeah.

Gary:

The only way you're going to function from contribution is through choice, possibility, and question. You've already got the target of contribution. It's not about how contribution has to be added to this; that's what you and everybody else desires as a being—to be a contribution.

If you start to function from "different," different things can show up in your life. You've got to create a different reality rather than trying to change this reality. Don't try to be the fix-it man.

Class Participant:

When I try to change me to have things work better or to fit in better, is that where I lose myself?

Gary:

Yeah, that's where you lose yourself, because you're not doing or being something different; you're changing so you fit better. It's like you've changed your outfit. You're dressed for the role. You're not dressed for success.

Class Participant:

This gives me so much awareness of what I have been choosing that I have never been aware of. I'm truly grateful for this.

Dain:

It explains a lot of areas where we, as men, have not been able to be men, and it explains a lot of the non-maleness we've tried to function from.

Gary:

Because you try to adjust you and change you to fit the cut-out cardboard universe of change.

Class Participant:

Exactly. I have been asking myself, "How can I change so it works better for someone else?" instead of asking, "What's going to work for me?" and "What can I do different that would work for me and maybe for the other person as well?"

Have You Ever Been Encouraged to Be a Man?

Class Participant:

I'm sorry that I'm having trouble getting this and being what I can be as a man. I'm so grateful for the Gentlemen's Club.

Gary:

So can I ask you a question?

Class Participant:

Yes.

Gary:

Have you ever been encouraged to be a man?

Class Participant:

No, not at all.

Gary:

Has anybody on this call been encouraged to be a man?

Class Participant:

Now you are making me cry.

Gary:

I was never encouraged to be a man. I was encouraged to be a man that women would choose to marry.

Class Participant:

I've never seen a man who has chosen to be a man. They've just been trying to be whatever works for their woman or their wife.

Class Participant:

Thank you, guys, for being willing to deal with us.

Gary:

We like you. We like you better than you like you.

Dain:

Yes, exactly! We like you a lot more than you like you.

Gary:

We want you to step up to being something different.

Class Participant:

Different is my new word.

Gary:

All right you guys, take care. I love you lots.

Class Participant:

Thanks, guys.

Gary:

Bye-bye.

Dain:

Bye-bye.

2

CREATING SEX AND RELATIONSHIP FROM AN AWARENESS OF WHAT IS

*You have a tendency to look for the rightness of your
limited point of view,
not the truth of what you can perceive, know, be, and receive,
and you end up in relationships that don't work.*

Gary:

Hello, gentlemen. Does anyone have a question?

Creation vs. Invention

Class Participant:

At the moment, I haven't got time to deal with the man thing. All my energy is going into making money and doing my business. There's no time for this gentlemen stuff. All of these other things are way more important. What am I creating with that? What can I do or be that will create something different for me so I can have it all?

Gary:

You have to be clear that there's a difference between creation and invention. Invention is when you watch television and you see people doing things, and you try to invent that what they're doing is actually real, so you say the same words and do the same actions, thinking you're going to create what they have. But you're not creating anything. It's a total invention of what reality is. It's not an awareness of what reality is.

We'd like to get you to a place where you have a different kind of choice so you can start to look at what is and ask, "How would I like to use this?" and "How can I create this?"

Once when we were in Costa Rica, I was watching a movie on TV. Everything was in Spanish, and I didn't fully understand it, but I got the gist of what was going on. They wanted to portray "passion," so they showed somebody's undies falling to the floor. The person was wearing Nikes and low-top socks. I might have thought "passion" if it had been panties falling on high heels. I might have thought "passion" if had known whether it was a male or female wearing the Nikes, but as it was, it didn't work for me as "passion." Watching it, I realized that we *invent* the thoughts, feelings, emotions, sex and no sex that we function from. We don't *generate* and *create* the true elements of what will give us everything we want. For example, what percentage of your sex life is invented according to the visual cortex of this reality?

Dain:

The visual cortex is the part of the brain that processes visual information. You see somebody who matches your visual cortex's invention of what a person is supposed to be and you invent that it means this, this, and this. What you see doesn't mean any of that, but you cut off your awareness in favor of going with the limitation of invention.

The Way It Looks vs. The Way It Is

Gary:

You, as an infinite being, perceive, know, be, and receive, right?

The lower harmonic of perceiving, knowing, being, and receiving is functioning from thoughts, feelings, emotions, and sex or no sex. When you're doing that, everything is delineated as what you, the limited being, visually see in the world. You have a totally limited point of view of what can actually be. For example, when you try to do something from the visual aspect, you can only see the way it looks—not the way it is.

You have a tendency to look for the rightness of your limited point of view, not the truth of what you can perceive, know, be, and receive, and you end up in relationships that don't work.

What stupidity are you using to create the invention of the signs, seals, symbols, emblems, and significances of sex, copulation, and relationship as the wrongness, the refusal of success, the elimination of receiving, and the losing you are choosing? Everything that is times a godzillion, will you destroy and uncreate it all? Right and Wrong, Good and Bad, POD and POC, All Nine, Shorts, Boys, and Beyonds.

The signs, seals, symbols, and emblems, and significances are the badges you wear that have nothing to do with who you are. You look for the signs, seals, symbols, emblems, and significances of sex, copulation, and relationship.

The signs, seals, symbols, emblems, and significances of copulation are "They look like my type," "They don't look like my type," "They might be fun," "They might not be fun," "I can watch them do this, but I don't have to be involved in it." It's all the weird places you go, where instead of having choice, you have the elimination of possibility.

The signs, seals, symbols, emblems, and significances of relationship are "Oh, they like me," "Oh, they don't like me," "Oh, they want to be with me," "They don't want to be with me," "Oh, I want somebody in my life," "I don't want somebody in my life."

How many times do you look at somebody and say, "This is the person I want to be with," yet you have no idea who the hell that person is? You have no awareness of what they really want, and you cut off all of your awareness of what they're going to ask of you because you don't want anybody to ask anything of you that you're not willing to give. How's that working?

Class Participant:

Not at all. It's like a caveman autopilot thing. It seems fundamental to being a man (speaking in a caveman voice), "Uh, that looks good, go."

The Rule of Dick

Gary:

The fundamental thing about being a man is you're supposed to be ruled by your dick. Whether you're a gay man or a straight man, dick rules. Is that truth or is that invention?

Class Participant:

Invention.

Gary:

How many of you have invented the rule of dick? Everywhere you've invented the rule of dick, will you now destroy and uncreate all of that? Right and Wrong, Good and Bad, POD and POC, All Nine, Shorts, Boys, and Beyonds.

Dain:

That's awesome. The rule of dick.

Gary:

How many of you have had that place where you invented that you were a "duh" kind of guy?

Dain:

Every time someone attractive walks by!

Gary:

Anytime you're attracted to anyone, you go into "duh."

Everything you've done to invent you as a "duh" kind of guy, will you destroy and uncreate all of that? Right and Wrong, Good and Bad, POD and POC, All Nine, Shorts, Boys, and Beyonds.

Dain:

"Duh, can I have that, please? Can I have one of those? Okay, thank you. Can I have another one please? Okay, thank you." It's like nothing else matters. You become a "duh."

Gary:

You become a single digit IQ.

Everything you've done to invent you as a single digit IQ, meaning your dick rules, will you destroy and uncreate all of that? Right and Wrong, Good and Bad, POD and POC, All Nine, Shorts, Boys, and Beyonds.

Dain:

Wow. I like this call already.

Gary:

I do too.

Dain:

What stupidity are you using to create the invention of the signs, seals, symbols, emblems, and significances of sex, copulation, and relationship as the wrongness, the refusal of success, the elimination of receiving, and the losing you are choosing? Everything that is times a godzillion, will you destroy and uncreate it all? Right and Wrong, Good and Bad, POD and POC, All Nine, Shorts, Boys, and Beyonds.

If You're a Man, You're Wrong

Gary:

Have you ever had the idea that you were wrong when you were with somebody that you thought was cute, good looking, and the right person for you?

Class Participant:

Yeah, but we're also wrong if we're not with that person.

Gary:

Well, of course! If your snake doesn't point in the right direction, you're wrong. If it points in a direction, you're wrong. If it points at all, you're wrong.

Dain:

And if it doesn't point, you're even more wrong.

Gary:

Everything you've done to invent that as your reality, will you destroy and uncreate it all? Right and Wrong, Good and Bad, POD and POC, All Nine, Shorts, Boys, and Beyonds.

Dain:

I've noticed, in getting ready to go out with different girls for dinner or sex or whatever, that I would be thinking, "Does this look okay? Oh jeez, did I manscape correctly? Let me brush my teeth another time. Uh, I need to make sure I have deodorant on. Let me make sure to wash this." There was an intensity of judgment about how I was going to be wrong, how I was already wrong, and how if I could look perfect enough, or sound perfect enough, or say something perfect enough, that would somehow undo the wrongness. It took me a long time to realize that I was perceiving what was in their world.

Everything that is that you've done to invent you as the needing to be the perfection of a sex partner, will you destroy and uncreate all of that? Right and Wrong, Good and Bad, POD and POC, All Nine, Shorts, Boys, and Beyonds.

Apparently all of you guys have been trying to do "perfect sex partner."

Gary:

If you're a man, you're wrong. If you're a man with men, you're still wrong. If you think about having sex with men, you're wrong. If you think about having sex with women, you're wrong. The good news is you're just frigging wrong.

Everything you've done to invent that as your reality, will you destroy and uncreate it all? Right and Wrong, Good and Bad, POD and POC, All Nine, Shorts, Boys, and Beyonds.

Dain:

What stupidity are you using to create the invention of the signs, seals, symbols, emblems, and significances of sex, copulation, and relationship as the wrongness, the refusal of success, the elimination of receiving, and the losing you are choosing? Everything that is times a godzillion, will you destroy and uncreate it all? Right and Wrong, Good and Bad, POD and POC, All Nine, Shorts, Boys, and Beyonds.

Gary:

Lordy, lordy. The good news is you guys have wrongness down to a fine science.

Dain:

It's good to be right at something.

Gary:

Yes, it's always good to be right at being wrong. It's like automatically, because you're a man, you're wrong.

Dain:

You're right.

Gary:

I know, but if I'm right, you're wrong, and if I'm wrong, you're right and if I'm a man, I'm wrong no matter what.

Everything you've invented about that point of view, will you destroy and uncreate it all? Right and Wrong, Good and Bad, POD and POC, All Nine, Shorts, Boys, and Beyonds.

Class Participant:

Do we think we're going to be right if we get the woman, so to speak?

Gary:

Well, you think that if you get her, you're finally going to prove you have the right signs, seals, symbols, emblems, and significances. Most of you are only willing to have the red badge of courage or the red letter "A," which means you're an adulterer and an asshole. What if you were the person who could activate and actualize a different reality? Are you choosing that or avoiding that? How many times have you invented you as a loser even before you start? More than a godzillion, or less?

Class Participant:

More.

Gary:

> Everything that is times a godzillion, will you destroy and uncreate it all? Right and Wrong, Good and Bad, POD and POC, All Nine, Shorts, Boys, and Beyonds.

Isn't that great? You've lost before you even open your mouth. Would that make it a little hard to create relationship or copulation? Yeah! That's not in your best interest.

The Invention of Contraception

Dain:

> What stupidity are you using to create the invention of the signs, seals, symbols, emblems, and significances of sex, copulation, and relationship as the wrongness, the refusal of success, the elimination of receiving, and the losing you are choosing? Everything that is times a godzillion, will you destroy and uncreate it all? Right and Wrong, Good and Bad, POD and POC, All Nine, Shorts, Boys, and Beyonds.

The signs, seals, symbols, emblems, and significances are inventions that keep you from giving birth to your awareness. They're like the ultimate contraception. You have sex, copulation, and relationship as things that create the wrongness, the refusal of success, the elimination of receiving, and the making sure to lose. You try to get the right sex, the right copulation, and the right relationship so that you can stop feeling like a loser, a not winner, and somebody who can receive and not be wrong.

Class Participant:

> When Dain said, "The signs, seals, symbols, emblems, and significances are inventions that keep you from giving birth to your awareness," it read for me. What is that?

Gary:

How much of the inventions of sex, copulation, and relationship are a way to eliminate and not to give birth to awareness but to abort awareness?

Class Participant:

All of it.

Gary:

How much of the sex you've had has been based on aborting all of your awareness? A lot? A little? Or megatons? Right and Wrong, Good and Bad, POD and POC, All Nine, Shorts, Boys, and Beyonds.

Dain:

What stupidity are you using to create the invention of the signs, seals, symbols, emblems, and significances of sex, copulation, and relationship as the wrongness, the refusal of success, the elimination of receiving, and the losing you are choosing? Everything that is times a godzillion, will you destroy and uncreate it all? Right and Wrong, Good and Bad, POD and POC, All Nine, Shorts, Boys, and Beyonds.

Gary:

Do you actually believe it's possible for you to lose? Everything you've done to create that belief, will you destroy and uncreate it all? Right and Wrong, Good and Bad, POD and POC, All Nine, Shorts, Boys, and Beyonds.

There are no losers. The difference between a loser and a winner is the difference between somebody who will try, regardless, and someone who won't even bother to try so that he doesn't lose.

How much of what you've created yourself as has been an invention so that you won't actually have to succeed, receive, or lose, but so you can always prove that you were wrong for not choosing different? Everything that is times a godzillion, will you destroy and uncreate it all? Right and Wrong, Good and Bad, POD and POC, All Nine, Shorts, Boys, and Beyonds.

Here's the process you guys need to start running:

What physical actualization of creating the sex, copulation, and success am I now capable of generating, creating, and instituting? Everything that doesn't allow that to show up times a godzillion, will you destroy and uncreate it all?

What If Success Is Just a Choice?

Class Participant:

You said, "sex, copulation, and success." How is success part of that equation? It seems out of left field.

Gary:

Well, if you achieve having sex with somebody, do you feel more successful?

Class Participant:

Yes.

Gary:

If you achieve a sense of having more money, do you feel more successful?

Class Participant:

Yes.

Gary:

Are they actually different?

Class Participant:

They're different energies, but the satisfaction or the success is there.

Gary:

The success is still there, regardless. That's why I'm giving you this process to run.

What physical actualization of creating the sex, copulation, and success am I now capable of generating, creating, and instituting? Everything that doesn't allow that to show up times a godzillion, will you destroy and uncreate it all?

Class Participant:

I keep coming back to success. It is such a loaded word for me. It's all about a validation of me, and it's just about judgment.

Gary:

Success is always a judgment. What if you didn't have to worry about judgment? What if success is just a choice?

Class Participant:

Could you just choose success without judgment?

Gary:

Yeah.

Class Participant:

Can you explain that?

Gary:

Yeah. Success with judgment is the idea that you're going to have sex with somebody. Success with judgment is the idea that you're going to create something as a result of it. Do you really need that? What if you were willing to look at something without a sense of success? What would it be like if you were willing to have everything you were capable of having? The things we look at as success, sex, copulation, and romance, are contrived. They're an invented reality.

You Can Create—or You Can Invent

Dain:

Because you can either *create* or you can *invent,* which goes back to the very beginning of this conversation.

Gary:

How much of your success with romance, sex, and copulation is invented to the point where it stifles you and destroys you? A lot? A little? Or megatons? Everything that is times a godzillion, will you destroy and uncreate it all? Right and Wrong, Good and Bad, POD and POC, All Nine, Shorts, Boys, and Beyonds.

Invention is when you look at somebody and you try to create an emotional connection. You try to create your sex and your copulation from that, but it doesn't work because it doesn't have any substance to it. You, as the being you are, have a lot more substance in life and unfortunately if you have serious substance, you have a tendency to scare the people you're interested in.

Dain:

You scare them rather dynamically. So you learn from a very early time to tone down everything that's intense about you. Everything that's great about you. Everything that's weird about you. Everything that's different about you, which by the way, is everything that makes you, you. It's everything that makes you attractive to somebody who would be fun to be with. You tone down all of those things and you try to invent you as something that would be attractive to the person you've invented that you have to be attracted to.

Gary:

How's that working for you?

Class Participant:

Not at all.

Gary:

You've got to get real about what you want to create. If you take the point of view "I want somebody to be in my life," what does that mean? Something? Nothing? Anything? Or is it so amorphous you don't have to see what will actually work for you?

How much of what you've decided "being with somebody" is, is an invention of the amorphous reality of nothingness?

Dain:

What stupidity are you using to create the invention of the signs, seals, symbols, emblems, and significances of sex, copulation, and relationship as the wrongness, the refusal of success, the elimination of receiving, and the losing you are choosing? Everything that is times a godzillion, will you destroy and uncreate it all? Right and Wrong, Good and Bad, POD and POC, All Nine, Shorts, Boys, and Beyonds.

What physical actualization of creating the sex, copulation, and success are you now capable of generating, creating, and instituting? Everything that doesn't allow that to show up times a godzillion, will you destroy and uncreate it all? Right and Wrong, Good and Bad, POD and POC, All Nine, Shorts, Boys, and Beyonds.

Creating Something That Is Different

Gary:

Do you guys understand that we're talking about creating something that is different? You have to get what you would like something to be. Ask:

- Will it be easy?
- Will it be fun?
- Will it be expansive for me?
- Will it be nurturing for me?
- Will I learn something?

If not, all you're doing is asking for somebody who will fuck you. And if you ask for somebody who will fuck you, lots of people will fuck you—and not always in a good way.

Dain:

True story.

Gary:

Does that make sense to you?

Class Participant:

Yes.

Gary:

How many of you have been fucked—and not in a good way— by someone you decided you wanted to be with? Everywhere you made that decision, because every time you do a decision, a judgment, a computation, or a conclusion about anybody you're going to have sex or copulation with, you've sealed your coffin and you're going to die in the situation. Everything that is times a godzillion, will you destroy and uncreate it all? Right and Wrong, Good and Bad, POD and POC, All Nine, Shorts, Boys, and Beyonds.

Dain:

What stupidity are you using to create the invention of the signs, seals, symbols, emblems, and significances of sex, copulation, and relationship as the wrongness, the refusal of success, the elimination of receiving, and losing you are choosing? Everything that is times a godzillion, will you destroy and uncreate it all? Right and Wrong, Good and Bad, POD and POC, All Nine, Shorts, Boys, and Beyonds.

What physical actualization of creating the sex, copulation, and success are you now capable of generating, creating, and instituting? Everything that doesn't allow that to show up times a godzillion, will you destroy and uncreate it all? Right and Wrong, Good and Bad, POD and POC, All Nine, Shorts, Boys, and Beyonds.

What stupidity are you using to create the invention of the rule of dick are you choosing? Everything that doesn't allow that to show up times a godzillion, will you destroy and uncreate it all? Right and Wrong, Good and Bad, POD and POC, All Nine, Shorts, Boys, and Beyonds.

Gary:

How many of you think your dick is ruling everything, including you? Everything you've done to give your dick rule over you, will you destroy and uncreate all of that? Right and Wrong, Good and Bad, POD and POC, All Nine, Shorts, Boys, and Beyonds.

Are You Making Yourself Less Sexual?

Dain:

> How many of you, in an effort to *not* have your dick run your life, have made yourselves totally asexual? Everything that is times a godzillion, will you destroy and uncreate it all? Right and Wrong, Good and Bad, POD and POC, All Nine, Shorts, Boys, and Beyonds.

Gary:

Wow. It's not that they've made themselves asexual. They've made themselves less sexual so that they can be received by those who don't like sex.

Dain:

Oh yeah, I did that for a long, long time.

Class Participant:

Oh my God.

Gary:

> Everything you've done to make you less sexual so you can be received by those who don't like sex, will you destroy and uncreate all of that, times a godzillion? Right and Wrong, Good and Bad, POD and POC, All Nine, Shorts, Boys, and Beyonds.

Class Participant:

We learn to do that as kids. Yesterday I took my son to his mom's, and it was interesting to watch how he completely shut off all of his sexualness so she could receive him.

Gary:

Yeah, you realize you're going to be vilified and made mincemeat of if you have that kind of sexualness.

What stupidity are you using to create the invention of the wrongness of your sexualness as the perfection of the judgments of your sexualness and the need to provide sexual energy for those who are dead and dying are you choosing? Everything that is times a godzillion, will you destroy and uncreate it all? Right and Wrong, Good and Bad, POD and POC, All Nine, Shorts, Boys, and Beyonds.

Dain:

Wow. Wow. Have I mentioned "wow"?

Are You Trying to Heal
Those Who Are Dying from a Lack of Sexual Energy?

Gary:

That's a good process. It's got a ton of charge. Apparently most of you have been cutting your sexual energy down so you can heal those that are dying from lack of sexual energy.

Class Participant:

Oh my God.

Dain:

What stupidity are you using to create the invention of the wrongness of your sexualness as the perfection of the judgments of your sexualness and the need to provide sexual energy for those who are dead and dying are you choosing? Everything that is times a godzillion, will you destroy and uncreate it all? Right and Wrong, Good and Bad, POD and POC, All Nine, Shorts, Boys, and Beyonds.

Hey, I've got a question. Is this why, when you're around somebody who has sexual energy, especially another guy, you freak out and do weird competitive shit? You'd rather pick some woman or some mate who's dead and dying and try to bring them to life, and you're pissed if some other guy is interested in bringing them to life instead of you?

What stupidity are you using to create the invention of the wrongness of your sexualness as the perfection of the judgments of your sexualness, you bad, bad boy, and the need to provide sexual energy for those who are dead and dying are you choosing? Everything that is times a godzillion, will you destroy and uncreate it all? Right and Wrong, Good and Bad, POD and POC, All Nine, Shorts, Boys, and Beyonds.

Gary:

Can I just say that injecting your sperm into somebody does not create life and living?

Everywhere you've tried to create that and everything you've invented that will actually create life and living, will you destroy and uncreate all of that please, times a godzillion? Right and Wrong, Good and Bad, POD and POC, All Nine, Shorts, Boys, and Beyonds.

Class Participant:

What if you inject it *on* them?

(Laughter)

Dain:

I love you. I love you.

What stupidity are you using to create the invention of the wrongness of your sexualness as the perfection of the judgments of your sexualness, because what else are you going to do with all of your time and energy and the need to provide sexual energy for those who are dead and dying are you choosing? Everything that is times a godzillion, will you destroy and uncreate it all? Right and Wrong, Good and Bad, POD and POC, All Nine, Shorts, Boys, and Beyonds.

Gary:

How many of you have actually invented that the people you have sex with who are dead and dying are the people who need the sex you can provide? Everything you've done to create that instead of actually enjoying the fuck out of yourselves, will you destroy and uncreate all of that? Right and Wrong, Good and Bad, POD and POC, All Nine, Shorts, Boys, and Beyonds.

Dain:

What stupidity are you using to create the invention of the wrongness of your sexualness as the perfection of the judgments of your sexualness and the need to provide sexual energy for those who are dead and dying are you choosing? Everything that is times a godzillion, will you destroy and uncreate it all? Right and Wrong, Good and Bad, POD and POC, All Nine, Shorts, Boys, and Beyonds.

Gary:

Have you decided you're the dead and dying that you have to provide sexual energy for?

Dain:

And that you can actually get sexual energy from people who are dead and dying?

Gary:

Everything you did to create that invention as real, will you destroy and uncreate it all? Right and Wrong, Good and Bad, POD and POC, All Nine, Shorts, Boys, and Beyonds.

Class Participant:

It seems like a measure of success to be able to prop up someone who's dead and dying.

Dain:

There's nothing there, and you say, "I will bring you to life! Therefore, I am strong. I am a success because I brought you to life."

What stupidity are you using to create the invention of the wrongness of your sexualness as the perfection of the judgments of your sexualness and the need to provide sexual energy for those who are dead and dying are you choosing? Everything that is times a godzillion, will you destroy and uncreate it all? Right and Wrong, Good and Bad, POD and POC, All Nine, Shorts, Boys, and Beyonds.

Gary:

Everything that doesn't allow you to see where you've chosen the dead and dying to have sex with instead of choosing the people who would actually be fun, will you destroy and uncreate all of that? Right and Wrong, Good and Bad, POD and POC, All Nine, Shorts, Boys, and Beyonds.

Dain:

Everything that makes this about where you have to become the dead and dying so someone will come and give you energy, will you destroy and uncreate all of that please? Right and Wrong, Good and Bad, POD and POC, All Nine, Shorts, Boys, and Beyonds.

Sexual Attraction

Gary: Is that what you call sexual attraction?

Dain:

Wow.

Gary:

That's what you've invented as sexual attraction. If you get somebody who's dead and dying, they're attracted to you. If you're dead and
dying, you will be attractive to somebody else.

Everything that is times a godzillion, will you destroy and
uncreate it all? Right and Wrong, Good and Bad, POD and POC,
All Nine, Shorts, Boys, and Beyonds.

What percentage of your sexual attraction is an invention
to get you to see or be the wrongness of you? A lot? A little? Or
megatons? Everything that is times a godzillion, will you destroy
and uncreate it all? Right and Wrong, Good and Bad, POD and
POC, All Nine, Shorts, Boys, and Beyonds.

Dain:

What stupidity are you using to create the invention of the
wrongness of your sexualness as the perfection of the judgments
of your sexualness and the need to provide sexual energy for those
who are dead and dying are you choosing? Everything that is
times a godzillion, will you destroy and uncreate it all? Right and
Wrong, Good and Bad, POD and POC, All Nine, Shorts, Boys,
and Beyonds.

Gary:

Wow, this is even more intense than I was hoping for.

Class Participant:

I'm really grateful.

Dain:

Man, this is really amazing. And I thought the other one was a
never-ending process.

What stupidity are you using to create the invention of the
wrongness of your sexualness as the perfection of the judgments

of your sexualness and the need to provide sexual energy for those who are dead and dying are you choosing? Everything that is times a godzillion, will you destroy and uncreate it all? Right and Wrong, Good and Bad, POD and POC, All Nine, Shorts, Boys, and Beyonds.

Gary:

What if you had more sexual energy than the other people around you?

How many of you are sexual healers and want others to be sexual healers for you? That's the one that's killing you. You want others to be sexual healers for you. Every invention you created in that world, will you destroy and uncreate it all? Right and Wrong, Good and Bad, POD and POC, All Nine, Shorts, Boys, and Beyonds.

Focus on the Creation

You try to *invent* that something is going to happen rather than *creating* it so it does happen.

If you want to be successful, you've got to look at what you're capable of creating. You've got to focus on the creation of getting together with somebody sexually.

Dain:

When you invent that something is going to happen and it doesn't happen, you're left with the wrongness of you for not being able to create what you invented that you should be able to create. You're willing to spend a lot of time and energy on who or what you might have sex with, or get laid by, or however you want to put it, except how much energy are you willing to put into creating success in every area of your life?

Gary:

You tend to use sex as the identification of success. You're successful if you have sexual energy that is attractive to large numbers of people. What if that's the lie that's keeping you trapped?

Everything you've done to buy the lie that sexual energy will be the sign of success and that sexual energy will get you laid, will you destroy and uncreate all of that? Right and Wrong, Good and Bad, POD and POC, All Nine, Shorts, Boys, and Beyonds.

Class Participant:

Hey, Gary, you say it's a lie, but it feels so true. I've bought hook, line, and sinker the idea that if you have sexual energy, you will be successful.

Gary:

Is that true, or is that what you're doing against you?

Dain:

Or is it what you're inventing against you?

Gary:

Everything you've done to use that energy against you rather than for you, will you destroy and uncreate all of that? Right and Wrong, Good and Bad, POD and POC, All Nine, Shorts, Boys, and Beyonds.

Going on Vacation

Dain:

All of these inventions are a huge part of what's standing in the way of sex ever being fun, because it's based on all of these inventions. It's also one of the places where you keep you from the success that's available. Think of the amount of energy you put into sex and getting laid—or avoiding getting laid—and ask, "If I put that amount of energy into my business, what would I have created in the last year?" Maybe you could consider the possibility of changing that so you start putting that energy into your business.

There was a time in my life where women were the thing. At one point, I went on a date one morning, and there was another girl I had sex with later that day. I spent the night with her, and I had another girl come over the next afternoon and she and I had sex. I had a two-and-half day vacation, if you will.

Gary:

That's what we call it now, "Dain goes on vacation."

Dain:

Yeah, "I'm going on vacation!" That was where I turned my mind off. It was my vacation from consciousness, awareness, and creating my business.

Gary:

What physical actualization of sex and copulation as "on vacation" are you now capable of generating, creating, and instituting? Everything that doesn't allow that to show up times a godzillion, will you destroy and uncreate it all? Right and Wrong, Good and Bad, POD and POC, All Nine, Shorts, Boys, and Beyonds.

Dain:

I was really grateful for having that experience because I realized I was putting huge amounts of energy into people's universes to bring them to life and to make sex the place where I could undo their judgments, get their bodies turned on, and have a level of intensity that I like. I looked at it and I said, "Man, if I had put that amount of energy into my business, my business would have taken off this weekend instead of just lurching forward a little bit." I had taken so much energy away from it. It's not that you have a finite amount of energy, but when you have the idea, "This is what's creative, this is what's generative, and very little else is," you take yourself away from the success you could create.

Gary:

Do you know how I used to bypass that? In the old days when I did drugs, sex, and rock and roll, I would have two joints before I had sex with somebody so I could bypass all of their judgments. It worked really well.

Dain:

If you can have that awareness and ask, "Am I actually destroying my success here by the choices I'm making?" you might find that you can make a different choice. You might say, "Okay, what would it take for this to be creative and generative? All of the inventions I have that are creating me going here right now, destroy and uncreate them."

What Would It Be Like to Create Sex and Relationship from a Totally Different Reality?

Gary:

This coming week, I'd like you to look at what it would be like if you were willing to generate and create sex and relationship from a totally different reality. Put this question on a loop and listen to it nonstop:

What physical actualization of sex, copulation, relationship, and success from a reality beyond this reality am I now capable of generating, creating and instituting? Everything that is times a godzillion, will you destroy and uncreate it all? Right and Wrong, Good and Bad, POD and POC, All Nine, Shorts, Boys, and Beyonds.

Dain:

Okay, beautiful men.

Class Participant:

I just want to say I'm so grateful for these calls. They're amazing. Thank you very much.

Class Participant:

Thank you so much.

Dain:

Thank you. How does it get any better than that?

Gary:

Thank you, guys. Love you a lot.

3

You Are the Valuable Product

I'm no longer making others the valuable product.
I've become the valuable product,
and there's more available for me than there has
been ever before.

Gary:

Hello, Gentlemen. Let's start with some questions.

Demons of Necessity

I'm so grateful for The Gentlemen's Club. For the first time in my life, I'm happy about being a man and being in a man's body. I've been asking the question, "How does it get any better than this?" and about ninety percent of the time I hear, "It doesn't." I don't know whether that's my thought, someone else's thought, or an entity's thought.

I've also been asking, "What stupidity am I using to create the total eradication and elimination of 'How does it get any better than this?' am I choosing?" Can you give me some clarity on this, please?

Gary:

You've got to ask: Demons of separation? And tell them it's time to leave. You say: Demons, go back to from whence you came, never to return to me or this reality again.

Anybody or anything that tells you that you can't do something is a demon. An entity is a being that would gladly take on a new body. A demon is an entity that has been given the job of getting power over someone or something. It will lock you up and keep you diminished. We want to get you to a place where that is not the case. Demons come whenever you become a follower of someone, because you're trying to get power from the person you're following. Have any of you ever given power over to a woman?

Class Participants:

(Laughter)

Gary:

That would be a yes. Let's start with this process:

What stupidity are you using to create the inventions, the artificial intensities, and the demons of necessity of following the opposite sex are you choosing? Everything that is times a godzillion, will you destroy and uncreate it all? Right and Wrong, Good and Bad, POD and POC, All Nine, Shorts, Boys, and Beyonds.

Class Participant:

Could you talk about what artificial intensity is?

Gary:

When you really want to have something, you take the point of view, "This is a really good idea!" You make it intense. You say, "I so need this!" It's an invented point of view. It's artificial. You use intensity to create the belief that you're going to create something good.

Every time you want to follow a woman, or the golden vagina, you're creating a place where you become the effect of demons. And if you were a woman in some lifetime, you'll try to follow men. Whenever you make yourself a follower of someone, you invite the demons in to control you.

Class Participant:

When you follow a guru, are you trying to get power over him?

Gary:

You follow a guru because you want him to see you as the brilliant person you are. You invite the demons in to see you and recognize how brilliant you are. The demons activate any time you try to follow somebody.

Class Participant:

This is so interesting.

Gary:

What stupidity are you using to create the inventions, the artificial intensities, and the demons of necessity of following the opposite sex are you choosing? Everything that is times a godzillion, will you destroy and uncreate it all? Right and Wrong, Good and Bad, POD and POC, All Nine, Shorts, Boys, and Beyonds.

You invent that demons are a source of power and that artificial intensity is a source of power. Of course, none of you have been artificially intense. Or have you?

What stupidity are you using to create the inventions, the artificial intensities, and the demons of necessity of following the opposite sex are you choosing? Everything that is times a godzillion, will you destroy and uncreate it all? Right and Wrong, Good and Bad, POD and POC, All Nine, Shorts, Boys, and Beyonds.

Whenever you try to follow something or someone, you're inviting what will create the worst result into your life. The idea of following is the idea that somebody needs to have control over you or that they can have control over you and that it's more important for someone to have control over you than it is for you to be you.

What stupidity are you using to create the inventions, the artificial intensities, and the demons of necessity of following the opposite sex are you choosing? Everything that is times a godzillion, will you destroy and uncreate it all? Right and Wrong, Good and Bad, POD and POC, All Nine, Shorts, Boys, and Beyonds.

Class Participant:

I'm having great difficulty in staying present with this call. I just don't want to be here. I want to rip my ear phones off. Is this demon stuff or something else?

Gary:

Demons always try to make you go away from anything that's going to give you freedom from them. So right now, all of you, tell all the demons that you've ever chosen in order to have the opposite sex or to be the opposite sex: Go back to from whence you came, never to return to me or this reality ever again.

Class Participant:

Wow, that's cool.

Class Participant:

Thank you.

Gary:

Is that feeling better for anyone?

Class Participant:

Yes!

Gary:

What stupidity are you using to create the inventions, the artificial intensities, and the demons of necessity of following the opposite sex are you choosing? Everything that is times a godzillion, will you destroy and uncreate it all? Right and Wrong, Good and Bad, POD and POC, All Nine, Shorts, Boys, and Beyonds.

Are you more able to stay present now?

Class Participant:

I'm much more present now. My body is almost shaking.

Gary:

Good. Is that shaking—or is that being the energy that your body can actually be? You invite entities and demons into your body and your reality so you can be the demon in bed you're supposed to be. This is where you're supposed to demand sex of a woman and she's expected to give it because she's supposed to follow you, but you're already following her, so who's in charge, and how's it working?

Class Participant:

It doesn't.

Class Participant:

Gary, I heard you say on a call the other day, and it was the first time I heard you say it, that the more conscious we become, the more we wake up these demons.

Gary:

The more conscious you become, the more you wake up the demons and entities because when you're no longer willing to be the effect of things, it becomes more difficult for them to maintain their jobs.

Class Participant:

I've noticed, as I've run this demon process, that some days the voices are gone and some days they're there times ten.

Permeating Consciousness into a Demon's World

Gary:

> Yeah, because a new set of them is waking up. You can run:

> What stupidity am I using to avoid the permeable conscious-ness I could be choosing? Everything that doesn't allow that to show up times a godzillion, will you destroy and uncreate it all? Right and Wrong, Good and Bad, POD and POC, All Nine, Shorts, Boys, and Beyonds.

If you permeate consciousness into a demon's world, it cannot maintain itself here. Demons have been doing the job of creating fol-lowers and creating people as the effect for trillions of years, and they don't really want to do it anymore. They don't like where they are; they don't like where they're stuck any more than you like them being stuck on you. The more consciousness that comes to light on planet Earth, the more their job is of no value. In India and most of the Middle East, for example, they've worshipped demon gods for centuries. And in other parts of the world, people practice black magic.

The idea that you, as a being, need something outside of you is an invented reality. People say things like, "Oh, the demon rum" or "The demons made me do it" or "The devil made me do it." Those are ways we invite demons into existence, but they can't maintain their job in the face of consciousness. So keep running:

> What stupidity am I using to avoid the permeable conscious-ness I could be choosing? Everything that doesn't allow that to show up times a godzillion, will you destroy and uncreate it all? Right and Wrong, Good and Bad, POD and POC, All Nine, Shorts, Boys, and Beyonds.

Class Participant:

> Is there a demon of money?

Gary:

Yeah. Money's considered a demon. People consider money the demon that keeps them from having a life. "Money is the root of all evil" or "The love of money is the root of all evil." No matter how you put it, money is delineated as evil, not as something that's easy, joyful, or valuable to have. Do you see how this works?

What stupidity are you using to avoid being the permeable laws of consciousness you could be choosing? Everything that doesn't allow that to show up times a godzillion, will you destroy and uncreate it all? Right and Wrong, Good and Bad, POD and POC, All Nine, Shorts, Boys, and Beyonds.

Here is another process you may want to run:

What physical actualization of being the permeable laws of consciousness are you now capable of generating, creating, and instituting? Everything that doesn't allow that to show up times a godzillion, will you destroy and uncreate it all? Right and Wrong, Good and Bad, POD and POC, All Nine, Shorts, Boys, and Beyonds.

If you put these two processes on a loop, they will start to change things in every aspect of your life, not just with relationships and women.

Are You Making Someone Righteous?

Class Participant:

I'm struggling with what I want from my life. I'm second guessing myself constantly.

Gary:

Let's try this process:

What stupidity are you using to create the inventions, the artificial intensities, and the demons that guard and protect the righteous I am following am I choosing? Everything that is times a godzillion, will you destroy and uncreate it all? Right and Wrong, Good and Bad, POD and POC, All Nine, Shorts, Boys, and Beyonds.

Class Participant:

Did you say, "the righteous"? What is that?

Gary:

The righteous I am following am I choosing? Say you decide someone is a righteous person. They're not easy; they're not a slut. They're not going to give themselves away easily. So you decide they're righteous, and righteous means better than you. Whenever you decide someone is better than you, you have to make you wrong about anything you choose. Then you have to look at how fucked up you are that the person didn't choose you.

Not that men do this with women. Oh yeah, they do! Let's run this one again.

What stupidity are you using to create the inventions, the artificial intensities, and the demons that guard and protect the righteous I am following am I choosing? Everything that is times a godzillion, will you destroy and uncreate it all? Right and Wrong, Good and Bad, POD and POC, All Nine, Shorts, Boys, and Beyonds.

Have you ever noticed how you say, "She's the perfect girl?" That's making her righteous. "This girl is perfect. She's so beautiful." Righteous. This is the way you make someone righteous rather than having you as valuable.

Everything that is times a godzillion, will you destroy and uncreate it all? Right and Wrong, Good and Bad, POD and POC, All Nine, Shorts, Boys, and Beyonds.

What stupidity are you using to create the inventions, the artificial intensities, and the demons that guard and protect the righteous you are following are you choosing? Everything that is times a godzillion, will you destroy and uncreate it all? Right and Wrong, Good and Bad, POD and POC, All Nine, Shorts, Boys, and Beyonds.

Class Participant:

When I called you last week, you gave me a clearing about choosing for me instead of choosing for everybody else. I've started to do that more, especially with my partner, and it has created a lot of very intense situations, because she has been used to me choosing her first or us first and never me.

Gary:

Well, she does have a golden vagina.

Class Participant:

(Laughing) Absolutely. All of what has happened in the last two weeks matches the energy of everything you are saying today. Can you help me to clarify what I'm not seeing here?

Gary:

What stupidity are you using to create the golden vagina you are choosing? Everything that is times a godzillion, will you destroy and uncreate it all? Right and Wrong, Good and Bad, POD and POC, All Nine, Shorts, Boys, and Beyonds.

Deal and Deliver

Class Participant:

She reacts strongly when I choose to do or be something different than before.

Gary:

You're changing things. You never did a Deal and Deliver with each other did you?

Class Participant:

No, absolutely not.

Gary:

A relationship is a business deal, so you have to do Deal and Deliver, as you would in any business deal. Difficulties in business interactions and relationships arise because most people have no idea what they would like. They believe that if they're kind and nice, people will deliver kind and nice things to them.

You're not willing to see what people want to deliver, what they're going to deliver, and what the deal is for them. You have a godzillion fantasies about what's supposed to happen, which means that you're not looking at what's actually going to occur. You've got to do Deal and Deliver or there won't be place from which to increase your reality. You've got to get clear on exactly what you need and desire and what the other person needs and desires. Ask:

- What is the deal?
- What are you going to deliver?
- What do you expect me to deliver?
- Exactly what is this going to look like and how is that going to work?
- What am I going to have to be for you?

You've got to say, "Hey, sweetheart. Can we do a Deal and Deliver here? What do you expect from me?" If you call her "sweetheart" instead of "sweetie" or "hon," she'll have to be kinder, to live up to the title you have given her.

Class Participant:

Cool. Have I created demons with my choices around her?

Gary:

Yes. How many demons do you have that create your following her at all times? A lot, a little, or megatons?

Class Participant:

Megatons.

Gary:

Have you made her the guru of your life? How many of you men have made women the guru you are supposed to follow? Everything you've done to create the demons that keep you following her and her orders and doing what she says and everything that is times a godzillion, will you destroy and uncreate it all? Right and Wrong, Good and Bad, POD and POC, All Nine, Shorts, Boys, and Beyonds.

Class Participant:

This matches the question I asked you about whether following somebody was trying to get power over them.

Will This Expand My Agenda?

Gary:

For several years, whenever Dain and I were considering doing something, we would ask the question, "Will this expand my agenda?"

The idea was that if doing something would expand our agenda, we should go for it.

It was very shocking to find out that all men's penises are named Agenda, and if there's a woman involved, all of you think your agenda is going to expand. In fact, you know it is.

Class Participants:

(Laughter)

Gary:

Your agenda is that thing that hangs between your legs. Every time you think about sex, you are expanding your agenda. Dain and I found that a way to get around asking about our agenda is:

- If I choose this, what will my life be like in five years?
- If I don't choose this, what will my life be like in five years?

It's the only way you're going to find out what you would like to create, which would be expanding your agenda.

Class Participant:

How come five years? That's quite far away. Why isn't it just a year?

Gary:

Five years is so far into the future that you can't invent what something's going to be like. Putting it at five years makes it possible for you to perceive something energetically rather than from your thoughts, feelings, and emotions.

Class Participant:

Thank you.

When You're the Leader, You Become the Valuable Product

Class Participant:

The thing of following the righteous describes the way I've always done my sexual relationships with men. I see a guy and I say, "Yes, he's the one." The one-digit IQ kicks in, and away we go. I give him all my power, as you say, and make him right, and if he doesn't choose me, then I'm wrong. Can you show me a different way to do this?

Gary:

Yeah. You've got to ask, "Why am I following instead of leading?"

What stupidity are you choosing to avoid the leading you could be choosing? Everything that is times a godzillion, will you destroy and uncreate it all? Right and Wrong, Good and Bad, POD and POC, All Nine, Shorts, Boys, and Beyonds.

Class Participant:

What does that look like?

Gary:

Well, when you're the leader, you become the valuable product. In Access Consciousness, women come up to Dain and say, "Oh, I'd love to have sex with you." Do they really mean that?

Class Participant:

No.

Gary:

No. What do they mean?

Class Participant:

They want power over him. They want to be significant.

Gary:

Yes. They want to be significant and they want to have a relationship. I got a note this weekend from a lady. It said, "I'd love to go out
to dinner with you and have good times and more." She is nice looking, but she is a demon bitch from hell.

Class Participant:

Isn't that right up your alley, Gary? Isn't that what you like?

Gary:

That's what I used to like. I discovered that following the golden
vagina usually works out badly for me. I'm no longer making others
the valuable product. I've become the valuable product, and there's
more available for me than there has been ever before.

What stupidity are you using to avoid being the valuable
product and the leader you could be choosing? Everything that is
times a godzillion, will you destroy and uncreate it all? Right and
Wrong, Good and Bad, POD and POC, All Nine, Shorts, Boys,
and Beyonds.

Most of you think that if someone is *willing* to have you, or have
sex with you, they can't be valuable. And if they're not willing to have
sex with you, you're not valuable. Why do you devalue you?

Everything that is times a godzillion, will you destroy and
uncreate it all? Right and Wrong, Good and Bad, POD and POC,
All Nine, Shorts, Boys, and Beyonds.

Class Participant:

I recently met a woman and it was as if she was saying, "We have
to have sex now, before we leave."

Gary:

It has to be about her desire, her reality, what she chooses, and
what she wants to create. What does that have to do with what you
desire?

Class Participant:

Nothing.

Gary:

Most people function from what other people desire and require rather than choosing what works for them.

Class Participant:

How come she has the same lack thing in her universe?

Gary:

She too is trying to find a person she can follow. Notice that the first process I gave you was not about man or woman, but the opposite sex:

What stupidity are you using to create the inventions, the artificial intensities, and the demons of necessity of following the opposite sex are you choosing? Everything that is times a godzillion, will you destroy and uncreate it all? Right and Wrong, Good and Bad, POD and POC, All Nine, Shorts, Boys, and Beyonds.

It applies to both sides of the game. That's the thing you've got to be aware of. How do you play both sides of the game? When you find somebody who has an insanity that matches yours, you'll find yourself very attracted to him or her. Isn't that cute? Your matching insanity attracts you to each other.

Class Participants:

(Laughter)

Class Participant:

And what is it when we want to kill people we know from other lifetimes? Is that another thing?

Gary:

When you have those really intense attractions where you cannot separate from the person, it's usually this. It's when you say, "I'd really like to do blah, blah, blah" or "It's really important to me that we get together" or "I know that we've been together lots of lifetimes."

Class Participant:

Recently I'm beginning to do different things. I haven't been going into those old patterns as much as before. Something has really shifted.

Gary:

Cool, we're on the way. And that's what we want to look for: On the way.

The Wrongness around Desiring Sex

Class Participant:

Could you talk about demons with regards to the wrongness around desiring to have sex?

Gary:

First of all, sex and copulation have always been a wrongness.

How many lifetimes have you chosen demons and asked for the help of the Lord or anyone who could stop you from wanting sex? How many demons do you have cutting off sexual energy?

Class Participant:

A lot.

Gary:

Everything that is times a godzillion, will you now demand that they go back to from whence they came, never to return to you or your reality for all eternity?

Class Participant:

Yeah.

Gary:

Everything that doesn't allow that to show up times a godzillion, on three: One... two... three! Thank you.

Have you ever said, "Please God, don't make me want to have sex all of the time, because I'm so wrong for wanting to have sex all of the time" or "I've got to have sex. Can somebody help me so I can have sex?" Either one invites the demons in. Either one takes away your power. You need to have choice and the willingness to receive.

Total Presence in Sex and Copulation

Class Participant:

What's going on when you leave your body during sex? Is that related to demons?

Gary:

Well, usually leaving your body during sex is a way to be present without being present. You're trying to leave your expanding agenda in place without showing up as you. So it doesn't work, does it?

Class Participant:

No.

Gary:

What would it be like if you were totally present?

What stupidity are you using to avoid total presence during sex and copulation are you choosing? Everything that is times a godzillion, will you destroy and uncreate it all? Right and Wrong, Good and Bad, POD and POC, All Nine, Shorts, Boys, and Beyonds.

Cultural Entrainment

Class Participant:

I'm Asian, and it seems to me that Asian people are more conservative about sex.

Gary:

No, they're more suppressed about sex.

Class Participant:

Is this cultural programming?

Gary:

Yes.

Class Participant:

I am single and I have problems approaching girls. I don't know what the real issue is. Sometimes it's like a feeling of fear or anxiety.

Gary:

Guys, you have to get that you're aware. There's as much fear and anxiety in the woman's world as there is in yours, if not more. You might want to ask, "Is this mine?" because a lot of times, the girl has as many problems as you do.

When I was in high school, there was a girl who was considered the most beautiful woman in the school. No one would talk to her or ask her out. They were afraid to because they were certain she would turn them down. I finally screwed up my courage and asked her out. She turned out to be the most boring person I've ever been out with. After that, I chose ugly people to go out with because at least they were interesting. I got clear that somebody who's really pretty has as much anxiety about being asked out as somebody who is ugly. You have to ask, "Is this fear or anxiety or whatever it is mine? Or is this theirs?" so you know what's going on.

Class Participant:

How can I overcome this regardless of everyone else's judgments about approaching girls?

Gary:

You can recognize that you're the valuable product.

Class Participant:

I attended the three-day body class and I wanted to exchange body processes with girls, but I have been taught by society and my mother that touching girls' bodies is wrong.

Gary:

You've been taught that touching girls' bodies is wrong. You're wrong if you touch them and you're wrong if you don't. That's cultural entrainment. Cultural entrainment is everything you buy from everybody else. It's everything your society and your culture say. All those things are erroneous piles of debris. Try running this:

What stupidity am I using to create the cultural entrainment I am choosing? Everything that is times a godzillion, will you destroy and uncreate it all? Right and Wrong, Good and Bad, POD and POC, All Nine, Shorts, Boys, and Beyonds.

Class Participant:

Does that cover religions too?

Gary:

Yes, religion is always a cultural entrainment. How many lifetimes have you been a priest and broken your vows and had sex with somebody, usually a boy, but we won't talk about that. It's not normal to be chaste.

Everything that is times a godzillion and all of the lifetimes in which you have judged yourself for breaking your vows to be chaste, will you destroy and uncreate it all? Right and Wrong, Good and Bad, POD and POC, All Nine, Shorts, Boys, and Beyonds.

What stupidity are you using to create the unsexing you are choosing? Everything that is times a godzillion, will you destroy and uncreate it all? Right and Wrong, Good and Bad, POD and POC, All Nine, Shorts, Boys, and Beyonds.

Being the Sexual Energy You Are

Class Participant:

Gary, what is unsexing?

Gary:

Unsexing is where, instead of being the sexual being you are, you try to deny it, suppress it, not be it, and find ways to eliminate it.

Class Participant:

Ah. Right.

Gary:

What stupidity are you using to create the unsexing and uncopulating you are choosing? Everything that is times a godzillion, will you destroy and uncreate it all? Right and Wrong, Good and Bad, POD and POC, All Nine, Shorts, Boys, and Beyonds.

You guys are putting so much energy into unsexing and uncopulating! It's amazing you ever get laid.

What stupidity are you using to create the unsexing and uncopulating you are choosing? Everything that is times a godzillion, will you destroy and uncreate it all? Right and Wrong, Good and Bad, POD and POC, All Nine, Shorts, Boys, and Beyonds.

You've been trying to unsex and uncopulate yourself forever! I don't go out and have sex, but I have plenty of opportunities, and I always ask the questions:

- Will it be easy?
- Will it be fun?
- Will I learn something?

Usually when I ask, "Will I learn something?" I get "Yeah, I'll learn how bad it's going to be!" So I don't go there. I used to figure as long as my agenda was expanding, it must be right to do it. None of you have that point of view, do you?

What stupidity are you using to create the inventions, the artificial intensities, and the demons of your penis always being the source of expanding your agenda are you choosing? Everything that is times a godzillion, will you destroy and uncreate it all? Right and Wrong, Good and Bad, POD and POC, All Nine, Shorts, Boys, and Beyonds.

How much of what is sexual energy are you suppressing?

Class Participant:

It's the following thing again, isn't it? You'll change or suppress your sexual energy based on what you think the woman likes.

Gary:

Yeah, rather than actually being you. If you're really being the sexual energy, you're being everything you are. If you're being everything you are, you become more intensely exciting, more valuable, and more desirable.

Everything that is times a godzillion, will you destroy and uncreate it all? Right and Wrong, Good and Bad, POD and POC, All Nine, Shorts, Boys, and Beyonds.

Class Participant:

I got confused there because I've been asking myself, "What does this person require of me?" and "What is she willing to receive?" I got what she was willing to receive and I decided to be that—but she was not willing to receive very much.

What Would I Like to Create for Me?

Gary:

That's what most of us do. We try to only give what other people can receive and we make them right. What if, instead of assuming the rightness of the other person, or the righteousness of them, or the goodness of them, you were willing to look at it and say, "I would really like to create something different here. What would I like to create for me?"

If you started to look at what you could create for you, would you create and generate more—or less? Would you create people in your life who were more willing to receive if you were doing what worked for you?

I was talking with Dain recently and I said, "You've got to stop looking for what women desire and start asking for what you desire. Your expanded agenda has no consciousness."

Does your expanded agenda desire more than what comes in the beginning? Everything that brings up times a godzillion, will you destroy and uncreate all of that? Right and Wrong, Good and Bad, POD and POC, All Nine, Shorts, Boys, and Beyonds.

What stupidity are you using to create the wrongness of being a man are you choosing? Everything that is times a godzillion, will you destroy and uncreate it all? Right and Wrong, Good and Bad, POD and POC, All Nine, Shorts, Boys, and Beyonds.

A man is soft when he's hard and hard when he's soft. Do you know what that means?

Class Participant:

No.

Orgasm by Contraction/Orgasm by Expansion

Gary:

If you have a hard-on for somebody, you will give them whatever they want. When you don't give them what they want, when you get what you want, all of a sudden, you have no further interest. This is the way the body works. It's not a wrongness or a rightness. If you go for sex, for the idea of the orgasm, and you do orgasm by contraction, which is how most people do it, having sex does not stimulate you to continue to live. If you go for contraction to create orgasm, you are not creating the generative energy of living, which is what you get when you do expansion to create orgasm.

Everything that just made you not understand a word of what I just said, will you destroy and uncreate all of that? Right and Wrong, Good and Bad, POD and POC, All Nine, Shorts, Boys, and Beyonds.

When you were a kid, you might have gone into the bathroom to masturbate. You would get it over with as quickly as possible because you didn't want anybody to know what you were doing. Most likely, your parents didn't encourage you to enjoy yourself. Very few mothers or fathers say, "Take your sweet time. Enjoy yourself and enjoy your penis." They ask, "What are you doing in there?"

If you really want to increase your sexual energy, I highly recommend you start by doing masturbation differently. You can do it with your girl or without her. She might enjoy it if you actually took time to masturbate. Decide that you're not going to get off in the first three and a half minutes; you're going to take longer than that. Be willing to spend an hour playing with your penis in a soft and gentle way, and every time you feel like you're getting close, instead of going faster so you get off, slow down. Do it more slowly and gently. Add some lubricant if you want to, but do it slow and gentle. Be easy, sweet, and kind. Every time you feel yourself contract, say "no" and expand out.

You may lose your hard-on during the process, but go back to playing with your penis gently until your hard-on comes back. Continue to stroke gently and easily. If you do this, you'll get to the point where a) you'll become a better lover, b) you'll become willing to allow yourself to have lovers who will take that kind of time with you and for you, and c) instead of exploding with a burst of energy that becomes a limitation, you'll start to create an orgasm that generates energy. After having an orgasm like that—expanded and not contracted—you'll want to go to work, you'll want to have a good time, you'll want to do more than go to sleep.

If you've ever had the experience of wanting to go to sleep right after you've gotten off, you've been doing contraction to create orgasm. Using contraction to create orgasm always lessens your body's generative and creative energies in favor of the orgasm.

Class Participant:

Is the artificial intensity we are creating from excitement through porn?

Gary:

When you create stroking your thing as fast as you can to get off, you're creating an artificial intensity to get off on.

Class Participant:

Cool.

Gary:

You're inventing that as the only way you can get off, then when you have sex with a woman, you have to go fast and hard all the time, as if fast and hard is the only way she's going to be satisfied. First of all, why is it always about how she is satisfied, not about how you are satisfied? When you're willing to function from expansion instead of pushing to orgasm, you invite the orgasm. You invite whoever you're having sex with to a different possibility and a different choice.

Class Participant:

The woman I'm seeing did that with me the other day. She was stroking my penis and sucking and licking, and I was falling asleep. I even snored several times. What is that? Is that just the body getting relaxed?

Gary:

Yeah, because the body should be relaxed. Have you ever woken up with a hard-on?

Class Participant:

When I'm relaxed, I get really hard hard-ons.

Gary:

Exactly! Relaxation is the source of what creates the hard-on. Relaxation is the source for excitation. That's the reason I want you to practice this. Take away the idea that you're trying to create orgasm. Instead you're shooting for the ability to create a more sustained hard-on, a more enjoyable hard-on. It's enjoying your hard-on just for being a hard-on. This will start to make you better when you are in bed with someone.

It will also take you to a place where you have a choice of what you want to create and the way you want to create it, which makes you the valuable product. Right now most of you would be very happy just to have a moist, warm place to stick your penis. That's pretty much enough for most men. And because that's pretty much enough for most men, women begin to think men are selfish. They think men are too fast; they don't go slow enough. A lot of women have the point of view that sex is just pound, pound, pound. They think, "Will you just get it over with and cum so we can stop?" It's not about inviting the women to an expansive life and living through the orgasmic quality of sex. It's about getting you off or getting them off. Neither of those should be the target.

Class Participant:

Do you have a clearing connected with moving from contracting into orgasm versus expanding?

Gary:

Unfortunately I can't create that. You have to practice, because you've learned to do it the other way. It's not that it's wrong. It's just not going to create what I think most of you would like to have. Am I mistaken?

Class Participant:

No.

Gary:

You'd like sex to be something that invigorates you and expands your life—not just your agenda. There's a different possibility here, as far as I can see. What possibility would you most like to have? The more expansive version of sex and copulation or the more contractive version of it?

Class Participant:

The more expansive version.

Class Participant:

Gary, you gave me a question that has been very helpful: What can I relax into that would create a greater possibility in sex and copulation than I never knew existed?

Gary:

Thank you for that. I'd forgotten about that question. That will help, but really, it's not about asking a question. You have to be willing to practice it. When I gave you that question, it was because no one would let me talk long enough to explain what you need to do. So practice—and use that question. What was it again?

Class Participant:

What can I relax into that would create a greater possibility in sex and copulation than I never knew existed?

Gary:

What physical actualization of total relaxation into sex and copulation are you now capable of generating, creating, and instituting? Everything that doesn't allow that to show up times a godzillion, will you destroy and uncreate it all? Right and Wrong, Good and Bad, POD and POC, All Nine, Shorts, Boys, and Beyonds.

Class Participant:

When I'm working and it's getting intense, sometimes I go and masturbate in that contractive manner. What is that?

Gary:

You think that getting off will relax you. But do you want to get off—or do you want to expand your life?

Class Participant:

The second one.

Gary:

When you're feeling that kind of tension, go to the bathroom and stroke yourself for fifteen minutes instead of three and a half, and do it without getting off, then go back to work and see how you do. The thing is, in order to be hard, you have to relax.

Class Participant:

Oftentimes I realize that the intensity is not mine.

Gary:

The intensity is not yours, but you want to relax into non-orgasmic playing with your penis, and then when you go out, people will look at the bulge in your pants and start to want you. That will do more to expand your agenda than anything else.

Integrity with Self

Class Participant:

When I walk down the street, I often avoid people and contract my sexual energy. I can actually feel myself disappear. Is it just a matter of expanding that sexualness or being present?

Gary:

Is it that you contract your sexual energy and make yourself disappear? Or is it that other people can't be sexual at all?

Class Participant:

The second one, yeah.

Gary:

Are you trying to entrain to the people around you?

Class Participant:

Yes.

Gary:

What stupidity are you using to entrain to the vibrational dis-integrity around you are you choosing? Everything that is times a godzillion, will you destroy and uncreate it all? Right and Wrong, Good and Bad, POD and POC, All Nine, Shorts, Boys, and Beyonds.

Class Participant:

What does *disintegrity* mean? How does that work?

Gary:

Do people function from integrity—or do they function from conclusion and judgment?

Class Participant:

Conclusion and judgment.

Gary:

Okay, is that where you want to function from?

Class Participant:

No. I should be functioning from integrity, then?

Gary:

Yes. Integrity with self. You entrain with the vibrations around you as though the vibrations around you are what you should be. But what you should really be is you regardless of anything else. Integrity is stepping into the greatness of you without a judgment. Integrity is being true to you.

What stupidity are you using to create the vibrational entrainment with the disintegrous realities other people are using are you choosing? Everything that is times a godzillion, will you destroy and uncreate it all? Right and Wrong, Good and Bad, POD and POC, All Nine, Shorts, Boys, and Beyonds.

Class Participant:

Does this come back to what you were saying about demons? Are you saying that when I'm around people and I make them greater than me, I'm inviting demons?

Gary:

If you make anyone greater than you instead of just different than you, you have to determine whether you're being a follower. Truth, are you a good follower? I said "truth" before I asked that question, so you have to admit what's true.

Class Participant:

No, not really.

Gary:

Nope, you're a crap follower, which is why, when you're in a relationship, you always get to the point where you are pissed off. Or you make the other person get pissed off so you can be in the rightness of you.

Class Participant:

Can we change that now?

Gary:

Everything you've done to have that as your reality, will you destroy and uncreate it all? Right and Wrong, Good and Bad, POD and POC, All Nine, Shorts, Boys, and Beyonds.

What would it be like if you were in integrity with you and you were being everything you are with no apology? Would you be more attractive or less attractive?

Class Participant:

Who'd give a fuck?

Gary:

Exactly! You wouldn't give a fuck, and because you wouldn't give a fuck, everybody would find you very desirable. As long as you give a fuck, they'll look at how they can use you, how they can talk you into becoming what they want you to be, and how they can convince you that you should do what they want you to do.

Class Participant:

Thank you for all of that. I just got that energy, and it's "Wow!"

Gary:

Well, guys. I think we're done here.

Class Participants:

Thank you, Gary.

Gary:

All right, my friends, take care. Love you lots. Talk to you soon.

4

BECOME THE KING OF POSSIBILITIES

What if you actually are what you've been pretending not to be?
What if you actually are the king of possibility?

Gary:

Hello, gentlemen. Dr. Dain is with us today.

The Eternal Season of Discontent

Dain:

Hello everyone. I'm happy to be on this call. I have to say that before we started doing these calls, I was as resistant to connecting with other men as you guys are, so I think something is changing in our world. Something is definitely changing in mine. I hope it's changing in yours too.

On the one hand, you know you're here to change things in the world; on the other hand, there's a familiar discontent that comes up in the presence of other men. You think it won't be there with women, but it's even more magnified with women. You don't want to see it because women tend to have other attributes you find…interesting, shall we say.

Gary:

What stupidity are you using to create the inventions, the artificial intensities, and the demons of the eternal season of discontent you are choosing? Everything that is times a godzillion, will you destroy and uncreate it all? Right and Wrong, Good and Bad, POD and POC, All Nine, Shorts, Boys, and Beyonds.

Dain:

Oh, the joy.

Gary:

Oh, the misery.

Dain:

I wonder what we could actually create together if we got over the idea that our separation was more valuable to us than the connection of the possibilities we could create.

What stupidity are you using to create the inventions, the artificial intensities, and the demons of the eternal season of discontent you are choosing? Everything that is times a godzillion, will you destroy and uncreate it all? Right and Wrong, Good and Bad, POD and POC, All Nine, Shorts, Boys, and Beyonds.

Class Participant:

What do you mean by *discontent*?

Gary:

It means you're never truly satisfied with anything. You know you're supposed to be, but you don't actually feel that way, and you keep trying to find how you could feel satisfied or how it ought to be that way, because that's the way you're supposed to feel, which actually isn't real to you.

Class Participant:

Oh, that one.

Gary:

It's like believing "Now that I have a woman, I will be happy." You guys are always trying to be content with what you've got and you never are. Why would you want to be content? What would be the value of that?

Class Participant:

It's like there's no good answer to that.

Gary:

Why do you keep seeking contentment instead of awareness? *Contentment* is the idea that you should be satisfied with what you can get. There is not a single one of you who cannot get a golden vagina in your life—and you're supposed to be content with the fact that you have a vagina available to you upon demand. You never ask: What choices do I have here that I haven't even considered?

Everything that brought up times a godzillion, will you destroy and uncreate it all? Right and Wrong, Good and Bad, POD and POC, All Nine, Shorts, Boys, and Beyonds.

Dain:

What stupidity are you using to create the inventions, the artificial intensities, and the demons of the eternal season of discontent you are choosing? Everything that is times a godzillion, will you destroy and uncreate it all? Right and Wrong, Good and Bad, POD and POC, All Nine, Shorts, Boys, and Beyonds.

Gary:

Have you ever noticed that you think you're going to be content when you have a woman in your life—except that seldom works because the woman is dedicated to making sure you are never content? As soon as you're feeling content about things, the woman will say, "Honey, we must have a talk," which means, what? "You're wrong, you're fucked, you're screwed," and not in a good way.

What stupidity are you using to create the inventions, the artificial intensities, and the demons of the eternal season of discontent you are choosing? Everything that is times a godzillion, will you destroy and uncreate it all? Right and Wrong, Good and Bad, POD and POC, All Nine, Shorts, Boys, and Beyonds.

Men think that women are going to be content with them, but they never are. Men are always looking for how they can create contentment with a woman, because they think that once the woman is content, they will finally have contentment, as well. It doesn't work!

A Twisted Discontent That Creates Separation between Men

Dain:

I've noticed a strange energy between men that relates to this. It's like a twisted discontent that creates separation between them and other men. Gary, I know that you don't have it with other guys, but I've noticed that a lot of other guys have it with me. I'll meet a guy and I can perceive that energy.

The best way I can describe it is this: Gary told me that once he was working with a guy, who said, "I have a problem with Dain. I'm competing with him." What Gary finally got with him was that the guy really wanted to have sex with me, and he was creating competition with me from that place. He'd try to bring me down. He'd make me wrong and badmouth me behind my back.

Can you guys imagine what else we would have available to us if this were to totally disappear? I don't know about you, but this is one of the places where I destroy the capacities and potency I have available. It's the ability to walk with my head up high and a sense of ease. I don't claim to have a path through this; I'm just bringing it up because it's something other guys aren't willing to be aware of or talk about. I'm saying, "You know what? It's time to talk about it, it's time to be aware of it, and it's time to fucking change it, because if you're separating from other guys, you're also creating a separation between you and you."

If you woke up tomorrow and you were no longer straight, no longer gay, or no longer whatever sexuality you've defined yourself as, do you realize how much freedom that would create for you? If you didn't have to wake up and do the search for the woman or a search for the man, if you didn't have to do the search for sex, what else could you put your energy into? What could you create and generate that would create a different possibility?

Gary:

And why would you separate you from you? The thing is, in order to have a fixed point of view, you have to create a separation of you from you.

How much of what you've tried to create as your sexuality is actually the place in which you created a necessity of being as unaware of what is possible as you can possibly be? Everything that is times a godzillion, will you destroy and uncreate it all? Right and Wrong, Good and Bad, POD and POC, All Nine, Shorts, Boys, and Beyonds.

Dain:

What stupidity are you using to create personality and sexuality as the choice of all choices for being are you choosing? Everything that is times a godzillion, will you destroy and uncreate it all? Right and Wrong, Good and Bad, POD and POC, All Nine, Shorts, Boys, and Beyonds.

What If There Was No Sense of Need in Your Life?

Gary:

That would be a different place to function from. It would be a recognition that there is no need in your life. When you come out of the sense of need, you no longer have to create a place in which there is limitation. Limitation is based on need. Why? Because need is always about creating the smallest common denominator you can. It's about inventing things. Whenever you invent something, you use it to create an upset.

What invention are you using to create the sexuality you are choosing? Everything that is times a godzillion, will you destroy and uncreate it all? Right and Wrong, Good and Bad, POD and POC, All Nine, Shorts, Boys, and Beyonds.

What invention are you using to create the upset with women you are choosing? Everything that is times a godzillion, will you destroy and uncreate it all? Right and Wrong, Good and Bad, POD and POC, All Nine, Shorts, Boys, and Beyonds.

What stupidity are you using to create the inventions, the artificial intensities, and the demons of the eternal season of discontent you are choosing? Everything that is times a godzillion, will you destroy and uncreate it all? Right and Wrong, Good and Bad, POD and POC, All Nine, Shorts, Boys, and Beyonds.

That sense of discontent is why men are always looking for a new woman. It's why relationships can't exist. You always have to be discontented with what you have. You assume that if you had what you thought you should have, you'd have a different result, which is why you can never be happy with just one woman. And why a woman can never be happy with just you.

Everything that is times a godzillion, will you destroy and uncreate it all? Right and Wrong, Good and Bad, POD and POC, All Nine, Shorts, Boys, and Beyonds.

Dain:

What stupidity are you using to create the inventions, the artificial intensities, and the demons of the eternal season of discontent you are choosing? Everything that is times a godzillion, will you destroy and uncreate it all? Right and Wrong, Good and Bad, POD and POC, All Nine, Shorts, Boys, and Beyonds.

Gary:

How many of you have tried to be content with one woman, yet you are always looking for another woman at the same time?

When I was married, I kept thinking, "There's got to be something greater," then I ran into a past life experience where I had been a famous guy and there was a woman who kept seeking me. I realized I had the point of view that eventually there would be a woman who truly loved me, truly wanted me for me, and truly thought I was wonderful. Unfortunately, that doesn't actually occur. That's the fantasy world of the insanity of possibility rather than the truth of reality.

What stupidity are you using to create the inventions, the artificial intensities, and the demons of the eternal season of discontent you are choosing? Everything that is times a godzillion, will you destroy and uncreate it all? Right and Wrong, Good and Bad, POD and POC, All Nine, Shorts, Boys, and Beyonds.

Luckily none of you guys have had that point of view.

Class Participant:

(Laughter) No.

Gary:

Yeah you have. You're so cute. I love you all.

Dain:

What stupidity are you using to create the inventions, the artificial intensities, and the demons of the eternal season of discontent you are choosing? Everything that is times a godzillion, will you destroy and uncreate it all? Right and Wrong, Good and Bad, POD and POC, All Nine, Shorts, Boys, and Beyonds.

I've got a question. If you see another guy that you judge as being similar to you and you see him choosing more than you, what does that do in your world?

Class Participant:

It makes me feel pathetic.

Dain:

It makes you feel pathetic, and so you create a separation where you're less-than.

Class Participant:

Yes.

Gary:

What invention are you using to create you as less than women are you choosing? Everything that is times a godzillion, will you destroy and uncreate it all? Right and Wrong, Good and Bad, POD and POC, All Nine, Shorts, Boys, and Beyonds.

Class Participant:

Wow.

Dain:

What invention are you using to create you as less than women are you choosing? Everything that is times a godzillion, will you destroy and uncreate it all? Right and Wrong, Good and Bad, POD and POC, All Nine, Shorts, Boys, and Beyonds.

Gary:

Wow, I'm going to change that:

What invention are you using to create you as less valuable than women are you choosing? Everything that is times a godzillion, will you destroy and uncreate it all? Right and Wrong, Good and Bad, POD and POC, All Nine, Shorts, Boys, and Beyonds.

Being Undefended

Dain:

Wow. That about describes it.

What invention are you using to create you as less valuable than women are you choosing? Everything that is times a godzillion, will you destroy and uncreate it all? Right and Wrong, Good and Bad, POD and POC, All Nine, Shorts, Boys, and Beyonds.

There are two other pieces of this you can look at. One is the invention. Ask: What invention am I using to create the problem with approaching women I am choosing?

The other thing is that we defend a position, and if you have anything to defend, you'll have trouble walking up to anyone and having a conversation with them unless you think you're well defended against them.

One of the things that attract women the most is a guy who is willing to be there totally undefended. They say, "Oh my God, where did you come from?" Everyone else goes up to them with the attitude, "Hey, I'm so cool because of this, and I'm so cool because of that. You should see how cool I am." Women are used to that, and there's a certain amount of trickery in it that can be entertaining to them, but you are far more attractive to them when you're there, totally undefended.

Undefended doesn't mean you're a pathetic little wimp. It means you have so much awareness of you available that you don't have to defend against anything. You just walk up and say, "Hi, I know you might kick me in the nuts. I know you may not like me. I know you may laugh at me, but all of that is fine with me because I know once I walk away from here I'm going to have as much of me as I had when I was talking to you." When you have to defend a position, you don't have that as one of your choices.

What defended position are you choosing that you truly could be refusing, that if you refused to defend it, would give you the freedom to be? Everything that is times a godzillion, will you destroy and uncreate it all? Right and Wrong, Good and Bad, POD and POC, All Nine, Shorts, Boys, and Beyonds.

Will She Make Me a Valuable Product?

As long as you're doing the sexuality of things, you don't have the freedom to be. You don't have the freedom or the ease, because most of the time, even before you even think about walking up to somebody, you're looking at, "Does she match all of the criteria that will make me a valuable product?" That's the only reason you talk to her in the first place. Ninety percent of the time, ninety percent of the guys aren't even interested in her. It's more like "Wow, let me see. Will this one make me valuable? Will that one make me valuable? Will that one over there make me valuable?" Not "Wow, this would be fun for me."

We take joy and fun out of the equation and choose to do what will make us valuable. When I was in college a long, long time ago, I met a girl. She was the one girl I knew I definitely could have sex with, and I hadn't had sex in a really long time, so I flirted with her, and I turned her on. She was not a girl who would make me a valuable product. She was fun to have sex with, but she didn't have the qualities that would make me a valuable product, so after we had sex, I tried to get her out of the house without waking anybody up so they wouldn't…

Gary:

Realize how ugly she was?

Dain:

Yeah, so they wouldn't realize how ugly she was and how mean she turned out to be. The thing I realized in that was "This has nothing to do with me having fun. I'm looking for a pre-determined outcome and I'm trying to find someone who matches it. It has nothing to do with me and nothing to do with her." How much of your sex and relationships have you created from that place?

The Avoidance of the Joy of Sex and Copulation

Gary:

What stupidity are you using to create the absolute and total avoidance of the joy of sex and copulation are you choosing? Everything that is times a godzillion, will you destroy and uncreate it all? Right and Wrong, Good and Bad, POD and POC, All Nine, Shorts, Boys, and Beyonds.

Back in the 1970s, I met a girl from Sweden. The Swedes were supposedly so much more sexually free than anybody else in the world that I thought we'd have a fun time together—except she was so frigging judgmental and rigid in her points of view. Where's the freedom in that?

Class Participant:

The avoidance of the joy of sex and copulation. Is this about the standards of morality and all the other crap that show up in my universe?

Gary:

Everyone has the standards. They all have the morality. Luckily for you if you're cute enough, you can overcome all standards and all morality. But if you aren't cute enough and sexy enough, you can't overcome them. One day I want to teach you how to walk so you can overcome your own rigidity.

Class Participant:

What do you mean?

Gary:

You don't walk like you're enjoying your body or you really want to fuck. You don't walk like you really want to have sex. You look like you're the image of what would want to have sex, not *somebody who actually likes sex.*

You eliminate a certain kind of energy flow in the body so that you cannot be that which invites the *joy of sex.* You can only be that which invites the *possibility of sex.* So you invite the possibility and then you get to have two or three women a night, which is fine. It's great. It's wonderful, but where are you in the computation?

Class Participant:

That's right. I'm not even there.

Gary:

That's the part that has to change.

What stupidity are you using to create you as the prince charming who never gets laid are you choosing? Everything that is times a godzillion, will you destroy and uncreate it all? Right and Wrong, Good and Bad, POD and POC, All Nine, Shorts, Boys, and Beyonds.

What invention are you using to avoid being the king you are choosing? Everything that is times a godzillion, will you destroy and uncreate it all? Right and Wrong, Good and Bad, POD and POC, All Nine, Shorts, Boys, and Beyonds.

The Turn-On You Are

How many of you, when you were a kid, got inappropriately aroused at different times without having a clue why you were aroused?

Class Participant:

Yes. Lots of times.

Gary:

Yeah.

Everything you did to suppress and repress all of that, will you destroy and uncreate all of that? Right and Wrong, Good and Bad, POD and POC, All Nine, Shorts, Boys, and Beyonds.

The reason you get aroused is because you arouse others. When you are the sexual energy of you, you arouse sexual energy in other people's bodies. You turn other people on, and because you turn them on, you get turned on, or at least your body does.

How much of the turn-on you've received at one time or another is a place where you invalidated your awareness of the turn-on you were and the turn-on other people were toward you? Everything that is times a godzillion, will you destroy and uncreate it all? Right and Wrong, Good and Bad, POD and POC, All Nine, Shorts, Boys, and Beyonds.

There's serious unconsciousness attached to that. When I was fifteen, I used to get turned on in my algebra class every day, and the teacher would call on me. What's the turn-on in algebra? For years, I thought I was just frigging strange that algebra made me horny. And then one day I looked at it and said, "Wow!" I didn't realize my math teacher was gay and I was a turn-on to him. Once I was hard, he would try to get me to stand up and go to the blackboard to do an equation.

Everywhere you're unwilling to acknowledge the fact that you're just as horny as you were when you were fifteen, and everything you've done to try and suppress and repress it, will you destroy and uncreate all of that? Right and Wrong, Good and Bad, POD and POC, All Nine, Shorts, Boys, and Beyonds.

Class Participant:

I've got a question. Sometimes when I'm with a woman and there's a really nice space between us, I get an erection. It creates a really funky, weird place in my universe like "I'm not a man here."

Gary:

So when you're out with a woman and there's a really nice space between you but you're not turned on, do you ever acknowledge that she may not be willing to have sex? Or that she's willing to have sex, but you and your body have no desire? You think that if a woman wants you, you have to deliver.

Class Participant:

True.

Gary:

That's because you're a complete and total slut.

Dain:

Gary said it like it's a bad thing, but I don't think it is.

Gary:

I do not have a point of view that being a slut is a bad thing, but unless you acknowledge that you're a slut, when somebody wants you, you'll go there no matter what they look like. Dain was talking about the girl that he had sex with because he knew it would be easy. Easy means it doesn't cost you anything, so you go there. You guys keep trying to say, "Yes, but she must meet my standards." Your standards are the things you use to avoid what you could choose.

What invention of standards are you using to avoid what you could be choosing that would be easy and fun? Everything that is times a godzillion, will you destroy and uncreate it all? Right and Wrong, Good and Bad, POD and POC, All Nine, Shorts, Boys, and Beyonds.

Class Participant:

This thing about thinking that you have to deliver, does that have to do with a standard too?

Gary:

No, that has to do more with being a prince charming. If you're not married, you have to be a prince. Once you're married, you're a slave. You never get to be king.

Class Participant:

Unfortunately.

Gary:

What stupidity are you using to avoid being the king you could be choosing? The nice thing about being a king is that kings can be dirty, they can be smelly, they can be all kinds of things, and they still get whatever they want.

Everything that is times a godzillion, will you destroy and uncreate it all? Right and Wrong, Good and Bad, POD and POC, All Nine, Shorts, Boys, and Beyonds.

Class Participant:

We're talking about hard-ons and erections and feeling sexual. I had my bars run yesterday by an older lady, and I had a really nice erection while she was running my bars. This happens a lot of times. Does this mean that she would like to have sex with me? Or is it that I'm arousing her or that I'm aroused by her? What do you make of that?

Dain:

Yes.

Gary:

That's correct, yes. I'm sorry. You're a man. You have a penis. You're breathing. You want to get an erection. It's a given. When are you most useful? When you're hard as a rock. When are you useless? When you're not. Most men try to avoid that kind of sexual energy. The older lady was looking at you and thinking, "Could I please have this?" and your body went, "Ooh, thanks. Here, I'll show you how good it would be," so you got a hard-on. It's not that you wanted her. It's the fact that she wanted you and you were willing to receive it from her because she's not your standard.

Dain:

It's also part of the energy of living. When you're living, you're turned on. When you're dying, you're not. Most people on the planet are dying, so we don't know what it is to be turned on as a matter of course and a matter of life and living. Really, it is the energy of living no matter how much someone or something else has tried to beat it out of you.

Class Participant:

Going back to when we were fifteen, I used to get hard-ons all the time—on the bus, going home on the train, wherever. I was just turned on by life and living. Now it seems to be more irregular. It doesn't happen as much. It would be great to go back to that time when I got hard-ons more regularly and I was more aroused by life and living.

The Ultimate Arousal

Gary:

Yes, that's the ultimate arousal—life and living. The ultimate arousal is someone who's willing to live. The older lady was willing to live and she looked at you as a possibility for living even better. When you're fifteen, there are a lot of people who lust after you and you don't notice because you're not supposed to notice that kind of stuff; you think it means you'd have to do something about it. But it doesn't mean you have to do anything about it. It just means that people are lusting after you.

How much energy are you using to make sure lust never comes after you and never permeates your life, your living, your reality, or your hard-on? Everything that is times a godzillion, will you destroy and uncreate it all? Right and Wrong, Good and Bad, POD and POC, All Nine, Shorts, Boys, and Beyonds.

Dain:

It would be bad if you actually had lust permeate your reality again. When you were a teenager, it was out of control. And you were like Gary in his algebra class, going, "Oh my God!" He was thinking, "Oh no! Got another hard-on," and then of course, the teacher would call on him and he'd think, "No! I don't understand math."

Gary:

"I don't know the answer. I have no idea. No, I can't do that problem." I made myself inept in that area of my life. I was algebraically challenged because I didn't want to stand up and show my hard-on.

Dain:

What would have been cool is living in a reality where he could have stood up and showed his hard-on. "Hey, I have a cool thing going on right now. I have such a hard-on I am just about to lose it all over everyone. What was it you wanted to know about quadratic equations again?" What if we lived in a reality where that were possible? When you consider that possibility, you realize how far we are from being able to have and be whatever is going on for us and our bodies at the moment. We are so dynamically cut off from our bodies. If we didn't have to do that, what else would be possible?

Gary:

What invention am I using to avoid the hard-on I could be choosing? Everything that is times a godzillion, will you destroy and uncreate it all? Right and Wrong, Good and Bad, POD and POC, All Nine, Shorts, Boys, and Beyonds.

Class Participant:

This call is making me feel really turned on.

Gary:

If you had a hard-on for life and living, would that give you more creation and more generation than you currently have?

Class Participant:

Oh, hell yeah!

Gary:

If you're not willing to have that place where lust, the joy of living, and the joy of copulation are part of your reality, you're not willing to have a way of living in a generative and creative capacity. An orgasmic quality of living comes from a willingness to have the intensity of lust and the creative juices that come with orgasm.

What invention are you using to avoid the hard-on you could be choosing? Everything that is times a godzillion, will you destroy and uncreate it all? Right and Wrong, Good and Bad, POD and POC, All Nine, Shorts, Boys, and Beyonds.

Have any of you noticed you might be getting just a little bit excited about life and living?

Class Participant:

Yes.

Gary:

How many of you have noticed that when you have a hard-on, it makes you really feel good?

Dain:

It's kind of a happy time. It's like "Oh, hi!"

Gary:

It's a happy, sloppy time.

Dain:

What stupidity are you using to create the inventions, the artificial intensities, and the demons of the eternal season of discontent are you choosing? Everything that is times a godzillion, will you destroy and uncreate it all? Right and Wrong, Good and Bad, POD and POC, All Nine, Shorts, Boys, and Beyonds.

What invention are you using to avoid the hard-on you could be choosing? Everything that is times a godzillion, will you destroy and uncreate it all? Right and Wrong, Good and Bad, POD and POC, All Nine, Shorts, Boys, and Beyonds.

What invention are you using to create the suppression and repression of sexual energy are you choosing? Everything that is times a godzillion, will you destroy and uncreate it all? Right and Wrong, Good and Bad, POD and POC, All Nine, Shorts, Boys, and Beyonds.

What invention are you using to create you as "not the king" are you choosing? Everything that is times a godzillion, will you

destroy and uncreate it all? Right and Wrong, Good and Bad, POD and POC, All Nine, Shorts, Boys, and Beyonds.

What stupidity are you using to create you as the prince charming that never gets laid are you choosing? Everything that is times a godzillion, will you destroy and uncreate it all? Right and Wrong, Good and Bad, POD and POC, All Nine, Shorts, Boys, and Beyonds.

Gary:

Well, you would add that part! You only get laid by princesses instead of anybody who's smart enough to have fun with you. You know, princesses are all virgins and they don't know how to give—and they certainly don't know how to give blow jobs.

Everything that is times a godzillion, will you destroy and uncreate it all? Right and Wrong, Good and Bad, POD and POC, All Nine, Shorts, Boys, and Beyonds.

Dain:

What invention are you using to create you as less valuable than the women you are choosing? Everything that is times a godzillion, will you destroy and uncreate it all? Right and Wrong, Good and Bad, POD and POC, All Nine, Shorts, Boys, and Beyonds.

What invention are you using to avoid the hard-on you could be choosing? Everything that is times a godzillion, will you destroy and uncreate it all? Right and Wrong, Good and Bad, POD and POC, All Nine, Shorts, Boys, and Beyonds.

Gary:

Did you notice how excited your body got when we ran that one?

Class Participant:

Yes.

Gary:

So whatever you do, don't put that on a loop and listen to it for the next thirty days. Please don't do that, or you may find yourself getting excited about life and living in general.

Dain:

And that would be bad.

Gary:

When you're fifteen, you're excited about life and depressed at the same time. You're grateful when you have a hard-on, and the rest of it seems less important as long as you have a hard-on. What if you used that as a generative energy in your life instead of a wrongness?

What invention are you using to avoid the hard-on you could be choosing? Everything that is times a godzillion, will you destroy and uncreate it all? Right and Wrong, Good and Bad, POD and POC, All Nine, Shorts, Boys, and Beyonds.

Sex Is a Life Force

Class Participant:

That's like my life at the moment. When I'm not having sex, or not masturbating, or not having a hard-on, everything else seems to pale in significance.

Gary:

Yes I know. Why is that? Do you have any clue?

Class Participant:

No, why is that?

Gary:

When you get a hard-on, you get the life force that exists with you and your body. Sex is a life force. It's something that gives you the awareness of possibilities of creating and generating beyond the limits of this reality—but that's not the way it's presented to us in this reality. It's presented as a rightness or a wrongness, not as an energy that insists on life and living. Sex is treated as something that requires us to limit life and living.

Class Participant:

This is doing my head in.

Gary:

That's a good thing. Now if it did both your big head and your little head in…

Dain:

That would be awesome.

Gary:

Everything that brought up times a godzillion, will you destroy and uncreate it all? Right and Wrong, Good and Bad, POD and POC, All Nine, Shorts, Boys, and Beyonds.

What invention are you using to override your little head with your big head are you choosing?

Class Participant:

I've got a big head. Which one are you talking about?

Gary:

Both of them. If your little head is as big as your big head, you need to be doing porn flicks, dude.

Dain:

What invention are you using to override your little head with your big head you are choosing? Everything that is times a godzillion, will you destroy and uncreate it all? Right and Wrong, Good and Bad, POD and POC, All Nine, Shorts, Boys, and Beyonds.

What invention are you using to avoid the expanding of your agenda you could be choosing? Everything that is times a godzillion, will you destroy and uncreate it all? Right and Wrong, Good and Bad, POD and POC, All Nine, Shorts, Boys, and Beyonds.

Seeing You as Valuable

Class Participant:

Lately I've been waiting for women to choose instead of choosing for me. Will these clearings help with that?

Gary:

The clearing about being valuable, "What invention are you using to create women as more valuable than you are you choosing?" will create the most change. This is where you can change the places where you look to how the woman is valuable instead of you. You don't see you as valuable.

Class Participant:

I know.

Gary:

When you don't see you as valuable, you come at women with a disgusting, slutty kind of energy that is pernicious and not nice. It gives women the point of view that you're some kind of pervert. It's not an invitation for them to come to you. It's like you're trying to go to them. Does that make sense?

Class Participant:

I met a woman and in the beginning, I was the valuable product. I was pulling energy and I was just me, and then after a while it was "Oh, I'm back to my old patterns again." I don't know how to get around that.

Gary:

You might want to run:

What invention am I using to create the problem with this lady I am choosing? Everything that is times a godzillion, will you destroy and uncreate it all? Right and Wrong, Good and Bad, POD and POC, All Nine, Shorts, Boys, and Beyonds.

What Will It Take for This Relationship to Work?

Class Participant:

Thank you. I listened to a Gentlemen's Club call from Australia, and somebody asked, "How do I create a relationship?" You said something like, "The woman creates her idea of the relationship and the man creates his idea of the relationship, and if they try to make them go together, it doesn't work."

Gary:

Basically what it boils down to is this: You try to see how you fit into the woman's world in order to create a relationship with her. She tries to see how you could fit into her world, which is relationship to her, and none of it is about being present with "What's actually going to work here?"

You begin to invent beautiful, romantic pictures of the two of you together. You're smiling and kissing, and everything is perfect. You say, "Oh, she's perfect. This is going to be perfect." Are those questions? No! "Everything's going to work out fine. I can't wait to see how this works out." None of it is a question. The invention of the idea of a perfect relationship is not the awareness of the relationship you actually do have. You're creating an upset for you or an upset for her, one of the two, rather than seeing what's actually possible.

You've got to ask:

- What will it take for this relationship to work?
- What's going on here and what would I like this to be?

The Subtlety of Awareness You Actually Have

Dain:

It's based on conclusion rather than the subtlety of awareness you actually have. You have a subtlety of awareness. It's the awareness of every subtlety of energy that is. It's an awareness of what is possible, what is not possible, what's possible with someone, and what isn't.

We've been taught to go to conclusion instead of awareness, and when you go to conclusion, you cut off all of the subtleties of awareness that you have; you cut off all you can see and all you can perceive. All you can do is function from the conclusion you have. When you think about a girl, if you allow yourself to ask a question, you'll have a lightness, you'll have a heaviness, or you'll have a sort of twisting thing that goes on, and you can ask, "Okay, is this the subtlety of my awareness?" If it is, then it becomes detective work to find out what that something is. If you see that you've come to a lot of conclusions, you can ask: What can I change now to make this different? Or is this even capable of being changed?

Gary:

This is the question you have to go to. Most guys go to conclusion: "Oh, this woman is wonderful. This woman is great. She's everything I ever wanted," and what question is that?

Class Participant:

None.

Gary:

Not having question is more real to us. We invent the idea that this is the way something has to be rather than asking, "What can this be? What would I really like it to be that I haven't even perceived?"

Class Participant:

Recently I was listening to *The Place* for the second time, and I just cried. It was "I know this is possible. How the hell do I get there?"

Gary:

Yeah, I know. For me, that's the reality too. Ask: What is really possible I haven't considered here?

Dain:

And what if it were possible to actually create it as a living, breathing reality rather than all of the stuff we've tried to make real that we all know is not real?

The Hard-On You Could Be Choosing

Gary:

What invention are you using to avoid the hard-on you could be choosing? Everything that is times a godzillion, will you destroy and uncreate it all? Right and Wrong, Good and Bad, POD and POC, All Nine, Shorts, Boys, and Beyonds.

Why is that the question that creates the most joy in your bodies?

Dain:

That's the one that just keeps going, and going, and going.

Gary:

The gift that keeps on giving. A hard-on.

Dain:

What invention are you using to avoid the hard-on you could be choosing? Everything that is times a godzillion, will you destroy and uncreate it all? Right and Wrong, Good and Bad, POD and POC, All Nine, Shorts, Boys, and Beyonds.

Gary:

Isn't that amazing? *Being* a hard-on, even more than *having* a hard-on, is what the reality is. When you have a hard-on, it is the one time you're most willing to go after something like having a greater life. You're always looking for "Where can I put this thing? What else can I do with this?" The only time you go into question is when you have a hard-on.

Dain:

But it's also the one time you go into absolutely no question.

Gary:

It's the time where you come to serious frigging conclusions, as well.

Class Participant:

It's a very strong demand when you have a hard-on.

Gary:

Yes. It's a very strong demand. What if you were willing to have your desire and not your demand? What would that be like?

Gary:

If you used that same energy to create a different possibility, what would life be like?

Dain:

What invention are you using to avoid the hard-on you could be choosing? Everything that is times a godzillion, will you destroy and uncreate it all? Right and Wrong, Good and Bad, POD and POC, All Nine, Shorts, Boys, and Beyonds.

This could be the process that runs forever.

Gary:

This is the forever process. Put this on a loop, especially if you're sleeping next to a woman. She might get a hard-on and get after you in the morning. If she gets a hard-on and it's a hard-on in her clit, she'll want to have sex with you.

What invention are you using to avoid the hard-on you could be choosing? Everything that is times a godzillion, will you destroy and uncreate it all? Right and Wrong, Good and Bad, POD and POC, All Nine, Shorts, Boys, and Beyonds.

I can feel all of your bodies saying, "Yeah! Yeah! Yeah!" Do you realize how much of your body you're trying to turn off? That's how we create aging. That's why you're never an eternal boy—you're using the turning off of your hard-on to age your body and make it less real and less valuable to have one. Do you want to youthenize? Run this process.

Dain:

What invention are you using to create the avoidance of the hard-on you could be choosing? Everything that is times a godzillion, will you destroy and uncreate it all? Right and Wrong, Good and Bad, POD and POC, All Nine, Shorts, Boys, and Beyonds.

That's interesting. We were doing "What stupidity are you using?" now we're doing "What invention are you using?"

Gary:

You've made yourself unaware of things, but now it's not just the unawareness that we choose; it's the place where we invent things we have chosen as somehow more real than our capacity to choose something different, so that's part of it, but it's slightly different too.

What invention are you using to avoid the hard-on you could be choosing? Everything that is times a godzillion, will you destroy and uncreate it all? Right and Wrong, Good and Bad, POD and POC, All Nine, Shorts, Boys, and Beyonds.

Any of you feel like you have more blood coursing through your body?

Class Participant:

There's something about suppressing the life energy, and all of that that comes up because it would be inappropriate to have a hard-on all of the time.

Gary:

You are wrong. It would not be inappropriate for you to have a hard-on all the time. It would be an invitation for more women to use you.

Dain:

Aha.

Gary:

If you don't have a hard-on, you're not useful, are you?

Class Participant:

No.

Gary:

If you don't avoid the hard-on you are, you become a more useful person in other people's lives, and in order for you to see yourself as not valuable you have to become useless, right? So you might get that avoiding the hard-on you could be choosing is affecting all areas of your life.

Class Participant:

It totally does. It's like I am keeping it until it can be unleashed in the appropriate moment. Not all of life. Like the image of standard morality in men.

Gary:

Like having a hard-on for life is different from having a sexually hard rod, as it were. There are so many areas of your life that you suppress because it is not acceptable for you to have a hard-on. You won't let yourself have that enthusiastic element in your life and living, which means you won't allow yourself to be.

Class Participant:

Exactly. Wow.

Gary:

What invention are you using to avoid the hard-on you could be choosing? Everything that is times a godzillion, will you destroy and uncreate it all? Right and Wrong, Good and Bad, POD and POC, All Nine, Shorts, Boys, and Beyonds.

If you're willing to be a hard-on, you're willing to be the energy that creates a hard-on. You're being the energy that creates and generates. If you're being less than that, you're trying to institute whatever the woman wants you to do or be, which isn't choosing to be you.

This is the place where men cut themselves off from being an energy that gives what can be received but doesn't have to give what

BECOME THE KING OF POSSIBILITIES   133

can't be received, which is what you are if you're willing to be that hard-on. If you're not willing to be that, then you have to defend her point of view, refuse to give what she can receive, and refuse to be what can be received.

If you're willing to be the kind of energy that is an invitation—because having a hard-on is an invitation. If the person can receive it, great. If the person can't receive it, is it wrong that you have a hard-on?

For some reason you don't seem to get that being a hard-on is an invitation. It doesn't mean that people have to take it. It just means it's an invitation. What if you were just hot and that was the beginning of the possibility of the energy of sex, copulation, and the hard dick? If you had that kind of energy of being "I'm ready to go when you're ready to go" would that be a different energy and a different invitation than "There's something wrong with me because I have a hard dick"?

Class Participant:

Yeah. Can you talk more about that?

Gary:

Yeah. You have that available to you when you're willing to have that kind of energy flow. But you've turned it into "a hard dick to be able to fuck somebody." You have to be willing to create what will create something greater.

Step into the Role of the King

Dain:

When you are willing to create something greater, you take yourself out of the role of the prince. The prince is the one who gets to play around and let the world happen around him, and if he gets laid, he's happy and that's enough. You have to step into the role of the king. That's where you realize it's up to you to create the reality around you. Nobody else is going to do it for you. Nobody else is going to be responsible for you. They will try to bring you down and they will judge you, but it's irrelevant. You're the fucking king. And so instead of living your life believing that you are flotsam and jetsam and that as long as you get laid, everything is okay, you ask, "What am I creating here?"

If you're willing to be the king and the hard-on that you've been refusing to be, you realize you are a creative force and a creative control in the world that you've been refusing to be. If you look at how much crap we do about women—whether they like us, whether we're getting laid, whether somebody else is getting laid more than we are, whether we're getting laid less, and blah, blah, blah—all of that is the crap we use to keep us from being the creative, generative being we actually are.

What invention are you using to create you as not the creative, generative source, force, and control you could be choosing? Everything that is times a godzillion, will you destroy and uncreate it all? Right and Wrong, Good and Bad, POD and POC, All Nine, Shorts, Boys, and Beyonds.

Gary:

There's something else we need to add: "source, force, control, and generative energy."

Dain:

What stupidity are you using to create the inventions, the artificial intensities, and the demons of never being the creative, generative, source, force, control, contribution, and generative capacity you are choosing? Everything that is times a godzillion, will you destroy and uncreate it all? Right and Wrong, Good and Bad, POD and POC, All Nine, Shorts, Boys, and Beyonds.

Class Participant:

Wow. That one is a rocket.

Class Participant:

Is this also connected to the image thing?

Gary:

You try to create yourself as somebody who *looks like* rather than somebody *who is.* You want to look like a shag master. You want to look like what you think a woman is going to want. You want to look like somebody who is successful. You want to look like somebody who is valuable, but *being* those things and *looking like* them are two different worlds.

What If You Were Willing to Be the King of Possibilities?

Dain:

You have to be aware that the world is going to look at you in all kinds of different ways. People, are going to look at you in all kinds of ways. You have to know what your aim is, what your target is, and what's actually true for you.

I don't know about you guys, but I've been doing the prince charming thing for a long time. It seemed like an ideal place to be, and I'm realizing at this point that it's not enough for me. I don't know if it's enough for you. I don't know if you've looked at the place I was functioning from and said, "Wow, that would be enough for me. Let me take his spot."

What if you could realize that in your own world, even in comparing yourselves to whomever you compare yourselves to—the comparisons to me, the comparisons to Gary, the comparisons to anybody else? Are those enough for you? Maybe there's something far greater in being the creative, generative source, force, control, and capacity we are that takes us beyond the prince thing we've been doing, where we're happy to have any woman who will have us.

What if we were being the king of possibilities?

Gary:

Oh! Good one!

What stupidity are you using to create the invention and the artificial intensity of avoiding being the king of possibilities you could be choosing? Everything that is times a godzillion, will you destroy and uncreate it all? Right and Wrong, Good and Bad, POD and POC, All Nine, Shorts, Boys, and Beyonds.

Have I told you how much I love it when you open your mouth, Dain?

Class Participant:

Is this also where we create separation and competition between men, when we look at someone else and say, "Ooh, wow!" and we make ourselves smaller?

Dain:

Yes, because if you realized you were the king of possibilities, you would have a totally different view of you. It would be "I'm sorry. I would compete with whom?" You'd be able to see where other kings in their own right could be a contribution, a gifting, and a receiving in this creative, generative capacity and the force, source, and control of something different.

We don't usually use the words *force, source,* and *control* as something to embrace, but this is a place where we men haven't been willing to embrace our natural capacities. If you did embrace those capacities, what else would be possible? And what if the way out of the competition you've been doing with me, other men in Access Consciousness, or men outside of Access is to recognize that you have a greater capacity than you've been willing to acknowledge? What if you actually are what you've been pretending not to be? What if you actually are the king of possibilities? And if you are willing to be that, would that eliminate the competition with other men in your world?

Gary:

There is no real competition. Competition is a lie. Competition is what you do on the playing field for sports. More than anything else, competition between men is a way you never have to claim the totality of you. It's a way you guarantee you don't have to choose the greatness of you. It is a place where you get to choose against other men as though doing that is finding you, rather than seeing what's actually possible and how you could work for you.

Have you ever had the experience of working with another man, and it was so cohesive and easy that you got everything done really quickly?

Class Participant:

Yeah.

Gary:

That's because there is no real competition. If there were, there would never be a situation where men could cooperate with one another. And I see many instances of men cooperating with men very easily. What would it be like if you were willing to have a whole different world? I'd like you all to put this on a loop:

What energy, space, and consciousness can I be that would allow me to be the king of possibilities I truly be for all eternity? Everything that doesn't allow that times a godzillion, will you destroy and uncreate it all? Right and Wrong, Good and Bad, POD and POC, All Nine, Shorts, Boys, and Beyonds.

Dain:

Let's play, gentlemen. Let's create a different reality.

Gary:

Yeah. Let's have a whole bunch of kings of possibilities instead of queens of stupidity.

Dain:

And princes of inanity.

Gary:

And princes of invisibility.

Dain:

So please run these processes, guys. Thank you so much for you. What else is possible for us to create together?

Gary:

Thanks so much for being on this call. You guys rock.

Class Participants:

Thank you!

5

THE PHENOMENAL SEX, COPULATION, AND RELATIONSHIP YOU COULD BE CHOOSING

If you were willing to work from the point of view of the greatest possibility and the greatest choice rather than from the wrongness of your point of view, what else might be possible?

Gary:

Hello, gentlemen.

Creating Demon-Augmented Occurrences

Recently Dain and I noticed that when women go after men, the guys cut off their awareness in order to get laid. They never question whether it's what they want or whether it will make their life better.

You say things like, "Well, it just happened," "I couldn't help myself," "I slipped," or "It occurred by accident," but that's not the way it is. You think that if it can occur, it *should* occur; therefore, you invite demons in to make sure it *does* occur.

What stupidity are you using to create the demon-augmented occurrences you are choosing? Everything that is times a godzillion, will you destroy and uncreate it all? Right and Wrong, Good and Bad, POD and POC, All Nine, Shorts, Boys, and Beyonds.

Class Participant:

What do you mean by "invite demons in"?

Gary:

You must invite demons in, in order to create the power you have as powerlessness. None of you have been powerless in the face of your dick, have you?

Class Participant:

Yeah.

Gary:

It's like you're always powerless. As soon as your dick starts to get filled with energy, it's as if there is no brain available. You have a single digit IQ. This works on other areas of life too. Any time you say, "Well, this just occurred" or "I couldn't help it," you're inviting demons to make sure you're not responsible for anything that occurred. Anywhere you say, "Uh, I don't know how this happened," is a lie. That's what you do to make sure you are not in control and you have no capacity to create anything. You become the effect of everything that occurs around you.

What stupidity are you using to create the demon-augmented occurrences you are choosing? Everything that is times a godzillion, will you destroy and uncreate it all? Right and Wrong, Good and Bad, POD and POC, All Nine, Shorts, Boys, and Beyonds.

Well, the good news is you guys have been demon augmented ever since you got a penis!

Class Participant:

What does *augmented* mean?

Gary:

Augmented means the demons come in and help you with being stupid. They help you with being less aware. They help you put yourself in a bad situation. They help make sure that you don't have any idea what's really going to happen, which is why bad things occur that you're not happy with. It can be with money, it can be with sex—but usually for you guys, it's with sex. I love you all, and you're a bunch of dicks looking for a place to happen.

What stupidity are you using to create the demon-augmented occurrences you are choosing? Everything that is times a godzillion, will you destroy and uncreate it all? Right and Wrong, Good and Bad, POD and POC, All Nine, Shorts, Boys, and Beyonds.

Class Participant:

My partner and I are going our separate ways. We're moving house and stuff. After Dain's Energetic Synthesis of Being class, I was so clear on what I would like to create and generate, and I've come back to move out of the house my partner and I share. But when I walked into the house, I hit a brick wall. Is that a demon-augmented occurrence?

Gary:

Are you willing to see what's true for you? And remember I thought "truth" before I asked that.

Class Participant:

I was until I walked into the house, and now I'm unhappy.

Gary:

Yeah, because you have realized what you've been living with the whole time.

Class Participant:

Yeah.

Gary:

Once you get clear that you want to do something else, you suddenly become aware, finally, of all the things you've been shutting out of your awareness in order to maintain what you have. You have the occurrence of the relationship as it is, where you cut off your awareness to make sure you continue to have something the way it is.

Class Participant:

So I'm just more aware of where I've stuck myself?

Gary:

Yeah. You're aware of what you were refusing to be aware of before. Any time your penis is involved, any time you go into relationship of any kind, you go to the believable and credible relationship. You don't choose the unreal and unbelievable relationship. Why is it that you want a relationship that is credible and believable?

Class Participant:

Yeah, that just hooks you back into this reality.

Gary:

Yeah. It brings you back into this reality. It sticks you with this reality instead of giving you a choice of a different reality. Why would you not want a different choice?

Class Participant:

Oh, I do.

Gary:

If you had choice, if you were actually choosing and you had choice and awareness, you wouldn't let demon-augmented occurrences take control of your life. But you let demon-augmented occurrences control your life. You say, "Oh, I lost this money. I fell out of this money." You act like there is no choice when there is.

What stupidity are you using to create the demon-augmented occurrences you are choosing? Everything that is times a godzillion, will you destroy and uncreate it all? Right and Wrong, Good and Bad, POD and POC, All Nine, Shorts, Boys, and Beyonds.

What stupidity are you using to defend against the unreal, unbelievable, fantastic, and phenomenal sex, copulation, and relationships you could be choosing? Everything that is times a godzillion, will you destroy and uncreate it all? Right and Wrong, Good and Bad, POD and POC, All Nine, Shorts, Boys, and Beyonds.

Wow, you guys really don't want to have anything that's not ordinary, do you?

What stupidity are you using to create the defense against the unreal, unbelievable, fantastic, and phenomenal sex, copulation, and relationships you could be choosing? Everything that is times a godzillion, will you destroy and uncreate it all? Right and Wrong, Good and Bad, POD and POC, All Nine, Shorts, Boys, and Beyonds.

What stupidity are you using to create the demon-augmented occurrences you are choosing? Everything that is times a godzillion, will you destroy and uncreate it all? Right and Wrong, Good and Bad, POD and POC, All Nine, Shorts, Boys, and Beyonds.

It Didn't "Just Happen"

When you suddenly decide you want to have sex with somebody, it's not an accident. It's not something that just occurred. It didn't just happen. Those women go after you. Is that at all real to you? I watch people. The other day in a class, I watched a woman go after a guy. It was obvious she was after him, and it was ridiculously ugly the way things were being done. He couldn't see it at all because demons augmented the occurrence. He didn't have a clue that he could actually induce his own death by the choice he was making.

Class Participant:

Do we choose that from the moment a girl starts going after us?

Gary:

Yeah. You choose it when she starts putting her snail tracks on you. This guy and girl were going out to lunch. I saw them and I thought, "Oh, poor sucker. He is doomed." This girl was mean and evil and I knew she was going to do mean and evil things to him. But his agenda got hard, his brain went away, and he had a demon-augmented occurrence called "the love of the sex." He shined everybody else on to be with her. Everything he promised to do for others, he refused to do. Everything he said he was going to accomplish, everything that made up his business, his life, and his friendships with everybody in the world was lost in favor of the golden vagina that was sliming all over his world.

Class Participant:

Wow.

Gary:

Everything that is times a godzillion, will you destroy and uncreate it all? Right and Wrong, Good and Bad, POD and POC, All Nine, Shorts, Boys, and Beyonds.

Class Participant:

Have I been using my relationship to defend against women doing that to me?

Gary:

Well, you've been defending against it. First of all it's not whether women do it to you. Men will do it to you too.

Class Participant:

Yeah.

Gary:

You're defending against anything that would give you choice.

Class Participant:

I'm going cross-eyed now. What do you mean by that?

Gary:

If you define yourself as gay or straight, or if you have any particular sexuality, you create a set of judgments to guarantee that definition and make it real. You defend against anything that challenges that or puts you in a place where you could question it.

What if the best relationship you had was with a good friend? Years ago I had a friend I was really close with. We did everything together. It was really fun. He was smart and bright and funny, and we had a great time together. Then he got a girlfriend. He dumped me like some kind of cheap suit, and I said, "Uh, wait a minute! We were so close and now he can't even talk to me?"

They broke up and he called me. He wanted to get together to be friends again. He said, "Hey, let's rev up our friendship."

I said, "No, because the next time you get a girl, you'll dump me again. I'm not interested." He was willing to destroy his friendship with me in order to have an exclusive relationship with a girl. He thought that relationship was the most important.

Are you willing to shine on your friends for the vagina that's currently sliming you? That's what you do, whether you have a commitment to do something or not.

Class Participant:

And even the commitments to yourself.

Gary:

More than anything, the commitments to yourself. Going against what you committed to is like saying, "She's more important. Everything she has is more important than my own life."

Class Participant:

And once you lose that commitment to yourself...

Gary:

That's where you start to bring in death. That's where you induce death. Here's another process I want you guys to run on your own:

What seduction am I using to create the induction of death I am choosing? Everything that is times a godzillion, will you destroy and uncreate it all? Right and Wrong, Good and Bad, POD and POC, All Nine, Shorts, Boys, and Beyonds.

We allow ourselves to be seduced to die. The guy I was just talking about was seduced into giving up all of his other friends, people who had supported him and loved him, in favor of the woman. That's all she cared about. When she left him, she felt like a million dollars; he felt like a pile of shit.

What seduction am I using to create the induction of death I am choosing? Everything that is times a godzillion, will you destroy and uncreate it all? Right and Wrong, Good and Bad, POD and POC, All Nine, Shorts, Boys, and Beyonds.

Please put this on a loop and run it nonstop, gentlemen. You have to get to the place where you're not seduced into giving up your life for a woman just because she wants you.

"I Want Him to Give Up His Life for Me"

Years ago I was doing a class and a couple was there. I asked the woman, "What do you want of him?" and she said, "I want him to give up his life for me."

I said, "What?!" Everyone else in the room said, "Oh, isn't that sweet?"

I said, "Sweet? You want the guy to give up his life for you? Basically you're saying he should do everything you want, he should do whatever you require and desire, and he should have no life of his own."

She said, "Yeah."

This is the way most relationships are created. I asked, "Why do people think this is a good thing?" You have to be willing to see what you really want to have as your reality and what you want to have in a relationship.

Who or what are you willing to give you away to that if you didn't give you away to it, would give you all of you? Everything that is times a godzillion, will you destroy and uncreate it all? Right and Wrong, Good and Bad, POD and POC, All Nine, Shorts, Boys, and Beyonds.

Class Participant:

Do we create the seduction into the induction of death by giving ourselves away?

Gary:

Yeah. You give you away in order to create it.

What stupidity are you using to create the defense against the unreal, unbelievable, fantastic, and phenomenal sex, copulation, and relationships you could be choosing? Everything that is times a godzillion, will you destroy and uncreate it all? Right and Wrong, Good and Bad, POD and POC, All Nine, Shorts, Boys, and Beyonds.

Dain was with a lady the other day. She said, "I think we should spend a couple of days together."

He asked, "Why?"

She said, "So we can get to know each other better."

He said, "But I don't need to do that. I know you." He's willing to know. She was not willing to know. She wanted to spend time together because her point of view was you have to spend time to get to know somebody. What if you didn't have to spend time to get to know somebody? What if you could just know them?

Who or what are you willing to give you away for that if you didn't give you away for it, would give you all of you? Everything that is times a godzillion, will you destroy and uncreate it all? Right and Wrong, Good and Bad, POD and POC, All Nine, Shorts, Boys, and Beyonds.

Class Participant:

When we "spend a couple of days to get to know someone," isn't that where we find ways we can cut ourselves off to fit into their reality?

Gary:

Yeah. That's where you can induce your death in favor of their life.

How many of you would give up your life to have a woman? Everything that is times a godzillion, will you destroy and uncreate it all? Right and Wrong, Good and Bad, POD and POC, All Nine, Shorts, Boys, and Beyonds.

Romance

Class Participant:

Is giving yourself away what they call romance in this reality? Is that what's called romantic?

Gary:

Well, what is called romance is having the fun and the joy of doing what stimulates you and the woman you're with, who creates some illusion that you're going to have something greater. Romance is what you use as a stimulant for creating a woman's response.

I personally like romance. I like dinners and looking into their eyes longingly, giving them flowers, having nice wine and music, talking to them, and asking them questions about themselves nonstop and never telling them anything about me. At the end of the evening when they say, "Wow, you're the most interesting man I've ever met," I know I'm going to get laid. I'm more pragmatic than you guys. I know what my target is. You think your target is to get a woman. How many of you have gotten a woman and then been happy with her afterwards?

You do romance to stimulate a woman to let down her barriers and give you what you want. You don't give yourself up to get the woman. You guys would give up anything to get a vagina. If she says, "I want you to bark like a dog," you'll frigging bark like a dog. You'll do anything she asks because she has the vagina.

How much of you have you given up your whole life for a vagina? Everything that is times a godzillion, will you destroy and uncreate it all? Right and Wrong, Good and Bad, POD and POC, All Nine, Shorts, Boys, and Beyonds.

Who or what are you willing to give you up for, that if you weren't willing to give you up for it, would allow you to have all of you? Everything that is times a godzillion, will you destroy and uncreate it all? Right and Wrong, Good and Bad, POD and POC, All Nine, Shorts, Boys, and Beyonds.

"I Seem to Attract Married Women"

Class Participant:

I seem to attract married women who are seeking fun times with me and then I go into the wrongness of giving them my body. I go into the wrongness of what it will create afterwards with the husband, and so on. I would like to know what your take on this is and how you would deal with it.

Gary:

Married women who aren't happy in their lives will do anything to get a man they can have sex with. Are they actually going to leave their husbands for you? That would be a no. Why are they doing it? They are choosing you because you're safe and because you're not willing to make a commitment to them. The married women who are coming after you are more masculine in their point of view than they are feminine. Most women will go after another woman's husband. Are you a husband?

Class Participant:

No.

Gary:

Are you just a shag?

Class Participant:

Possibly, yes. I'd like to not go into the wrongness of it and have a bit of fun, but I keep thinking of what it could create afterwards for them and their...

Gary:

Are you a humanoid man?

Class Participant:

I believe so.

Gary:

Humanoid men don't like to go after married women because they don't want to screw up another man's gig.

Class Participant:

Yes.

Gary:

But you've got to look at it for real. Is the gig already screwed up? Yes or no?

Class Participant:

Yes.

Gary:

Is it real that you need to have a problem? Or are you trying to create a problem to justify that you, as the humanoid man you are, can't believe it can be right for you to have sex with a married woman?

Class Participant:

Yep, That's it.

Gary:

You're creating a demon-augmented occurrence. Here's a process you need to run. It will get you clear about the fact that if a married woman comes after you, it's because she has decided she wants out of her marriage and she's looking at you as the source. Now if that were the case, you'd have to have a load of money and a well-paying job and you'd have to appear to be somebody who had more than you have. Would that be accurate?

What seduction are you using to create the induction of death you are choosing?

Everything that is times a godzillion, will you destroy and uncreate it all? Right and Wrong, Good and Bad, POD and POC, All Nine, Shorts, Boys, and Beyonds.

Class Participant:

Well, I've got a really good job.

Gary:

Are you handy eye candy?

Class Participant:

It depends whose eyes are looking at me. Sure. Beauty is in the eye of the beholder. I don't know. I don't know about that. You'd have to ask them.

Gary:

You've got to admit what you are and stop trying to be what you think you're supposed to be. If you're just a dick that gets to be used, then be a dick that gets to be used and enjoy the fuck out of being used. In reality, that's what most young guys are. Married women tend to go after young guys that they consider a dick they can use. Why do they choose handy eye candy? Because they beat their husbands up so much at home that their husbands don't want to have sex anymore.

You have to be bluntly honest with yourself, guys, as to what you are. If you're a slut, you're a slut. It's not a wrongness; it's just something you are. Stop trying to create something that's not real for you. You have to look at what's real for you—not what's real for others.

What seduction are you using to induce the death you are choosing? Everything that is times a godzillion, will you destroy and uncreate it all? Right and Wrong, Good and Bad, POD and POC, All Nine, Shorts, Boys, and Beyonds.

Every time you go into judgment, you go into death. You're inducing death every time you go to judgment.

Are You Giving Up You?

Let's take the friend I was talking about. By the way, this is not Dain. This is a different friend. Everybody always thinks that when I talk about a friend, I'm talking about Dain. No, I'm not. When this guy went for it with that woman, he created upsets with all the people he had agreed to do things with and for. He gave up his own life in favor of her and her point of view of what she wanted. That stopped a lot of the forward motion in his life that was creating money, possibility, and choices. It took him about two years to turn things around.

Every time you choose to go against you, you can be seduced out of what is an awareness for you and you set things up in such a way that you end up giving up everything you've started in favor of what you've got. You lose your entire future when you do that.

What seduction are you using to induce the death you are choosing? Everything that is times a godzillion, will you destroy and uncreate it all? Right and Wrong, Good and Bad, POD and POC, All Nine, Shorts, Boys, and Beyonds.

Class Participant:

Gary, I'm having an "Oh my God" moment. Is that what I've been doing in the last year?

Gary:

Yeah, you've been trying to adjust yourself to the person you're with to make her happy. That's a justification; it is not real. You aren't doing it to make her happy. You're doing it to give you up. You're doing it to kill you. How much of you do you care about? Slim to none.

Class Participant:

Well, obviously I didn't.

Gary:

Everything that is times a godzillion, will you destroy and uncreate it all? Right and Wrong, Good and Bad, POD and POC, All Nine, Shorts, Boys, and Beyonds.

Class Participant:

Will this seduction process help get me back out there in the world to create and generate what I would like?

Gary:

Hopefully. You'll at least start to be able to see what you'd like. You won't be seduced into the idea that "She won't be happy with me if I do this." You won't seduce yourself into not doing something as though that's going to make her happy. It doesn't make her happy. Nothing makes a woman happy except when she decides to be happy. And nothing makes a man happy except giving himself up for a vagina. He thinks he's happy when he does that, but at the end of it, he's fucked up, miserable, and wants to kill himself. How's that working for you, gentlemen?

Class Participant:

Not well!

Gary:

What seduction are you using to induce the death you are choosing? Everything that is times a godzillion, will you destroy and uncreate it all? Right and Wrong, Good and Bad, POD and POC, All Nine, Shorts, Boys, and Beyonds.

Have any of you ever noticed that when you go into relationships, you get into a start-and-stop thing with your whole life? You'll start down some road, get invested in a woman, and then the next thing you know, you're giving up everything you started to create in favor of being with her. Why would you do that?

Who or what are you willing to give yourself away for or to, that if you didn't give yourself away for or to it, would allow you to have all of you? Everything that is times a godzillion, will you destroy and uncreate it all? Right and Wrong, Good and Bad, POD and POC, All Nine, Shorts, Boys, and Beyonds.

Why are you not complete without a woman?

What stupidity are you using to defend against choosing you over a woman or a sex partner are you choosing? Everything that is times a godzillion, will you destroy and uncreate it all? Right and Wrong, Good and Bad, POD and POC, All Nine, Shorts, Boys, and Beyonds.

Choose what you want to choose. Don't choose because she wants you to choose. Choose because you want to choose.

What stupidity are you using to create the seduction of the induction of death are you choosing? Everything that is times a godzillion, will you destroy and uncreate it all? Right and Wrong, Good and Bad, POD and POC, All Nine, Shorts, Boys, and Beyonds.

Inculcation of Realities

Class Participant:

Dain was talking to me the other day about the way I inculcate others' reality. I grab someone's reality and blend it through mine.

Gary:

Inculcating is where you put all of the parts and pieces of both of you together and place them in a blender and try to come out with the two of you being the same. It's the way most people try to create relationships.

We think we have to create a relationship by blending our realities and coming out with something that is palatable to both of us. Except the only part you get is her shit, and the only part she gets is your gold. You'll take her shit in exchange for your gold all the time. What?

Class Participant:

Is that what people do with families as well?

Gary:

That's what people do with families.

Class Participant:

Cults?

Gary:

Cults and religions—and anything where you try to fit in. Unfortunately, most of you are crap at fitting in, because you're way too willing to be leaders rather than followers. In reality, you're all like kittens. Nobody can control you, but you keep trying to pretend that somehow you can be controlled. It doesn't work, but if you're happy with it, fine. If it makes you happy, feel free. Fuck yourselves over and feel good about it.

There's also *exculcating*, which is where, instead of you and your partner trying to blend together all the parts and pieces of yourselves, you try to separate all that stuff. You are the oil and the water instead of the choice.

Intertwining of beingness is where you're so close to somebody that you hear and perceive what they're unwilling to hear and perceive.

Dain and I are very close, and when he refuses to see what's actually possible, I always get to see it and know it.

For me, it's seeing where the person needs to understand what's really going on and look from a different place. For example, I would pick up strange shit from the girls Dain was having sex with about how they didn't want him to be with anybody else. I would think "Oh my God. I don't want Dain to be with anybody else," and then I'd say, "But he's not with me! What is this?"

I knew what he wasn't willing to receive. I'm willing to know a lot of things. I knew that the guy who was in the class was being slimed by the woman. I could see exactly what was going on, but he wouldn't see it no matter what was said to him, so I kept my mouth shut and let him go down the road to killing himself so he could have that opportunity yet again. It wasn't his best choice. You don't want to go down those roads.

Class Participant:

And choice creates awareness.

Gary:

Choice does create awareness. He chose. He got a lot of awareness. It wasn't the awareness he wanted, but he got a lot of awareness.

What stupidity are you using to create the inculcation of realities as relationship are you choosing? Everything that is times a godzillion, will you destroy and uncreate it all? Right and Wrong, Good and Bad, POD and POC, All Nine, Shorts, Boys, and Beyonds.

Years ago when I got divorced, there was a lady who said, "I can't wait until we can spend time together."

I asked, "What do you mean?"

She said, "Well, I figure we'll spend seventy-five percent of our time together from here on out."

I said, "Seventy-five percent of our time? Let's see, in a twenty-four hour day that means I'm spending eighteen hours with you? I don't like to spend eighteen hours with anybody. I don't want to spend eighteen hours with somebody."

How many hours would you actually like to spend with somebody—and to be totally present with them the whole time? If you say more than two and a half hours, you're lying.

Class Participant:

Yeah. Two or three hours.

Class Participant:

Three and a half hours a week.

Gary:

The time you want to spend with someone is about ten percent of the time that you have in a day, because that means you're totally present for them. They're totally present for you. How many of you could be totally present for somebody where you are in no judgment, no conclusion, no consideration, but just being there, totally in question and in presence? How many of you can do that for longer than two and a half hours?

Class Participant:

Two and half hours seems pretty long.

Gary:

Most of you want to be with someone until you cum, then you're ready to go away.

What seduction are you using to induce the death you are choosing? Everything that is times a godzillion, will you destroy and uncreate it all? Right and Wrong, Good and Bad, POD and POC, All Nine, Shorts, Boys, and Beyonds.

Be Honest about Where You Are in Your Life

Gary:

Guys, be honest with yourself. If you're a dick looking for a place to happen, then you're a dick looking for a place to happen. That doesn't make it wrong or right or anything else. It's just that you're a dick looking for a place to happen.

You've got to be honest about where you are in life. What kind of person you are. What's really important to you. What you want to create. If you're willing to do that, you ask, "Okay, how can I use this?" instead of "How can I abuse me with this?" Being a shag master and a slut are considered bad things in this reality, but what if they were the greatest power you had available to you? If you were willing to work from the point of view of the greatest possibility and the greatest choice rather than from the wrongness of your point of view, what else might be possible?

Class Participant:

It's like I'm using "I'm a slut" as a justification to kill myself.

Gary:

Yeah, it's using "slut" as justification instead of saying, "Okay, I'm a slut. I will have sex with anybody. How can I use this to create my life?" It's not "How can I use this to destroy my life, to kill myself?"

Everything that is times a godzillion, will you destroy and uncreate it all? Right and Wrong, Good and Bad, POD and POC, All Nine, Shorts, Boys, and Beyonds.

You are a shag master. It's just what you are. You can use that to induce your death or you can use that to create your life. Which way have you been using it?

Class Participant:

To induce death.

Gary:

Yeah. Not your best choice, is it?

Class Participant:

To create life. What would that look like?

Gary:

Ask: How can I use being a slut to create more of a life, not less? Who can I shag that will expand my universe, give me the life I want, and make everything work? Instead of going to what will create your life, you go for what's going to get you laid, because shagging has become the valuable product—not the fact that you can shag, not the fact that you're cute and you entice people to shag, not the fact that you can enjoy the hell out of yourself. You make getting laid the end goal, the target of everything. Most men do.

Class Participant:

I'm laughing. I see that so clearly.

Gary:

Creation stops the moment you go to the completion of "This woman will have sex with me." You're not looking at "How can I use this to my advantage?" I hate to tell you this, gentlemen, but women like to get laid as much as men do. They just want the romance to be able to choose it.

How Can I Use Being a Sleaze Ball to My Advantage?

Gary:

For example, a few of you do sleaze ball. Does that usually work well for you? No, it doesn't. So you have to ask, "How can I use being a sleaze ball to my advantage?" If you added humor to it, you could use it to your advantage. If you saw the fun and games in it, if you saw the possibilities in it instead of the destruction in it, the badness in it, the awfulness in it, or any of that stuff, would a different reality show up?

Class Participant:

Can you give me an example of that?

Gary:

If you do sleaze ball with humor, people will think you're not really a sleaze ball. Sleaze ball means you slime on girls. You ask, "Hey, can I take off my pants and show you my penis? Don't you want it now that you've seen it?" and the women say, "Gross!" You have not looked at how you can use this in a different way. What if you did something different instead of sleazing all over women and saying, "You're going to want to have sex with me."

It's not about changing the fact that you do sleaze ball. It's about seeing how you can use it to your advantage. What I'm trying to tell you is that you do sleaze ball, and it doesn't get you the results you want. So what would you have to be or do different to get the results you really do want? How could you do or be different with it?

Ask: How can I use this in a different way? You've got to learn how to use it in a way that works for you. Right now you're using it in a way that isn't working. You have to get clear on what you want. Do you want a relationship? Do you just want to get laid? If you just want to get laid, make a bunch of money and hire a hooker. It's unencumbered. Or become gay, because that's unencumbered sex too.

It's the same with anything. If you have good looks, you've got to acknowledge that you have good looks and ask, "How do I use this to create my life?" not "How can I use this to get a woman?" You'll use your looks to get a woman and then destroy your life to have her. You'll use your looks to kill yourself. You're seduced by the fact that your good looks get you laid, so you seduce somebody into getting laid in order to kill yourself.

What seduction are you using to induce the death you are choosing? Everything that is times a godzillion, will you destroy and uncreate it all? Right and Wrong, Good and Bad, POD and POC, All Nine, Shorts, Boys, and Beyonds.

What stupidity are you using to create the defenses against the unreal, unbelievable, fantastic, and phenomenal you, you are rather than getting laid are you choosing? Everything that is times a godzillion, will you destroy and uncreate it all? Right and Wrong, Good and Bad, POD and POC, All Nine, Shorts, Boys, and Beyonds.

Using Your Sexual Energy

Class Participant:

I don't see myself as a shag master or a sleaze ball. Could you help me find what that is for me that I could use to create my life?

Gary:

Are you trying to create yourself as highly sexual or as asexual?

Class Participant:

Asexual at the moment.

Gary:

Okay, so everything you've done is to make yourself asexual. When you try to make yourself asexual, are you trying to put away the sexual energy you have so you are not seduced into a relationship that doesn't work anymore? Or are you trying to make yourself asexual so you don't create problems in other people's worlds?

Class Participant:

The last one.

Gary:

Everything that is times a godzillion, will you destroy and uncreate it all? Right and Wrong, Good and Bad, POD and POC, All Nine, Shorts, Boys, and Beyonds.

When you try to make yourself asexual as though it's not going to cause problems in people's worlds, you entice a whole lot of people to try and seduce you, which is the part you like. Don't you like it when people try to seduce you, and you get to say no?

Class Participant:

Yeah.

Gary:

You like being able to say no. "No, I'm not that kind of girl... I mean I'm not that kind of boy. I won't give it up that cheaply. I'm not a cheap slut. I'm not a sleaze ball. I'm not a shag master. I'm a good boy."

Class Participant:

So does doing asexual create people wanting to seduce you? Is that just intimidation?

Gary:

Total sexualness can be intimidation. If you're willing to be totally sexual and use your sexualness as a way of intimidating others, a whole new world opens up. I was doing a sex class once, and a really pretty young thing looked at me and said, "I could put my strap on and do you."

I asked, "Do you really think you can handle me, honey?" and she got totally interiorized. She was doing sex as force. She wasn't doing sex as reality. You have to get to where you recognize that sex as reality is a totally different universe. Sex as reality is "Who can I intimidate with my sexual energy? Who can I invite with my sexual energy? Who can I induce into my life that's not going to kill me? And who can I create with that that will create more of the life I'd really like to have?"

A lot of people use their sexual energy in order to create art and literature; they sublimate their sexual energy for copulation and instead use it in artistic ways, as though that handles things for them. Sexual energy is not the *source* of creation; it is a *contribution* to it. You want to expand your sexual energy so it can be a contribution to everything you're able to create, whether it's art, literature, painting, music, or anything else.

You've got to have the willingness to be intimidating sexually, which means instead of saying, "Oh, she wants me. Cool. I'm so glad she wants me. I'll let her leave her snail trail all over my body and nobody else will touch me," you ask, "Do you really think you satisfy me, babe? Bye. See you later. I've got things to do, people to see, and places to be!" not "Yes. I'll give up my life for you."

Everything that is times a godzillion, will you destroy and uncreate it all? Right and Wrong, Good and Bad, POD and POC, All Nine, Shorts, Boys, and Beyonds.

Most of you don't want to be sexually intimidating, because you figure if you're sexually intimidating, nobody will want you. No, the fun ones will want you.

When you are sexually intimidating, you are never willing to be less because someone else can't receive the sexualness you are. When you are sexually intimidating, people have to choose whether or not to be with you rather than you trying to seduce them into doing something they don't want to do. When you try not to be sexually intimidating, people try to figure out what it is you want from them instead of being able to choose what they want. If you're willing to be sexually intimidating, they know what you want from them and they get to choose whether they want to do that—or not.

How many times have you been unwilling to be sexually intimidating? And all the places where you've decided that being sexually intimidating is a wrongness, will you destroy and uncreate all of that? Right and Wrong, Good and Bad, POD and POC, All Nine, Shorts, Boys, and Beyonds.

Most of you, when you have a really good sexual experience, will dumb it down next time to make sure you don't lose the person.

Everything that is times a godzillion, will you destroy and uncreate it all? Right and Wrong, Good and Bad, POD and POC, All Nine, Shorts, Boys, and Beyonds.

You'd rather have some lame duck wanting you rather than somebody who would be fun and who would enjoy the fuck out of you, and enjoy fucking you. And if you said you didn't want to do what they wanted you to do, they would say, "Oh, okay. I'll do whatever you want."

Dain finally got sexually intimidating. When the lady said she wanted to spend two days with him, he said, "No, I don't want to spend two days with you." She texted him the next day and said, "You're right. I just want to be with you. Whatever time I get is such an invitation, such a contribution. I want to have that." If you're not willing to adjust to people's world, they will adjust to yours. Stop being pansies.

Everything you've done to create yourself as a pansy where anybody can sniff you or lick you, will you destroy and uncreate it all? Right and Wrong, Good and Bad, POD and POC, All Nine, Shorts, Boys, and Beyonds.

Class Participant:

So if I'm choosing asexualness, am I seducing myself into the induction of death?

Gary:

Yeah. You're seducing yourself to death. That's what asexualness is. You have no sexuality. You have neither man nor woman nor anything in your life. You have no sexual energy in your body. How can you heal your body if you have no sexual energy?

Class Participant:

You can't.

What Are You Creating with Your Sexual Energy?

Gary:

Sexual energy is creative energy. You need to turn the sexual energy back on, but you don't have to use it to get laid.

Class Participant:

No, I can use it to create and generate my life. So what questions can I be asking from here?

Gary:

Ask: What seduction am I using to induce the death I am choosing? You are seducing yourself into asexualness as though that's going to create your life. No, that's going to create your death.

You have to look at what you're creating with your sexual energy. If you're being a shag master, you think that as long as you're getting laid three times a day you're creating your life. No, you're creating your penis. You're not creating your life. Life is not a penis. It doesn't have to be hard all the time for you to enjoy it. You have to start looking at these things from a different place and begin to ask: What would I really like to create as my life?

When that lady said to me, "We can spend seventy-five percent of our time together," I had to look hard and long at it and ask, "Do I truly desire a relationship?" She did. She was married, by the way, and was going to leave her husband for me. When I looked, I realized she wasn't interested in me; she was interested in me being interested in her. What's the difference?

Class Participant:

That's the space of you not being willing to give yourself up.

Gary:

I'm not willing to give myself up for anybody, any amount of money, or anything else.

Who or what are you willing to give yourself up for that if you didn't give yourself up for it would allow you to have all of you? Everything that is times a godzillion, will you destroy and uncreate it all? Right and Wrong, Good and Bad, POD and POC, All Nine, Shorts, Boys, and Beyonds.

Great Sex

A guy was telling me about an experience of great sex that he had. He asked, "What would it take to have some more of that?" When you have experiences of great sex, instead of asking, "What would it take to have more of that in my life?" try "What would it take for me to perceive that energy in people?" You have to be willing to perceive the energy in people that creates great sex.

Class Participant:

And to choose it.

Gary:

Yes, and to choose what's going to create that. You guys create weird-ass standards based on somebody else's point of view about what an attractive person is. I can see a woman with a beautiful body or a man with a beautiful body and say, "Oh wow, beautiful! Would they be any fun to have sex with?" No? Okay. Beautiful body. Beautiful to look at. Incredibly seductive—and useless from my point of view.

You guys see a beautiful body, a beautiful set of tits, or whatever it is that turns you on and... Why is it you see something that turns you on instead of just being so turned on that you turn everybody else on?

Class Participant:

Is the first kind of turn-on the seduction into the induction of death?

Gary:

Yes. It's the seduction into the induction of death, because the person you're turned on by is the person who will induce death in you.

Everything that is times a godzillion, will you destroy and uncreate it all? Right and Wrong, Good and Bad, POD and POC, All Nine, Shorts, Boys, and Beyonds.

You're all very cute but you have a single digit IQ, and it hangs between your legs.

Class Participant:

I really appreciate this call. These calls are amazing.

Gary:

If I get two or three of you to the point where you can actually have some fun and create your life while still being able to be a shag master, a slut puppy, or a sleaze ball, then it will have been worth it.

Don't Make Other People's Judgments True

Guys! I love you, but you're just damn, frigging dumb. When somebody tries to make you wrong because you are what you are, don't make it wrong. Say, "Yeah, thanks" or "Holy shit! Are you kidding me?" You have been making yourself wrong for one of your best attributes. Instead of using it *for* you, you have been using it *against* you. When people told me I was a perverted, slut puppy, I said, "Yeah, I am!"

They said, "Well that's not a good thing."

And I said, "Based on what? It works for me."

Class Participant:

So we create the induction of death to validate somebody's point of view?

Gary:

Yes, to validate somebody's point of view that you're wrong. You're not wrong; you're just a slut. Slut is not wrong. Slut is just slut.

Class Participant:

Watch out! Here comes Slut Puppy!

Gary:

All right, now we're getting somewhere! I'll be calling you a slut puppy instead of asexual.

Class Participant:

All this is based on validating other people's judgments?

Gary:

It's all based on validating this reality's point of view—the judgments of other people's reality. I'd say, "Okay, so what if I'm a slut?" When people have a judgment of you, you make it real and true. I never went there. I would ask, "What? You would think that was good or bad or wrong or right, and you wouldn't see this other point of view for what reason?"

When I was in high school, I was a good dancer and I was good looking. I didn't know I was good looking, but I was. From the first year I was in high school, I got invited to every senior prom. I was invited by the ugliest girls in the world, but I didn't mind. I was going to be a virgin when I got married, and I was not tempted to have sex with ugly women. I would wine them and dine them, I would dance with them, and they would feel really special and beautiful and that was fine.

Everything that is times a godzillion, will you destroy and uncreate it all? Right and Wrong, Good and Bad, POD and POC, All Nine, Shorts, Boys, and Beyonds.

When I finally decided that I was going to give up my virginity and not wait till I got married, I went after the woman who was considered the greatest slut in the place where I worked. She put every guy down. She wasn't interested in any of them. So I entertained her. I smiled at her, I talked to her, I was funny, I was delightful, I was amazing. I pulled energy from her and I never asked her out. For three months I didn't ask her out. Then I finally asked her out. We had the best sex! I learned how to have sex in every position. In every car. On every piece of furniture. Anywhere at any time. It was wonderful. She was a girl who enjoyed sex, and I was interested in somebody who enjoyed sex. My criteria were: Will it be easy? Will it be fun? And will I learn something? Not: Can I give myself up and die for this woman so she will know how much I love her?

Please run this for the next month:

What seduction am I using to induce the death I am choosing? Everything that is times a godzillion, will you destroy and uncreate it all? Right and Wrong, Good and Bad, POD and POC, All Nine, Shorts, Boys, and Beyonds.

I can guarantee you that every woman you find so seductive you can't pass up is designed to induce your death. Yes, she will expand your agenda, but she is not designed to create your possibilities.

Use the questions:

- If I choose this what will my life be like in five years?

- If I don't choose this what will my life be like in five years?

And be honest for a change. You figure that if you're going to get laid, life is going to be better. No, it's not going to be better. It's going to be more of the same thing you've been creating that hasn't been working. Don't give up any part of your life for anybody else, because if you do, you give up every future you've started to create, and you'll have to start from ground zero all over again. Love you all. That's it for today.

Class Participants:

Thank you, Gary.

Gary:

Thank you. You guys are good. Now be bad. It's way more fun. Bye-bye.

6

WHAT DO YOU REALLY DESIRE?

Your awareness can create a relationship if you want.
It can create whatever you desire, but you have to desire it.
The question is: What do you really desire?

Gary:

Hello, gentlemen. Does anyone have a question?

What If Everyone Was Willing to Be a Slut?

Class Participant:

In the last call, you were saying that being a slut and a shag master is not a wrongness. I have always bought the point of view that being a slut or a shag master is wrong and that a nice, decent gentleman wouldn't be or do that. Could you talk about this some more?

Gary:

What makes you a gentleman? How softly you put it in while it's hard? If everybody was willing to be a slut, we would have a much easier world, but everybody tries to be in judgment about what "proper" things they're supposed to be. They think that if they could do the proper and correct thing, they wouldn't have problems. But the problems exist not because you're being a slut or shag master. The problems exist because of the judgments that people use as a weapon against you.

How many of you have had someone use their judgment of your sexual energy against you? Every time sexual energy comes up, the first thing you do is go into the wrongness of you, because the judgment has been that's what you have to do.

Everything that is times a godzillion, will you destroy and uncreate it all? Right and Wrong, Good and Bad, POD and POC, All Nine, Shorts, Boys, and Beyonds.

What Do You Want to Have in Your Life?

You have spent so much time being wrong for everything you chose. You don't ask, "What do I really want to create here?" What if you were willing to look at what is actually possible?

You have to ask, "Truth, do I desire to have a relationship? Or do I just like to have sex? And what am I willing to pay to have the sex I want?"

Dain:

If you ask, "Do I desire to have a relationship?" you may say, "Well, not necessarily, but I like the sex. I also like going out on dates and playing or cuddling. Once it gets to relationship, it's one heavy bitch. It's just a pile of obligations." I don't necessarily think sex is enough for a lot of us. We tend to like to hang out with people too, so where does that leave us?

Gary:

You have to look at what you'd really like to create for you. What do you want to have in your life? What would it be like if you were capable of having everything you desire?

Dain:

And what would that be? We tend to put it into "Do you just want sex or do you want relationship?" Isn't there something else? Isn't there a broader spectrum of possibilities?

Gary:

In this reality, there isn't a broader spectrum of reality.

Dain:

Right. Is that part of the reason we have such challenge and difficulty—because we keep thinking it shouldn't be an either/or, as that's where every male tends to put it?

Gary:

You think the only choice you have is to be the either/or of everybody else's point of view. You assume that some sort of problem or wrongness exists with the way you are. You've got to ask: What would be the most amazing thing I could have in life? Unfortunately, I see most people trying to figure out what they *shouldn't* have rather than what they *can* have.

Dain:

I think we all do that. There's some place in our worlds where we're going along, let's say in the area of sex and relationship, and we find somebody and we have sex with them. We have sex a few more times, then all of a sudden, before we realize it has happened, we're in a difficult place that is no fun. There are obligations. We say, "Wait a minute. How did we get here? Everything was easy just a moment ago, and now we are in this impossible place. What's going on?" We try to cut off more of us to undo the impossible place we find ourselves in rather than realizing that if we had acknowledged it ahead of time, we might not have had to go there.

Choosing Awareness

Gary:

Rather than choosing awareness, you choose to cut off your awareness.

Everywhere you have chosen to cut off your awareness rather than choosing it, as though cutting it off is a greater source of choice, will you destroy and uncreate all of that? Right and Wrong, Good and Bad, POD and POC, All Nine, Shorts, Boys, and Beyonds.

Everywhere you have chosen to cut off your awareness, as though that is a greater source of choice, will you destroy and uncreate all of that? Right and Wrong, Good and Bad, POD and POC, All Nine, Shorts, Boys, and Beyonds.

You make women unfathomable. How many of you have recognized that you tend to see women as some kind of unfathomable thing you can't figure out? You don't ask:

- What can I figure out with this woman?
- What can I be aware of?
- What can I know?

What stupidity are you using to defend totally against the unfathomable women, sex, copulation, and relationships you are choosing? Everything that is times a godzillion, will you destroy and uncreate it all? Right and Wrong, Good and Bad, POD and POC, All Nine, Shorts, Boys, and Beyonds.

You've spent your whole life trying to figure out how to deal with women, but you don't seem able to fathom, to go deep enough, to figure out what it is. It becomes an unfathomable place. You cannot go deep enough to understand or to get what they're talking about.

What stupidity are you using to defend totally against the unfathomable women, sex, copulation, and relationships you are choosing? Everything that is times a godzillion, will you destroy and uncreate it all? Right and Wrong, Good and Bad, POD and POC, All Nine, Shorts, Boys, and Beyonds.

It's an eternal defense. You have no choice but to defend against everything.

Dain:

When you did the process initially, Gary, you said, "the defense against," and then the next time you did it, you said, "the defense for." Are we doing both? Defending it *and* defending against it?

Gary:

Yeah, apparently so.

What stupidity are you using to create the eternal defense for and against the unfathomable men, women, sex, copulation, and relationships are you choosing? Everything that is times a godzillion, will you destroy and uncreate it all? Right and Wrong, Good and Bad, POD and POC, All Nine, Shorts, Boys, and Beyonds.

Class Participant:

You end up in a no-man's land.

Gary:

Well, isn't that pretty much where you feel you are most of the time? In some kind of no-man's land where you have no clue what is going on and why?

Class Participant:

Absolutely.

You Have to Desire It

Gary:

That's the whole situation in a nutshell. You have no idea what's occurring or why. All you know is somehow, something isn't right. And usually you are what isn't right. And because you've determined and decided you're not right and there's something wrong with you, you have to be in a constant state of looking at the wrongness of you. You don't look at the choice and awareness you are. You don't see you as the valuable product.

Your awareness can create a relationship if you want. It can create whatever you desire, but you have to desire it. The question is: What do you really desire? I was talking with a guy a while ago, and he was saying, "Well, I don't really want children, but I kind of maybe...." It was a whole lot of fantasy and blah, blah, blah.

I said, "You know what? You don't have a choice here. Truth, do you really want a relationship?"

He said, "It feels heavy."

I asked, "Do you want a fantasy relationship?"

He said, "Yeah, I do."

I asked, "Okay, can you create it?"

He said, "No, it wouldn't be good."

I asked, "How do you know? You haven't created it yet." Have any of you ever achieved the fantasy relationship you thought was possible?

Class Participant:

No.

Gary:

Right. You don't try to do it from awareness! You try to do it from the unfathomable relationship, sex, copulation, men, and women.

What stupidity are you using to create the eternal defense for and against the unfathomable men, women, sex, copulation, and relationships you are choosing? Everything that is times a godzillion, will you destroy and uncreate it all? Right and Wrong, Good and Bad, POD and POC, All Nine, Shorts, Boys, and Beyonds.

Class Participant:

That's like defending the foundation of this reality.

Are You Making Yourself Wrong for the Truth of You?

Gary:

Yes, it is the foundation of relationship, sex, and copulation in this reality. I would like to get you to the place where you start to look at the kind of relationship you would like to create instead of a relationship based on this reality.

Class Participant:

When I was in my early twenties I met a girl at a party, and her friend said to me, "You just want to fuck." I clearly remember saying, "Yes, and what?" Then I made myself wrong for what I truly am.

Gary:

Let's see, that was about fifteen years ago. The good news is that for fifteen years, you've made yourself wrong, when in truth what you had going for you was the truth your early years were.

What stupidity are you using to defend against the shag master, slut puppy you truly be are you choosing? Everything that is times a godzillion, will you destroy and uncreate it all? Right and Wrong, Good and Bad, POD and POC, All Nine, Shorts, Boys, and Beyonds.

How much of your awareness do you have to cut off to not recognize that what you really want to do is fuck? You make yourself wrong and then you spend all your time trying to prove that's not really what you want so other people will think you don't really want that when it really is what you want. But other people are psychic too, so they know you really want it. You have to lie to them and you have to lie to yourself doubly in order to prove that you're not really wanting what you really want, because that would be so bad and sad.

Everything that is times a godzillion, will you destroy and uncreate it all? Right and Wrong, Good and Bad, POD and POC, All Nine, Shorts, Boys, and Beyonds.

What stupidity are you using to create the eternal defense against being the shag master, slut puppy you truly be are you choosing? Everything that is times a godzillion, will you destroy and uncreate it all? Right and Wrong, Good and Bad, POD and POC, All Nine, Shorts, Boys, and Beyonds.

What stupidity are you using to create the eternal defense for and against the unfathomable men, women, sex, copulation, and relationship you are choosing? Everything that is times a godzillion, will you destroy and uncreate it all? Right and Wrong, Good and Bad, POD and POC, All Nine, Shorts, Boys, and Beyonds.

Class Participant:

What will it take to generate and create contribution where we go beyond the crap we invent as more real than who we really be?

Gary:

That's what this whole sequence of calls is about.

An Ideal Relationship with a Woman

Class Participant:

Would you be able to describe an ideal relationship with a woman?

Gary:

Yeah. She lives across the country. You visit each other for three days. I'm kidding.

You keep trying to create a relationship that's going to be an ideal relationship. If you're doing relationship from the viewpoint of an ideal relationship, are you looking at the person in front of you? Or are you looking at who you would like her to be, who you think she ought to be, and who you think she might be?

What stupidity are you using to create the defense for and against the utopian ideal of relationship you are choosing? Everything that is times a godzillion, will you destroy and uncreate it all? Right and Wrong, Good and Bad, POD and POC, All Nine, Shorts, Boys, and Beyonds.

The best relationship with a woman is where you can live with each other, and each one of you allows the other person to be who they are. You have no judgment, both of you enjoy the sex you have, whether it's a lot or a little, and you don't have to spend every moment together.

Spending Time Together

One of the things all of you need to look at is how much time you would like to spend with a woman. I personally like to spend about an hour to an hour and a half talking to her, and after that, I want to have sex with her.

What percentage of your life would you like to spend with a woman? Ten? Twenty? Thirty? Forty? Or what?

Class Participant:

Ten.

Gary:

Okay, so you want to spend two and a half hours a day with her.

Class Participant:

Yep.

Gary:

Two and a half hours a day is probably a good percentage. Any more than that, and you'll most likely get bored.

Class Participant:

It seems like women want to spend more time with me than I want to spend with them.

Gary:

Yes, because you never commit to being there even when you're spending ten percent of your time with them. And you're not willing to be intimidating. You tend to function from a total incapacity to intimidate them. What if you demanded of them that they spend more time with you?

Class Participant:

Would that be intimidating?

Gary:

Yes, because if a man demands that a woman spends time with him, guess what she wants to do? Go away. If you want to make a girl go away, demand more time with her.

Class Participant:

Can you give me an example of how to do that? Is it an energetic thing? Is it what I say?

Gary:

You have to start out with the energy of it. You have to look at her and say, "You know what? I don't think we're spending enough time together."

When you're away from her, call her and tell her how much you miss her. If you keep doing that, she'll suddenly find reasons not to be available. If she stops answering her phone, then you know you finally have control. How many of you have had women do that to you? They call you so often, and so much, that you don't want to even answer your phone.

Class Participant:

Yup.

Gary:

So why aren't you doing that to them? You resist being so demanding of them that *they* have to be quiet and good and calm around you instead of *you* being calm, good, and quiet around them.

Class Participant:

Yeah, holy moly!

Gary:

Do you want a woman to give you some space? That's another thing that most men want in a relationship—somebody who will give them space. How many of you realize that as a man you like your alone time?

Class Participant:

Yes.

Gary:

Men require down time. It's your process time. It's when you take all the things you've collected all day long, put your attention on them, and come to an awareness or a conclusion of what you want to do with the awareness of all of those things.

Everything that doesn't allow that to show up in your life, will you destroy and uncreate that? Right and Wrong, Good and Bad, POD and POC, All Nine, Shorts, Boys, and Beyonds.

Men have been taught that they have to do things to indicate that they love or care. They're trained to believe that doing equals caring. So they have to deal with all the stuff they've collected and ask, "What do I do with all this stuff?" until they come to "Oh! I see what I need to do." It's the way they come to an awareness of what they "need to do." But it's not actually an awareness—it's a conclusion, which doesn't give them the freedom awareness would.

Women can talk about something all day long and never have to come to conclusion. A man has to process something until he can come to conclusion and determine what he needs to do. It's a different way of dealing with life.

What's the Most Important Thing to Me?

Class Participant:

Would you talk more about creating our lives?

Gary:

Well, one thing you have to look at is: What would I like to have as my life? You have to ask questions like:

- What would I like my life to be like in five years?
- Do I want to travel?
- How much money do I want to make?
- What is it that's most important to me?

See if there's a relationship included in there. I find that most men get their lives going, and then they decide to add a relationship, which gets rid of half of their life. What if a relationship was an addition to your life, not a replacement for your life?

Everywhere you've made relationship a replacement for life and living, will you destroy and uncreate all of that? Right and Wrong, Good and Bad, POD and POC, All Nine, Shorts, Boys, and Beyonds.

Class Participant:

It seems that I have to make a commitment to myself with regard to asking, "What I would like?"

Gary:

Yes, you have to look at whether you really want a relationship and then make a commitment to what you'd like. Most of you get into relationship by default. Do you recognize that?

Class Participant:

Yeah.

Make a List: What I Would Like in a Partner?

You need to ask, "What would I like in a partner?" You've got to get clear about what you want in a relationship. The problem is you don't ask that. You look at somebody and you say, "Oh, I like her." You never ask, "Does she like me? Does she like men?" You assume, because you like her, that she's going to like you and she's going to like men and everything is going to be perfect.

Find out what you desire. How would you like your interactions with each other to be? What would it be like to interact with her? What do you want to create with her? Do you want someone who has a good sense of humor? Someone you can have a good conversation with?

By the way, there's a big difference between conversation and communication. Communication is "Get your dirty feet off the couch." That's an honest communication; it's a good communication, but it's not a conversation. Find out what you want to create with her. Make a list of what you'd like to have in a partner.

You Also Need an "I Don't Want to Have" List

Before I got together with my ex-wife, I made a list of all the things I *wanted* in a woman I was in a relationship with. She had all those things. What I didn't make is a list of all the things I *did not want* in that person. So I got everything I wanted, and I also got everything I didn't want.

Class Participant:

How specific does the "don't want" list have to be? Isn't that creating a limitation?

Gary:

It's not about limitation. You've got to look at it and say, "I do not wish to have a woman who's going to complain all the time" or "I don't want a woman who always argues." Have any of you noticed that you've chosen a woman who is very similar to the last woman you chose? It's as if she's the same women in a different body?

Class Participant:

Yes.

Gary:

You're choosing the same woman over and over again and expecting a different result. Who's the one person you can change?

Class Participant:

Me.

What Stupidity Are You
Using to Create the Women You Are Choosing?

Gary:

You've got to change *your* perspective. You can't change somebody else's. Have a look at your perspective. "I've chosen the same woman over and over again and I've got nothing I want out of it. Why would I do that?" If you're going to swim across the river and you take the same number of strokes in the same way all the time, are you going to get to a different place in the river? No. You're going to get to the same place you got to before. So ask: What stupidity am I using to create the woman I am choosing?

Class Participant:

I will do that.

Class Participant:

Last month I participated in Dain's Energetic Synthesis of Being through live streaming. Even though I wasn't physically there, I found that I was judging some of the women in the class. I couldn't stand the way they asked questions. It seemed to me they were just trying to get Dain's attention.

Gary:

Of course! He's the leader of the class. They want to get his attention. So what's the deal?

Everything you're unwilling to acknowledge about your awareness, will you destroy and uncreate all of that? Right and Wrong, Good and Bad, POD and POC, All Nine, Shorts, Boys, and Beyonds.

Class Participant:

I noticed that Dain was totally cool with them. He received them with no judgment regardless of what they said or what they asked. How can I be that? Receiving all girls and women for who they are. Are there any clearings we can do so we can do that too?

Gary:

What stupidity am I using to create the women I am choosing? Everything that is times a godzillion, will you destroy and uncreate it all? Right and Wrong, Good and Bad, POD and POC, All Nine, Shorts, Boys, and Beyonds.

Keep running that one.

Being Needless of a Woman

Class Participant:

In the past, I have heard you talk about needlessness. Can you talk some more about being needless when it comes to girls, women, sex, relationship, and copulation? This is a big one for me. If there weren't all these things I thought I needed, I could have the true value of me.

Gary:

The more you can function from the needlessness of it, whatever it is, the more you begin to recognize the choices you have to actually choose it. Recently I asked Dain, "Do you get that these women want you?" and he said, "No, I don't get that."

I said, "Yeah, you keep thinking you want them, but the reality is they want you."

When you're needless of a woman, she wants you all the time. The more needless you are, the more she wants you. You have a need to be needed, because you were taught that you needed to be able to fix things and do things for a woman to prove you loved her. You're trying to do proof of love instead of being needless of having love or giving love.

Class Participant:

Yeah.

Gary:

What stupidity are you using to defend against the needlessness you could be choosing? Everything that is times a godzillion, will you destroy and uncreate it all? Right and Wrong, Good and Bad, POD and POC, All Nine, Shorts, Boys, and Beyonds.

Class Participant:

When I first started looking for relationship, it had nothing to do with me. It was that I *needed* a relationship to be the valuable product. There are all these things we're told we need.

Gary:

Why do you need a relationship? You need a relationship to prove something. You need a relationship to prove that you're not a useless pile of debris. You need a relationship to prove that you're not gay. You need a relationship to prove that you have value. You need a relationship. Is any of that true?

Class Participant:

No, and it's the same with everything. We go into that place of need. "I need to have kids. I need to get married. I need to have this much money."

Gary:

That's where you complete a choice.

How much of your life have you done as the completion of choice based on the need to be something you're not? Everything that is times a godzillion, will you destroy and uncreate it all? Right and Wrong, Good and Bad, POD and POC, All Nine, Shorts, Boys, and Beyonds.

"I've Stopped Creating"

Class Participant:

I feel like I'm at a place now where I've stopped creating. Can you help me out with that?

Gary:

Did you stop creating because somebody else was doing all the creation?

Class Participant:

Hmm. Yeah.

Gary:

Did you stop creating because there was no need for you to create? And did you misidentify and misapply *no need as needless*?

Class Participant:

Yeah. I misidentified *no need as needless*.

Gary:

Everything that is times a godzillion, will you destroy and uncreate it all? Right and Wrong, Good and Bad, POD and POC, All Nine, Shorts, Boys, and Beyonds.

Class Participant:

Wow.

Class Participant:

Thank you for asking that question. It showed me the mess I created so I'd have something to do. And now I'm not creating.

Gary:

Your problem is that you've created need as the source of choice instead of choice as the creation of your life.

Class Participant:

Yeah.

Gary:

What physical actualization of creation through choice are you now capable of generating, creating, and instituting? Everything that doesn't allow that to show up times a godzillion, will you destroy and uncreate it all? Right and Wrong, Good and Bad, POD and POC, All Nine, Shorts, Boys, and Beyonds.

Abdicating Your Voice

Class Participant:

In the Right Voice for You facilitators class, you mentioned that men abdicate their voices.

Gary:

Yeah. Most of the men in the world think that it's important to be the strong, silent type. How much of your voice in the world have you abdicated so you can be strong and silent? A lot, a little, or megatons?

Class Participant:

Megatons.

Gary:

> Right and Wrong, Good and Bad, POD and POC, All Nine, Shorts, Boys, and Beyonds.

You abdicate your voice with regard to women because you don't want to get into an argument with them. You think that if you get in an argument, they'll go away. Women have a strange characteristic. They like to discuss everything and come to no conclusion. You, as a man, are always trying to come to conclusion about everything you say or do. So for you, an argument means conclusion. For a woman, it means "We're just discussing it, and you're wrong."

> Everything that is times a godzillion, will you destroy and uncreate it all? Right and Wrong, Good and Bad, POD and POC, All Nine, Shorts, Boys, and Beyonds.

Class Participant:

Is conclusion trying to work out what action to take?

Gary:

You only have to figure out what action to take based on the conclusion that you're wrong in the first place. (Not that you've never been made wrong in relationship!) This is where men abdicate their voice.

> What stupidity are you using to defend the rightness of abdicating your voice are you choosing? Everything that is times a godzillion, will you destroy and uncreate it all? Right and Wrong, Good and Bad, POD and POC, All Nine, Shorts, Boys, and Beyonds.

Well, the bad news, gentlemen, is that we're not done. The good news is you get to go out and practice. Remember, slip it in gently. That makes you a gentleman.

Class Participant:

I love it. We now have a definition of what it is to be a gentleman.

Dain:

Finally!

Class Participant:

You're wonderful, Gary. Thank you.

7

BEING GOOD IN BED

*I decided I'd better learn everything I could about
how to get a woman off,
so she would be satisfied no matter what I did.*

Gary:

Hello, gentlemen. Let's begin with a question.

Class Participant:

The Access Consciousness Level One manual says that being good in bed is one of the three elements of a good relationship. Can you talk about this? What do you mean by "good in bed"? Is there a criterion for what's good in bed?

Create a Galvanic Response in Her Body

Gary:

Yes, there are several criteria. Let's start by looking at the galvanic response of people's skin. It's about the way your touch creates an effect in the other person. Pull up your sleeve and run your hand about a half an inch over your arm and pull energy. You'll feel the hair begin to rise up off your arm to meet your hand. If you use this with somebody you're having sex with, they will see you as very different from their other lovers and they will be more excited. The galvanic responses you can create in someone's body are part of what creates your being good in bed. It's also part of what invites your partner's body to an orgasm, which also makes you better in bed. You have to ask, "How much time am I willing to take to have sex with this person?"

Go Slow

Most of us have been taught to get it over with fast. You learned to ejaculate based on looking at some pictures and pounding your pud as hard as you could in order to get it over with quickly, because somebody was going to knock on the door, come in, and catch you at any time. You have to overcome that point of view. It's about learning to go slow.

Learn about the Parts of a Woman's Body

The other thing is you want to learn about the parts of a woman's body. The clitoris is the most sensitive part of her body. Don't use harshness on the clitoris. Use the lightest butterfly touch with your tongue that you can possibly create and invite that clitoris to be like the hair on your arm wanting to reach up and grab your hand.

Touch the clitoris so lightly that it creates a tingling in the woman's body but also an awareness of you and what is making it tingle. Wait until the clitoris starts to come up to meet you. Lap down the sides and put your tongue in the vagina. And then go back to touching the clitoris very lightly. If you use your tongue like a butterfly on a woman's clitoris, you can usually bring her to orgasm within five to seven minutes. If she has two or three orgasms before you even enter her, she's going to think you're the best thing in bed ever. So use this technique.

What Kind of Touch Would She Like?

And ask: What kind of touch would this person like? What would create a dynamic galvanic response in her? When you do this rather than looking at how you can get it up, get it on, and get it in without messing up your hairdo, you'll start to get where she functions from and how she might do things. You want a different point of view. You want to look at the possibility of what *could* be—not what you *want* it to be or *don't want* it to be. That's really important.

Decreased Libido

Class Participant:

Do you know anything that will help males with sexual dysfunctions like decreased libido or premature ejaculation?

Gary:

You have a decreased libido because you have not chosen to have sex with people who desire to have sex with you. Our brain is the thing that creates the libido, not our body. What are you doing to stimulate your brain? Most men think that stimulating the brain means watching porn or something that is going to turn them on and make them want to have more sex. No. Look at the parts of a body that are a turn-on for you. Some women have a wonderful curve in their back, and some men have that too. Notice how a woman's butt moves and how her butt works. Those are things that stimulate in you a sense of the possibilities that might occur in working with that body.

What part of the body is most exciting to you? Most men have been trained to believe that tits and vagina are the sum total of sexual desire. I personally don't believe that. I find the way a woman walks is a great indication of whether she's going to be good in bed. She needs to be able to move those hips. She needs to be able to move them with you in bed.

And by the way, gentlemen, you need to be able to walk like that too. You need to know that you can move your hips in every direction possible. The purpose of having a good physique is so you can fuck better. Go out and create your physique for greater fucking, not for how you look in the mirror. You tend to focus on how you look in the mirror, and that's only to inspire other men to think you're not in competition with them—or to think you are. That's not necessarily your best choice. Notice how people move their hips. That probably wouldn't be true for a gay guy. He might want to see how somebody eats, because that's a greater indication of whether they'll eat him well.

If you have a decreased libido, you can do things like Viagra. There are also different kinds of natural substances that the Chinese have used for years to create greater and longer-lasting erections. You just have to find one that works with your body. Ask your body:

- Would this be good for you?
- Will you like this?
- How would this work for you?

It's not: "Oh good, this is going to get me hard." That's not the perspective. First of all, getting hard is one thing; creating a dynamic capacity in bed is a totally different universe. You have to ask: How do I create stimulation in this person's body? You want to get to the point where you're so present with how you have sex that you can feel the other person's body feeling what you're doing to their body, while your body is feeling it too, so that you get every direction. That would be the greatest stimulation you can do for your libido.

Class Participant:

Is there a clearing for that, Gary?

Gary:

What stupidity are you using to defend for and against the galvanic responses, the stimulating touches, and the invigorating possibilities that would alter your limited sexual capacities are you choosing? Everything that is times a godzillion, will you destroy and uncreate it all? Right and Wrong, Good and Bad, POD and POC, All Nine, Shorts, Boys, and Beyonds.

Class Participant:

I have a question about creating my body for better fucking. Is there a question or a clearing that would assist with that?

Gary:

What physical actualization of creating my body as a fucking machine could I be choosing that I'm not choosing? Everything that does not allow that to show up times a godzillion, destroy and uncreate it all? Right and Wrong, Good and Bad, POD and POC, All Nine, Shorts, Boys, and Beyonds.

Class Participant:

Gary, when you say, "fucking machine," what pops up in my mind is a rabbit. It's like you're doing rabbit sex.

Gary:

Have you judged yourself for doing rabbit sex because you came too quickly?

Class Participant:

Not because I came too quickly, but because I was enjoying it and the rawness in it.

Gary:

And who judged you for that?

Class Participant:

The woman and I.

Gary:

Was that looking at how you could use the galvanic response to create something different? No. Look at the galvanic response I told you about and how to use the clitoris. There's also the G-spot which is on the upper side of the vaginal area.

Class Participant:

Gary, can you explain that? I don't know what that is.

Gary:

The G-spot is on the upper side of the vaginal area. Go in from the front with your hand and move it around in little circles against the front side of the vagina, and you'll feel a hardness begin to occur. The same thing can occur on the bottom side of the vagina if you use that technique as well. Now, why would that occur? Because all of it is designed to go together. Just think about it. If you were entering from behind and you put your penis in—most penises have a tilt that goes up toward the body—and that tilt goes up and would hit some place in the vaginal cavity that would allow for a greater stimulation. And your balls slapping against the clitoris can have an effect on that. That's why some women really like to have it from behind.

Stimulating Her Body

When I first began having sex—and "sex" was three guys going behind the library and masturbating—we'd pop our puds to see who could get off the quickest. One of the guys had a twelve-inch dick that was about three inches in diameter, the other one had a ten-inch dick that was about three and a half inches in diameter, and I had about five and a half inches. I thought I was definitely a retarded child and that everybody had a ten-inch dick or a twelve-inch dick.

It was very interesting later in life to find out that wasn't so, but because I thought I was deprived in the penis department, I decided I'd better learn everything I could about how to get a woman off, so she would be satisfied no matter what I did. I learned about oral sex, I learned about how to give good head, I learned about the galvanic response, and I learned how to touch a woman's body to the point where she was screaming to have intercourse, not something else.

I started learning how the clitoris works and what part of her body to touch, and instead of just putting my penis in, I went slow. I spent a lot of time caressing the breasts, caressing the armpits, caressing the fold of the elbow on the front side, and touching different parts of the body. If you run your hands very slowly down the outside of the woman's body from her tits down to her knees, you can create enough galvanic response that she starts to get goose pimples, and you'll have amazing sex. You've got to get her to the point where she's willing to have that kind of stimulation within her body.

Most women have never learned to have that kind of stimulation in their body because the only reason they're having sex is to get a relationship. And men have only been taught to do sex. Neither of those things is loving sex.

What physical actualization of the sensual, sexual, copulation, and innervation am I now capable of generating, creating and instituting? Everything that doesn't allow that to show up times a godzillion, will you destroy and uncreate it all? Right and Wrong, Good and Bad, POD and POC, All Nine, Shorts, Boys, and Beyonds.

Masturbation

What if the purpose of masturbation was to create a greater sensitivity in your body so that you could be a greater lover?

Class Participant:

Then I should be the greatest lover on the planet!

Gary:

Yes, but have you been doing it for that purpose—or have you been doing it to get off?

Class Participant:

Ah, I've been doing it to get off.

Gary:

When the sole reason you masturbate is to get off, you're trying to dissipate the sexual energy that's part of life and living.

Class Participant:

When masturbating, what is the value, if any, of fantasizing about having sex or copulation with the various women who come into my life? For many years, I have had sex with women in my mind and my hand, and then I've felt that the act was completed.

Gary:

And it is. That's one of the reasons you do it. The question you're not asking is: Do these women wish to have sex with me? And if they do, ask: What would be the most pleasurable thing to give them?

If you're going to fantasize at all, think about what you would be doing to bring their body to a higher level of rev and vitality, because that's what the purpose of sex should be. That's why you don't want to go to masturbation to get completion; you want to get to the point where your body is stimulated and you feel more energy coming in. When that occurs, quit. Go off and do something else. That will do two things: Number one, it will start to create a place in your body where being sexually aroused is a valuable product, and number two, it will create more of a libido for you. Look at masturbation from the point of view of: What am I creating here? What am I doing this for?

If you're masturbating to just get off, you're not going to achieve a sense of the greater energy that can occur from copulation. The purpose of copulation should be to make you more stimulated to live, not to create the little death. The little death is what the French call ejaculation. So keep looking at: What is it that I'm trying to accomplish by what I'm doing?

Most people masturbate as a way of desensitizing their penis instead of sensitizing it. I know someone who took two Rockhards, which is a stimulant for the penis. He said, "All I had to do was brush my penis against something and I'd get a hard-on." That's a level of sensitivity most men can't handle and most women don't want to know you have. Another friend mentioned that he took a Rockhard when was wearing loose pants without underwear, and the pants just sort of rubbed around his body. He said, "I had to stop in the middle of the street and think of dead rabbits because I couldn't get rid of my hard-on." There are a different ways of sensitizing yourself. Ask: How can I sensitize myself so I'm ready to go at any time?

Try stimulating your nipples and the rest of your body by running your fingers down and doing the galvanic response until you get a hard-on. The next time you have sex with a woman, you're going to be a much better lover, because you're going to be more sensitive and more aware. You're also going to have a willingness to receive that is not currently in your repertoire. Most men don't know how to receive a blow job, and most women don't know how to give one. Now why is that?

Receiving

Class Participant:

It's about receiving, isn't it?

Gary:

Yes. You have never taught yourself to receive; you've taught yourself to get off. If you spend your life masturbating to get off, you're not increasing your capacity to receive, which also limits the amount of money you can have in your life. You've got to get your body sensitized again, because you have mostly cut it off. Most sports are about slamming into other guys. Is that what you call sensitivity? It's actually eliminating sensitivity. Ask: How do I sensitize my body so its galvanic responses create a galvanic response in others?

The galvanic response is a system that your body has that you may not be using. Your body has automatic systems in it. You have a somatic response everywhere in your body. The way your body responds to something is part of the information your body is supposed to get. You have elements in your body that allow you to "respond" in a different way to things. You can create a place in you and your body where your sensitivity and your sense of receiving are more extreme. For example, most men have never had their anus touched. It's one of the most sensitive parts of their body, but they won't even bother to touch it. They wipe it with toilet paper, but that's about as far as they go.

Learn how responsive each part of your body can be. It's not that you're going to go gay. It doesn't mean that a woman is going to put a strap on and fuck you in the ass, although that could be fun too. Recognize that there's a different possibility in the way your body receives. What would it be like if you were willing to have more of that and less of what you currently have? Is what you currently have enough? Is what you have what you want?

Seldom do people really get that there's a different choice. Most people have the idea "I have to do this" or "I have to do that" or "This is the only way it is" or "This is the way it's supposed to be." What if none of that was actually real?

Creating a Molecular
Vibration between You and the Woman

Class Participant:

You say that women usually do sex in order to get relationship and men usually do relationship in order to get sex. Instead of being bound by this reality, how can I have a different possibility? For example, how can I have sex without relationship? I have known quite a few people who are shag masters, but I can't seem to understand why or how they can be shag masters. It seems like it's so natural for them. How is that possible?

Gary:

What stupidity are you using to defend totally against being the shag master you could be are you choosing? Everything that is times a godzillion, will you destroy and uncreate it all? Right and Wrong, Good and Bad, POD and POC, All Nine, Shorts, Boys, and Beyonds.

Being a shag master is neither good nor bad. You have to ask questions: Does this woman really want to have sex with me or does she desire something else? More often than not, women who would like to have sex with you want something more from you than just sex, but you don't want to know that. You figure, "Okay, I can shag her" and you cut off your awareness in order to make sure you get to shag.

When you get really good at being a cunnilinguist, when you get really good at using your fingers in a woman's body and you get her off four or five times before you cum inside her, women will want to come and visit you again and again and again.

This is how you start creating the place where you become a valuable product. You've got to make yourself a valuable product by sensitizing your body enough that you can sense what her body is feeling and have your body feel what her body feels. Do the galvanic response stuff so you can get to the point where you can create communion between the molecular structures of your bodies. Ask: How can we create the molecular vibration between us as something greater than either one of us can have alone?

Class Participant:

That's what you are describing in *The Place* isn't it?

Gary:

Yes. That's what I'm describing in *The Place*. It's what I'm trying to get people to recognize: there is this place. Have I had this place personally? Yes. I was able to achieve it with a few different women.

It wasn't that I was a shag master. I used my silver tongue in more ways than one to get anything I wanted. I had roommates who were good looking, studly guys who used women. They'd get a girlfriend and they'd be bored with her after the first three times they had sex.

I'd ask, "What's boring about the way she has sex?"

Talk to Her

My roommates would say, "Uh, I'm just tired of having to talk to her." I realized that if you're willing to talk to somebody, you get a lot further than if you aren't. So I started talking to these girls, and I ended up going to bed with them. The funny part about it is that they all told me I was better than my roommates because it wasn't just about sticking it in. They said they enjoyed sex with me. You have to ask: What's going to be enjoyable for her? You can ask the woman, "What's the most enjoyable thing for you?"

I was a little different. When I was young, my point of view was I needed to learn everything I could because I wasn't adequately endowed, so I would try to find out what other people did. I would ask the women I was with, "So you were with this guy. What did he do that I haven't done?" or "What did he do that was really great?" The women were surprised I would ask, and they were thrilled to be able to tell. You have to be willing to ask, "What's the best thing anyone has ever done with you sexually?" Find out what it is and then ask, "Can you teach me how to do that?" Guess what? If you ask them to teach you, they'll start to contribute to you. This is how you get them on your team. "Teach me how to do the best thing you ever had. Teach me how to do it. Did I do it well enough or is there something I can improve?" You also ask the person's body, "What can I do different that would be an improvement of this?"

People Connect as Bodies

There's another thing about sensitizing your body. Recognize that people don't connect as beings; they connect as bodies. If you don't get that people connect as bodies instead of beings, your behavior won't make sense to you. We tend to look at the person we're with, or the person we would like to be with, based on where their body is and where they are in time. This is why, when somebody dies or when you lose a pet, for example, you miss them so much. You miss being able to touch them. When you feel separate from another, you no longer feel that your body is connected to their body.

When you go through the major changes that Access Consciousness creates for you, there will tend to be a sense of separation. That's where you ask: Have my body and I changed so much that we're no longer findable by other people's systems?

By systems, I mean the kinds of things people look for to have a sense of being connected to your body. They want to know where your body is in space and where you are in relationship to it. That's not necessarily the easiest or the best choice, but that's the way it's done here. As you go through these changes, your relationship with money changes as well—because is money for you, the being, or is money for the body? It's for the body.

"You're Mine"

Class Participant:

I went to a workshop where men and women paired up, and the woman was to ask the man for the touch she wanted. My partner asked me, "Can you touch me as if I'm yours?" She wanted me to touch her as if I owned her or she was my woman.

Gary:

What was that woman telling you? That she liked men? That she didn't like men? Or that she wanted to own one?

Class Participant:

She wanted to own one.

Gary:

Yeah. What people say is an indication of what is. Were you able to satisfy her?

Class Participant:

Actually I was, and it expanded my universe, because I hadn't been willing to go into that energy before. I had a judgment that the energy "You're mine" was bad.

Gary:

There's a difference between "You're mine" and "I own you."

Class Participant:

The energy was "You're mine." That was the energy she wanted to experience.

Gary:

This is what you have to be willing to look at:

- How do I own this woman forever?
- What can I do that would make her so thrilled sexually that she can't imagine doing without me?

What Does This Person Want?/What Do I Want?

Class Participant:

Dain talked about how sometimes we humanoid men like to cuddle and be romantic. Could you say some more about that? That was out of my universe. I am always getting into sex or relationship.

Gary:

It's not an either/or. You have to see what the person you're with wants. I ask: Will it be easy? Will it be fun? Will I learn something? What I learned is that many women just wanted to cuddle and not have sex, so I could go home. You've got to look at:

- What do I want?
- What did I come for?
- Why am I here?
- Why do I want to cum with this person?
- What is it I really desire?
- What is it I really require?
- Where is it I wish to go with this?

Most of us men never ask those questions. Personally, I realized, "I have all of these points of view about how I'm supposed to be as a man based on what women have told me I should be, not what was going to actually work for me. Oh! I need to look at what I really want and not try to figure it out according to what women want." Most men try to figure out what's going to be good for a woman and ignore what's going to be good for them.

What stupidity are you using to defend totally against being the man you can truly be are you choosing? Everything that is times a godzillion, will you destroy and uncreate it all? Right and Wrong, Good and Bad, POD and POC, All Nine, Shorts, Boys, and Beyonds.

You might want to run:

What physical actualization of a totally different sexual reality beyond this reality am I now capable of generating, creating, and instituting?

I've been trying to get you out of the place where you make women the authority, the reason, and the justification for everything. When you stop doing this, you start having a choice of being you, having you, and seeing you as valuable.

I'd also like to see you get to the point where, instead of choosing anyone who will have sex with you, you start looking for who would have sex with you that would actually be fun for you.

So it's not "Oh, she'll have sex with me" equals "I'll take her." Instead it's:

- Will this be fun for me?
- Will I enjoy this?
- Will this make my life greater?
- Will this make everything I desire more valuable, more phenomenal?

Do you see how different those questions are from "Will she actually have sex with me?" When you look at a woman and you say, "Oh, I'll bet she's it," that's a conclusion. That's not a question. A question is:

- Is she what I'm looking for?
- Is this going to be what I want it to be?

How many of you are settling for whatever you can get rather than knowing exactly what you want and not being willing to take less?

Everything that is times a godzillion, will you destroy and uncreate it all? Right and Wrong, Good and Bad, POD and POC, All Nine, Shorts, Boys, and Beyonds.

What commitment do you refuse to make to you that if you made it to you would give you the kind of sex and relationship you'd truly like to have? What stupidity are you using to defend for and against the sex and relationships you are choosing? Everything that is times a godzillion, will you destroy and uncreate it all? Right and Wrong, Good and Bad, POD and POC, All Nine, Shorts, Boys, and Beyonds.

Guys, you're not committing to you. You're committing to your women. Why is it more important to you to commit to a woman than to commit to yourself?

Nagging

Class Participant:

It's to keep her satisfied, so she's not nagging at me.

Gary:

In other words, you're expecting her to nag you. You expect women to nag you. Here's the problem with that: Because you're trying to avoid being nagged, you always pick women who will nag you. That applies to all of you.

Class Participant:

Can we clear that now, please?

Gary:

Everything that is times a godzillion, will you destroy and uncreate it all? Right and Wrong, Good and Bad, POD and POC, All Nine, Shorts, Boys, and Beyonds.

Class Participant:

That is funny, because in my relationship, the only thing I ever react to is her nagging at me. I don't care about anything else, but when she nags at me, I get really angry.

Gary:

But you always do what you can to create her nagging at you.

Class Participant:

What am I still defending for or against with my partner?

Gary:

Are you defending for her being a nag so you can choose to leave her while defending against her being a nag so you can love her?

Class Participant:

That's frightening.

Gary:

She's actually a perfect relationship for you. She's a girl who will nag you and nag you and nag you until you do what she wants, which means you can be mad at her for making you do what she wants, but at least she will nag you.

Let me ask you another question. Have you defined "nagging" as love?

Class Participant:

Apparently.

Gary:

Everything you've done to define nagging as love, and all of you guys who watched your mothers nag your fathers because you knew that when a woman was angry at a man and nagged at him, it was true love, will you destroy and uncreate all of that? Right and Wrong, Good and Bad, POD and POC, All Nine, Shorts, Boys, and Beyonds.

Class Participant:

That is awesome. How much are love and hate basically the same thing? They're different sides of the same coin. I have started to change a lot of that. I don't react to my partner anymore when she is nagging. I am in allowance of it and I choose something different for me, but for her, it's like I'm disappearing from her universe because I'm not reacting to it.

Gary:

Yes, I know. She has defined nagging as an act of love.

Class Participant:

What could I do different here? I don't know what to do or where to go.

Gary:

Well, what do you really want from her?

Class Participant:

That's a good question.

Gary:

You don't even know what you want. Let me ask you a question. What do you want with a woman? That. What was the energy that came up when I asked that question?

Class Participant:

What I get is "someone who is not in my way."

Gary:

So you want a woman who's not in your way. Would that be your partner?

Class Participant:

(Laughs) Yes.

Gary:

Everything that is times a godzillion, will you destroy and uncreate it all? Right and Wrong, Good and Bad, POD and POC, All Nine, Shorts, Boys, and Beyonds.

So what do you want with a woman? That.

Class Participant:

Somebody who is resisting or creating a resistance, so I have something to fight.

Gary:

Cool.

Everything that is times a godzillion, will you destroy and uncreate it all? Right and Wrong, Good and Bad, POD and POC, All Nine, Shorts, Boys, and Beyonds.

Class Participant:

Thank you, Gary. That was really helpful. Before you asked that question, I wasn't aware that I was looking for somebody who was creating some sort of resistance or fight. I thought I was doing something different.

Gary:

Everything that is times a godzillion, will you destroy and uncreate it all? Right and Wrong, Good and Bad, POD and POC, All Nine, Shorts, Boys, and Beyonds.

Gentlemen, I would like you all to run this process between now and our next call.

What stupidity am I using to create the (the name of the most recent relationship you've had or the person you're currently with) I am choosing?

So it's: What stupidity am I using to create the (person's name) I am choosing? Everything that is times a godzillion, will you destroy and uncreate it all? Right and Wrong, Good and Bad, POD and POC, All Nine, Shorts, Boys, and Beyonds.

Do that with the person you're with now or the last person you were with. You've chosen every woman you've ever had in your life because it matched some vibration. If you truly want to create a change in your life, you've got to find out what that vibration is. Okay, gentlemen, there you go. I'll talk with you on our next call. Take care, my friends. Bye-bye.

Class Participants:

Thank you so much!

8

WHAT IS A GENTLEMAN?

A gentleman comes from no conclusion,
and because he has no judgment,
he opens the door to possibilities for each and
every person he touches.

Gary:

Hello, gentlemen. Does anyone have a question?

Being a Gentleman

Class Participant:

When I think of the word *gentleman,* it feels heavy to me. I feel that being a gentleman is a limitation. In order to be a gentleman, there are things you should do and things you shouldn't do. What is your definition of *gentleman?*

Gary:

First of all, a gentleman is one who is willing to recognize what a woman needs and to deliver that.

Everything that doesn't allow that times a godzillion, will you destroy and uncreate it all? Right and Wrong, Good and Bad, POD and POC, All Nine, Shorts, Boys, and Beyonds.

Class Participant:

Is there more to that definition?

Gary:

If you're willing to be a gentleman, you're willing to see what a woman requires of you. A gentleman doesn't just take in a man's point of view. He is willing to see the woman's point of view, as well. He is willing to see what he can do that will create a different possibility. If you are not willing to see what you're capable of creating as a different possibility, are you truly able to create what you'd like to create?

As an example, I can be a gentleman and open the door for a woman when she's getting into a car. When I do this, she says, "You're such a gentleman." What that means from her point of view is what you're looking for, because in order to create a relationship or sex with anybody, you have to be what they're willing to have you be. If you're willing to be a gentleman, women look at you from a different point of view. Is that point of view judgment or no judgment? It's a point of view of no judgment. That's why being a gentleman is an operative state here.

Everything that is times a godzillion, will you destroy and uncreate it all? Right and Wrong, Good and Bad, POD and POC, All Nine, Shorts, Boys, and Beyonds.

If you have charge about being a gentleman, it means that you have been not a gentleman in way too many lifetimes.

Everywhere you've done "not a gentleman" and everywhere you've gone to judging yourself for not being a gentleman and everywhere you've tried to pretend that you actually don't care about being a gentleman, will you destroy and uncreate all of that? Right and Wrong, Good and Bad, POD and POC, All Nine, Shorts, Boys, and Beyonds.

Class Participant:

Can you talk about what it is to be a gentleman outside of the woman in relationship?

Gary:

If you're a gentleman, you realize the value of each and every person you're with. Gentlemen have no judgment of anyone. They only have the awareness of what might be possible for each and every person they're around. What if you were willing to have the awareness of everything that's possible instead of the judgment of what you should or shouldn't do?

Let's say you're a gentleman and you're out with a gay man and he's your friend. Do you flirt with him or do you not flirt with him?

Class Participant:

I flirt with him.

Gary:

Yeah, because that's what he requires and desires of you. Does it mean you're going to do anything?

Class Participant:

No.

Gary:

No. It means you're going to give him what he desires of you. You have to be willing to see what people desire of you. If you're not willing to be a gentleman, you're not willing to see what people desire of you. A gentleman always knows what is required and desired of him and he delivers whatever he chooses.

Class Participant:

How do you do that without divorcing yourself—because that's what I do?

Gary:

So you're out with a gay friend and you flirt with him. Do you have sex with him?

Class Participant:

Probably not. But I might. Who knows, actually?

Gary:

Good. You're always open to the possibility of what might occur rather than concluding and judging what can or cannot occur.

Class Participant:

What's the difference between a gentleman and a slut?

Gary:

A gentleman is a very good slut, because he has no judgment of what he does or what anybody else does. A gentleman doesn't come to conclusion or judgment. If you were going to look for the opposite of gentleman you might look for a sexist. That's close to being the opposite of gentleman.

A sexist is one who has determined what is right. He has decided that it's the way it's supposed to be and that's what you have to do. Being a gentleman means you're looking for the possibilities, you're not looking for the conclusions, and you're not looking for the judgment.

Class Participant:

Wow. I'm getting some acknowledgment or recognition here.

Gary:

It's the willingness to be something other people aren't willing to be.

Class Participant:

Wow.

Gary:

I'm seventy years old and women who are thirty tell me they would rather be with me than Dain because they know I would not hurt them and Dain would. Is that really true?

Class Participant:

No.

Gary:

No, the only thing that hurts anybody is when you don't give them what they want. Dain is more likely to give them what they think they want than I am. They think Dain is going to turn out to be the prince charming they thought they were looking for. They know I'm too old to be a prince charming, so what can I be? The old man who takes care of them with the elegance they deserve to be treated with.

A Gentleman Chooses Possibility over Judgment

People always choose judgment over possibility. And as a true gentleman, you will always choose possibility over judgment, which invites people to greater possibilities. Years ago I went out to dinner with a woman and her father, who was eighty-eight years old. He was a gentleman of the old school. He dressed elegantly and he looked elegant. There was a woman at dinner with us who was in her fifties and she was all over him. Why? Because he offered no judgment of her, only the possibility of what might actually show up.

A gentleman comes from no conclusion, and because he has no judgment, he opens the door to possibilities for each and every person he touches.

Everything that brought up for all of you, will you destroy and uncreate all of that? Right and Wrong, Good and Bad, POD and POC, All Nine, Shorts, Boys, and Beyonds.

Class Participant:

I have oftentimes heard women say, "Sean Connery is such a gentleman."

I ask, "Have you met him?"

The women say, "No, but he looks like a gentleman."

And I ask, "And I'm not?"

Ask Her to Step Up to a Greater Possibility

Gary:

Sean Connery is willing to be elegant in order to create a place in which people will choose more elegance. If you are a gentleman, you will always ask for everyone to become more of what they can be, not less. How many times have you had sex with a woman and asked her to become less of what she is? A lot, a little, or megatons? If you ask a woman to give herself to you, are you asking her to be all of her, or less of her?

Class Participant:

Less of her.

Gary:

Yeah. As a gentleman, you always ask her to step up to a greater possibility, and if you do that, possibility will occur. She will step up to a greater sexual energy than you've ever had before. Most of you ask for a woman to give herself to you, which is not asking her to be more of her. You don't ask her to step up to a greater possibility than she ever knew was possible. What if you were asking the women you have sex with to step up to something they wouldn't even know is possible?

Everything that is times a godzillion, will you destroy and uncreate it all? Right and Wrong, Good and Bad, POD and POC, All Nine, Shorts, Boys, and Beyonds.

Class Participant:

What would it look like to ask a woman to do that?

Gary:

It would be "Hey, can I do this for you?" Years ago, I would ask women, "What has somebody done for you that nobody else has ever done for you, that if it were done for you would give you more than you ever thought was possible?" I always wanted to know what others guys had done that I didn't do. Now why would I do that?

Class Participant:

To find out what she likes?

Gary:

Yeah! To find out what she likes, what makes her happy, and what makes her body sing. If you ask what some other man has done for her that nobody else has done, you will get the energy of it. When you're willing to deliver that energy, you're being a gentleman who's willing to give her everything she ever desired, everything she ever wanted, and everything she ever thought was great.

Everything that doesn't allow you to perceive, know, be, and receive that, will you destroy and uncreate it all? Right and Wrong, Good and Bad, POD and POC, All Nine, Shorts, Boys, and Beyonds.

Class Participant:

I'm not as fucked up as I thought I was.

Gary:

Is that you, Mr. Shag Master?

Class Participant:

Yeah. It's he who gives himself up to a woman instantaneously.

Gary:

Have you ever heard me tell you that you're not as fucked up as you think you are?

Class Participant:

Yeah. I've heard it a couple of times.

Gary:

Yeah, but you never believed me, did you?

Class Participant:

I've heard that maybe 2,000 times.

Gary:

The next time I see you, you have to give me a euro to prove that I wasn't wrong.

What you're capable of and what you do are two different things. What if they weren't two different things? Do you keep trying to see how you're wrong—or how you're right?

Class Participant:

How I'm wrong.

Gary:

What creation of sex and copulation are you using to validate other peoples' realities and invalidate your reality are you choosing? Everything that is times a godzillion, will you destroy and uncreate it all? Right and Wrong, Good and Bad, POD and POC, All Nine, Shorts, Boys, and Beyonds.

Class Participant:

Yeah, I jump into other people's reality.

Gary:

Do you want to know that you do that?

Class Participant:

Yes.

Gary:

No, you don't. You are always trying to figure out how you're not doing that rather than seeing how you are doing it. You have to be able to see what someone requires and desires of you.

For example, when you think you want to have sex with someone, do you cut off your awareness in order to have sex?

Class Participant:

Oftentimes, yes.

Gary:

Not oftentimes. All the fucking time!

What stupidity are you using to create the defense for and against the copulation others are choosing for you are you choosing? Everything that is times a godzillion, will you destroy and uncreate it all? Right and Wrong, Good and Bad, POD and POC, all Nine, Shorts, Boys, and Beyonds.

You Have to Create from Your Reality

Class Participant:

Gary, this has been an amazing series. Last night I had the most phenomenal sex. There is a desire for me to have more sex with this particular person and explore this more. Is it possible to have a Deal and Deliver with a woman about how to have more without creating a relationship?

Gary:

Thank God you have finally had this experience. Sexual energy is about the generative capacity of life and living and the orgasmic quality of life and living that most of us have never been willing or able to have. Do you all get this?

Is it possible to have more with a woman without creating relationship? Probably not. Would you like to believe it was? Absolutely. Are you completely delusional? Yeah, you're a man. You have to get that women look for a different thing than men do. Women aren't in the same universe as you. More often than not, they don't understand what you're asking for or what you're interested in.

There's a different possibility in life for how you create that. You have to create from your reality. Start running:

What energy, space, and consciousness can I be that will allow me to create the reality I know is possible can I truly be? Everything that doesn't allow that to show up times a godzillion, will you destroy and uncreate it all? Right and Wrong, Good and Bad, POD and POC, All Nine, Shorts, Boys, and Beyonds.

There's a new process I just came up with, which I think is appropriate for this:

What creation of sex and copulation are you using to subordinate, absolve, and resolve the choice and the awareness you have in favor of the reality of others are you choosing? Everything that doesn't allow that to show up, will you destroy and uncreate it all? Right and Wrong, Good and Bad, POD and POC, All Nine, Shorts, Boys, and Beyonds.

You keep trying to choose what will work for the woman. It's one of the things men do. They always try to choose what will work for the woman. Is there a reason for that? Yeah. You have been entrained and trained to believe that the woman is the most valuable product on the planet, not you.

Everything that is times a godzillion, will you destroy and uncreate it all? Right and Wrong, Good and Bad, POD and POC, All Nine, Shorts, Boys, and Beyonds.

What creation of sex and copulation are you using as the subordination, the absolution, and the resolution of your choice and your awareness in favor of other people's reality are you choosing? Everything that is times a godzillion, will you destroy and uncreate it all? Right and Wrong, Good and Bad, POD and POC, All Nine, Shorts, Boys, and Beyonds.

You keep assuming that you've got to give up your reality in favor of somebody else's. It's not even giving up your reality. It's that you have no point of view. You're a man. You have no point of view unless your penis is hard and pointing in a direction. The one thing I love about men is that they're completely insensitive to anybody else's awareness until their penis is pointing. Penile seeking is the direction you know how to follow.

Don't you find it interesting that you would always try to please and value somebody else before you'd ever try to see the value of you?

Class Participant:

Yes.

Gary:

Does that make sense?

Class Participant:

Well, no, it makes no sense.

Gary:

It's the non-sensible universe that you keep trying to create from. It doesn't work.

What Do You Want to Create?

Class Participant:

On the last call when we talked about sex, you said to get very good at cunnilingus and using our fingers. You said we would then have women who want to come and visit again and again, and that is how we start creating the place where we become a valuable product. It sounds to me like you're saying we are not valuable products, and that we need to do something in order to become a valuable product.

Gary:

Yes, in their eyes, you do.

Class Participant:

Isn't that beingness instead of being? You've said that *being* is you, the infinite being you are and that *beingness* is something you do to prove that you're being.

Gary:

You've got to look at what you're trying to create, not what you think it should be. You can have all kinds of wonderful points of view about what should be and what ought to be that isn't. You've got to look at what *is*—not what you *want it to be*.

Class Participant:

Can you please clarify this? It sounds like you're saying that men need women's acknowledgement to become the valuable product.

Gary:

To become the valuable product in a woman's world, you have to please the woman in ways that make her value the sex you like more than she does.

Class Participant:

Doesn't that make the woman more valuable?

Gary:

Yes. What's wrong with that?

Why Is Lust Considered a Wrongness?

Class Participant:

Last month a female friend posted a picture of us on Facebook where she was all dressed up and wearing make-up. She looked gorgeous, and many men were commenting on her picture. They praised her, and some tried to date her. When I saw that, I noticed I felt a bit angry. What am I missing here?

Gary:

Did you feel anger or did you feel envy? You have to get clear about the difference. My guess is you felt envy, because you wanted to be lusted after the way she was lusted after. How many of you are refusing to be lusted after because you think that makes you less?

Everything that is times a godzillion, will you destroy and uncreate it all? Right and Wrong, Good and Bad, POD and POC, All Nine, Shorts, Boys, and Beyonds.

Class Participant:

I had an awareness a few days later that she was trying to control the opposite sex with her looks and appearance. And the anger was because that's exactly what I haven't been willing to do.

Gary:

You mean you only get angry at what you yourself are doing or not doing?

Everything you've done to make it real and true for you that you can't be the lustful person you truly be, will you destroy and uncreate all of that? Right and Wrong, Good and Bad, POD and POC, All Nine, Shorts, Boys, and Beyonds.

What refusal of lust are you using to invalidate the being you could be choosing? Everything that is times a godzillion, will you destroy and uncreate it all? Right and Wrong, Good and Bad, POD and POC, All Nine, Shorts, Boys, and Beyonds.

Class Participant:

I have not been willing to take advantage of my looks. Most of the time I look normal, and sometimes I look quite sloppy.

Gary:

I'd say, my sweet friend, that you're choosing to be sloppy as often as you can because you don't want people to lust after you. Why is lust considered a wrongness? I do not understand that.

What creation of lust are you using to invalidate you and invalidate others are you choosing? Everything that is times a godzillion, will you destroy and uncreate it all? Right and Wrong, Good and Bad, POD and POC, All Nine, Shorts, Boys, and Beyonds.

What creation of lust are you using to invalidate your reality and invalidate other people's realities are you choosing? Everything that is times a godzillion, will you destroy and uncreate it all? Right and Wrong, Good and Bad, POD and POC, All Nine, Shorts, Boys, and Beyonds.

Class Participant:

I'm confused about this. Are you saying we lust after people to make us less valuable?

Gary:

Sometimes. The thing is, you're not willing to see the value of lust.

Class Participant:

So what's the value of lust?

Gary:

The value of lust is the place where you come out of judgment and go into "I'm going to do this no matter what it looks like. No matter what it takes. No matter what occurs." Lust is not a wrongness. Lust is a place in which you cannot overcome your unwillingness to be limited. You will choose lust over limitation every time. Instead of seeing that as an advantage and possibility, you see it as a wrongness. Why? Because you've been told forever that lust is wrong. Is it really wrong—or is it just where you sit?

When somebody wants to have sex with you, do you say, "Wow, this person wants to have sex with me. How cool is that?" Or do you go to the conclusion, "How can I do this and when can I do this?" You have to be willing to look at "And this person wants to have sex with me for what reason?"

Class Participant:

That would be a change for me.

Gary:

A lot of people would choose to have sex with you because a) you're a man, b) you're sexual, c) you actually like women, and d) you know how to do fairly good cunnilingus, but only fairly good, not good.

You boys need to learn how to do better cunnilingus, by the way, in case you didn't know that.

What stupidity are you using to create the defense for and against the sex somebody else wants to have with you are you choosing? Everything that is times a godzillion, will you destroy and uncreate it all? Right and Wrong, Good and Bad, POD and POC, All Nine, Shorts, Boys, and Beyonds.

Class Participant:

The other week, I got questioned by a woman who wanted to have a date with me. She was starting to defend that she wouldn't go to bed on the first date. So I just asked her "Are you playing hard to get or what?"

She asked, "Yeah, but who would you be or what would you do to get to that?"

I said, "Uh, I would be me."

She said, "Ah, you've got some self-esteem there, right?"

So then I said, "Off my list. Piss off."

Gary:

The female of the species is designed for what purpose? To have babies or have no babies?

Class Participant:

To have babies.

Gary:

Yeah, so who's she going to choose? A man who is good breeding stock. She'll look at one man and say, "He is good breeding stock; therefore, I will have sex with him." She'll look at another guy and say, "He might have a physical disability. He's not a good choice." She'll look at someone else and say, "He has a disease. I don't want him," or "He has an addiction, so he's not the best breeding stock." It's all about who can she choose for the best breeding stock.

Have you ever had a woman say to you, "We could make such beautiful children together?"

Class Participant:

Not so many, actually. It's oftentimes the other way around for me.

Gary:

You're the one who is saying it, right? But that's what she's feeding you to say to her so she can get you to choose to do that.

Who has another question?

Being Mean to Other Men

Class Participant:

I was once pissed off at another fellow and I said to him, "The body has four nervous systems—the central nervous system, the sympathetic nervous system, the apathetic nervous system, and the last one, which is the one that is most active in you." Damn. He got pissed off, and it was fun. Is that how men operate?

Gary:

No. You felt like having sex with him and the only way you could not have sex with him was to avoid it by saying something mean to him. Men do mean things to other men because they want to have sex with them.

Everything you're unwilling to perceive, know, be, and receive about that, will you destroy and uncreate it all? Right and Wrong, Good and Bad, POD and POC, All Nine, Shorts, Boys, and Beyonds.

Whenever you're being mean to another man, ask, "Am I choosing this because I would like to have sex with this guy?" It's not acceptable in this reality to have sex with another man, is it? No. Not if you're a heterosexual. So why do you have to be a heterosexual?

Class Participant:

That's the norm. To fit in.

Gary:

Everything you're doing to make that your reality rather than having choice, will you destroy and uncreate all of that? Right and Wrong, Good and Bad, POD and POC, All Nine, Shorts, Boys, and Beyonds.

By the way, I am not trying to get you to have sex with men. Please know that. A gay guy doesn't get mad with men. He gets sexual with them. You guys get mad with men.

Look back at all the places where you got mad at men that you actually wanted to have sex with.

Will you destroy and uncreate everything that doesn't allow you to perceive, know, be, and receive that you would have had a different response if you'd been willing to have sex? Right and Wrong, Good and Bad, POD and POC, All Nine, Shorts, Boys, and Beyonds.

I'm not advocating that you have sex with men. I'm trying to give you the freedom to look at what actually is, so you know where your choices are. The fact that you would be willing to have sex with a man means you would be willing to have somebody in your life who was willing to have sex with you.

Class Participant:

Isn't that a big part of receiving other men? Not the copulation part, but the receiving?

Gary:

Yeah. You have to receive when other men find you sexual as well as when you find you sexual. It's not that you need to have sex with men. What you need to have is the awareness that you're so sexual that you create in everyone around you the willingness to have sex.

Everything that is times a godzillion, will you destroy and uncreate it all? Right and Wrong, Good and Bad, POD and POC, All Nine, Shorts, Boys, and Beyonds.

Trying to Steal Other Men's Women

Class Participant:

You've said that humanoid men don't try to steal other men's women.

Gary:

Yeah.

Class Participant:

I think of myself as a humanoid, yet I can see that I've done that a couple of times. What is that?

Gary:

Were you really trying to steal their women or did their women want to make their men jealous?

Class Participant:

That one.

Gary:

When you're aware, you tend to look at things from the point of view of "What would this person want?" What would it be like if you were willing to see what would be possible with each and every person instead of trying to deliver what they want from you?

Class Participant:

And choose what works for me.

Gary:

Yeah, and the thing is, you're so psychically aware that when you go to steal another man's woman, it's because that woman wants to make the man jealous. Dain was with a woman one night and I was thinking, "I'm so jealous. I can't believe he's having sex with this woman." I said, "What? Wait a minute! Under the best of circumstances, that could not be my point of view. What is this?"

I realized it was her thought. She wanted jealousy in somebody's universe. The next morning, I asked Dain, "What happened last night? What was going on?" He said, "Well, she stayed the night because she was too drunk to drive home, but she called her boyfriend to say, 'Don't worry, I won't do anything,' and then she wasn't willing to sleep with me. She slept on the floor. I don't understand this woman at all. She said she wanted to have sex with me, but then she wouldn't."

I asked, "Do you think she might have been finding a way to make her boyfriend jealous by going with you and getting drunk so she couldn't drive home?"

Dain said, "Yes!"

Once that was spotted, I realized the jealousy I was aware of was what Dain wasn't willing to be aware of. The woman was trying to make her boyfriend jealous. She pretended she was going up to Dain's room to sleep with him, but she was doing it to get her boyfriend jealous so he would have a meltdown. If you're not willing to see where people are functioning from, you will always be the effect of their insanity.

Everything you've done to make yourself the effect of people's insanity instead of having the awareness of when they're being insane, will you destroy and uncreate all of that? Right and Wrong, Good and Bad, POD and POC, All Nine, Shorts, Boys, and Beyonds.

I have known this shit forever. Why don't others?

Class Participant:

Because you're weird.

Gary:

Yeah I know. It's because I'm weird.

Taxation

Have any of you ever had sex with someone and then felt you had to do something for them to make it okay?

Class Participant:

Yeah.

Gary:

That's a form of taxation. It's taxation—not choice, not possibility, and not creation and generation. Have you ever gone down on somebody and thought that they should go down on you?

Class Participant:

Yes.

Gary:

Or vice-versa?

Class Participant:

Is that taxation as well?

Gary:

Yes. "There is a tax I have to pay for what I got." Taxation is all the pieces and parts of what you have to pay, regardless of what else occurs. Doesn't that sound like fun?

Class Participant:

No. I'm over that.

Gary:

Cool. All right, next question.

A Sexual Reality beyond This Reality

Class Participant:

Throughout these calls, I've noticed the general tendency is for men to ask, "How do I get better sex and more sex?" Is that really what we're here for?

Gary:

Well, that's not what we're here for, but it's part of what's good about being here.

Class Participant:

From my point of view, my lady is very sexy and I adore her, but surely there is more than just getting my dick wet. From your point of view, what's beyond this that we haven't yet considered? What would it take to have that?

Gary:

What physical actualization of a sexual reality totally beyond this reality are you now willing to generate, create, and institute? Everything that is times a godzillion, will you destroy and uncreate it all? Right and Wrong, Good and Bad, POD and POC, All Nine, Shorts, Boys, and Beyonds.

It's All a Judgment of Receiving

Class Participant:

On these calls, there has been a lot of talk about women and sex. Are we talking about that because it's so interconnected to all the parts of our lives, and it's a way to...

Gary:

Unfortunately, we've spent a whole lot of time trying to determine whether we should have sex or shouldn't have sex, whether it's appropriate to have sex or not appropriate to have sex, whether we are going to get more if we have sex or not have more if we don't have sex. Is any of that judgment, or is all of that judgment?

Class Participant:

It's all about judgment, and does that correlate into all of the judgments we have in all areas, in the other parts of our lives as well?

Gary:

It's all a judgment of receiving. Remember, sex is about receiving.

Class Participant:

I know, I know.

Gary:

Let's say you're going to have sex with a woman. What are you willing to receive from her? Anything or nothing? Nothing.

Class Participant:

Nothing came up.

Gary:

Which is why you're trying to have sex with her, so you can give her everything you don't like about you.

Everything that is times a godzillion, will you destroy and uncreate it all? Right and Wrong, Good and Bad, POD and POC, All Nine, Shorts, Boys, and Beyonds.

Class Participant:

Is there anything to say about the opposite situation when you have more to give than the other person can receive?

Gary:

You're still in the computation of what you can give, not what you can receive. If you were willing to see somebody who could receive everything you are, would you be trapped by that?

Class Participant:

I got a *yes* on that.

Gary:

That's the problem. When you get somebody who can receive everything you are, you feel that somehow you're going to be trapped. Is that a truth, or is that the lie, or is that the insanity you keep trying to make real that actually isn't?

Class Participant:

Ah, shit!

Gary:

Everything that is times a godzillion, will you destroy and uncreate it all? Right and Wrong, Good and Bad, POD and POC, All Nine, Shorts, Boys, and Beyonds.

You're more interested in giving up choice than not.

What creation of life, living, and copulation are you using to enslave yourself to the anti-consciousness and unconsciousness you are choosing? Everything that is times a godzillion, will you

destroy and uncreate it all? Right and Wrong, Good and Bad, POD and POC, All Nine, Shorts, Boys, and Beyonds.

Please get that most of you have enslaved yourself to this reality. You haven't been willing to look at what your choices are. You're more interested in what choices you don't have. It's not your best choice.

Class Participant:

I've been seeing a beautiful woman and it has been really different this time. It has been very easy. The sex is amazing and so is the way I connect with her. It's just space. What is that? Is that me not receiving her?

Gary:

No, that's actually receiving,

Class Participant:

It's so different I almost don't know what to do with it. I'm so unused to it.

Gary:

Yeah, you've never chosen a woman who could actually receive from you, have you?

Class Participant:

No, I haven't.

Gary:

And have you ever chosen women who actually cared about you?

Class Participant:

No.

Gary:

Why? Why would you choose women who don't care about you? Is that so you don't actually have to care about them?

Class Participant:

Yeah.

Gary:

Everything you've done to choose women you don't have to care about, will you destroy and uncreate all of that? Right and Wrong, Good and Bad, POD and POC, All Nine, Shorts, Boys, and Beyonds.

Luckily, it's only you who does that.

Class Participant:

Yeah, right.

Gary:

Why do you choose a woman you don't have to care about in order to choose somebody to care about?

Class Participant:

That's a really good question. Is it to control myself out of not being greater?

Gary:

Is it to control yourself? Or is that the way you guarantee you'll never choose to be the greatness of you?

Class Participant:

The second one.

Gary:

Everything that is times a godzillion, will you destroy and uncreate it all? Right and Wrong, Good and Bad, POD and POC, All Nine, Shorts, Boys, and Beyonds.

Class Participant:

Thank you, Gary. These calls rock my world. I am so grateful for them.

Gary:

I'm so glad. Even if only six or eight of you start to choose greater, you guys may change the world, and I would really like to see what goes on here when sex and relationship are different.

Class Participant:

Let's change the world!

What Kind of Future Is She Trying to Create?

Gary:

Yeah. Originally, women's job was to be willing and able to create a future, because women are more willing to see it than most men are. It doesn't mean they're better. It just means they're more willing.

Class Participant:

Is that also because women are more likely to go out and conquer the world, and men are more likely to stay in the same place?

Gary:

Most humanoid men would rather have a comfortable life and create a nest for their children than go out in the world and conquer it.

Women want to create a future. The travesty done to women has been to make them believe that their desire for the future is about children, which is not actually so. They are not doing what they're doing for children. They're doing what they're doing for what will create a different possibility.

Everything that is times a godzillion, will you destroy and uncreate it all? Right and Wrong, Good and Bad, POD and POC, All Nine, Shorts, Boys, and Beyonds.

When you're with a woman, guys, you have to look at "What kind of future is she trying to create here?" If she is trying to create a future that is about having children, she's buying into this reality. Is that the reality you want to live by? If you get that she's trying to create babies, are you going to have the same kind of relationship with her that you would if she wasn't?

Class Participant:

No.

Gary:

If you start looking at what the future is that she is trying to create, you will no longer buy the wrongness of you. When a woman is willing to create a future that includes you, it's not going to make the wrongness of you more real than the choice you make.

What would you create if you knew what future she was trying to create? If she's trying to create a greater future than you're willing to have, can you be with her?

Class Participant:

I got a *no* for that.

Gary:

Yeah. That's a no. You have to be willing to create the future she's willing to have. How great a future is she willing to have? If you're willing to know that, you can create anything with her. You can create a relationship. Let's say you had a woman who desired to go out and conquer the world and you were perfectly happy being home, not doing a whole lot. If that was the case, could that woman stay with you?

Class Participant:

No.

Class Participant:

If that was the case, then what?

Gary:

Then you'd have to ask, "Can we create anything good?"

Class Participant:

Yeah.

Gary:

The only way you can create a relationship is if her desire for future and your capacity to go there can match. If you look at the relationships that haven't worked for you in the past, did the woman have a desire for a future that you had no desire for?

Class Participant:

Yes.

Gary:

That is why those relationships didn't work.

Everything that is times a godzillion, will you destroy and uncreate it all? Right and Wrong, Good and Bad, POD and POC, All Nine, Shorts, Boys, and Beyonds.

Class Participant:

That explains why I have bailed out, or pulled out, or chosen not to see a woman anymore. It's because I was aware of the future. I was aware of it but unwilling to see it and I made myself wrong for it.

Gary:

If the woman has a future in which you have to be a follower, are you going to be any good at that?

Class Participant:

No.

Gary:

No. You're not a follower. Are you willing to be a leader?

Class Participant:

Yes, I am.

Gary:

Or are you trying to avoid the leader you could be?

Class Participant:

Yeah, I am.

Gary:

Everything that is times a godzillion, will you destroy and uncreate it all? Right and Wrong, Good and Bad, POD and POC, All Nine, Shorts, Boys, and Beyonds.

Please know that I'm not trying to make you wrong. I want you to see what has not been working in your life so you can create something greater. It's very real to me that all of you have the ability to create something other people don't have the ability to create, but you get so involved with the women in your life. You keep thinking they're going to choose something that's going to make everything work more easily. Is that really possible?

Class Participant:

Not.

Stepping Out of Being Stoppable

Class Participant:

I contacted my father today. I haven't spoken to him for thirteen years.

Gary:

What were you aware of with your father that you didn't want to be aware of that kept you from talking to him?

Class Participant:

He missed me.

Gary:

That's nice, but that's not what you were aware of.

Class Participant:

I think he's sick as well.

Gary:

That's not what you were aware of. Was your father as sexual as you were? Or was he more sexual?

Class Participant:

More.

Gary:

Did your mother like that or hate that?

Class Participant:

She hated that.

Gary:

Did you like it or hate it?

Class Participant:

I liked it.

Gary:

So did you want to grow up to be like your father, but you resisted doing so?

Class Participant:

Yes.

Gary:

Everything that is times a godzillion, will you destroy and uncreate it all? Right and Wrong, Good and Bad, POD and POC, All Nine, Shorts, Boys, and Beyonds.

Class Participant:

It hangs together that since I was born, my mother has resisted me and rejected him.

Gary:

Were you willing to tone down your sexual energy to fit your mother's need?

Class Participant:

Absolutely.

Gary:

How much of your sexual energy have you toned down to fit other people's needs? A lot, a little, or megatons?

Class Participant:

The last one.

Gary:

Everything that is times a godzillion, will you destroy and uncreate it all? Right and Wrong, Good and Bad, POD and POC, All Nine, Shorts, Boys, and Beyonds.

How many of you have toned down your sexual energy to match something that was acceptable to your mothers, or not acceptable to your fathers, or too much like your fathers to be acceptable to your mothers? Everything that is times a godzillion, will you destroy and uncreate it all? Right and Wrong, Good and Bad, POD and POC, All Nine, Shorts, Boys, and Beyonds.

Just because you were capable of being as sexual as your father was, or as sexual as your mother was, or as sexual as they were together— that's the one. You are not willing to be as sexual as they were together because you assume that's what made you. I'm sorry. That isn't what made you. You slammed them together to make you the body you wanted. That didn't make you, the being. You were already you, the being.

Everything that is times a godzillion, will you destroy and uncreate it all? Right and Wrong, Good and Bad, POD and POC, All Nine, Shorts, Boys, and Beyonds.

You resist all of the sexual energy from your own life in order not to be as sexual as your father and your mother were together in order not to create somebody like you. That's cool, and of course that doesn't require any judgment of you, does it?

Class Participant:

Oh my God.

Gary:

Everything that is times a godzillion, will you destroy and uncreate it all? Right and Wrong, Good and Bad, POD and POC, All Nine, Shorts, Boys, and Beyonds.

It's amazing you guys can walk, talk, and chew gum, let alone get an erection.

Class Participant:

That also explains the reason why I'm looking for other things to judge, fix, or comb over.

Gary:

Why is it that you don't get that you are amazing? Why is seeing how amazing you are untenable, unfathomable, and inappropriate to you?

How much of you have you made inappropriate because you were concerned that you would be as sexual as your father and your mother were together, which is what you created in them in order to create your body? Are you not willing to create somebody as great as you and give them a body equal to what you got? That would be a yes.

Everything that is times a godzillion, will you destroy and uncreate it all? Right and Wrong, Good and Bad, POD and POC, All Nine, Shorts, Boys, and Beyonds.

Class Participant:

That would invalidate everybody else.

Gary:

Would it invalidate everybody else or would it inspire everybody else?

Class Participant:

Yeah, it would inspire.

Gary:

How many of you are refusing to inspire others dynamically so you can perspire yourself out of existence? Everything that is times a godzillion, will you destroy and uncreate it all? Right and Wrong, Good and Bad, POD and POC, All Nine, Shorts, Boys, and Beyonds.

Class Participant:

It's where we put up all of these inventions and standards and whatever we can come up with to box ourselves in.

Gary:

Well, is any of that actually yours?

Class Participant:

No.

Gary:

What creation of your sexuality are you refusing that you truly could be choosing that if you would choose it would create a whole different universe for you? Everything that is times a godzillion, will you destroy and uncreate it all? Right and Wrong, Good and Bad, POD and POC, All Nine, Shorts, Boys, and Beyonds.

Class Participant:

Oh, good Lord. Are you kidding me?

Gary:

What creation of your sexuality are you refusing that if you didn't refuse it would actually allow you to be everything you are? Everything that is times a godzillion, will you destroy and uncreate it all? Right and Wrong, Good and Bad, POD and POC, All Nine, Shorts, Boys, and Beyonds.

You guys are doing a lot to refuse your own sexual energy.

What sexual energy of you are you refusing in order to create the limitations you are choosing? Everything that is times a godzillion, will you destroy and uncreate it all? Right and Wrong, Good and Bad, POD and POC, All Nine, Shorts, Boys, and Beyonds.

Class Participant:

I've always refused my sexual energy.

Gary:

Why? Because nobody could receive it? Or because if you would be it, you'd have to be something you didn't think you were capable of?

Class Participant:

Oh, shit.

Class Participant:

When I listen to you talk about this, the word that comes up for me is unfathomable. It's unfathomable to step into that much sexualness.

Gary:

Do you mean stepping out of being stoppable?

Class Participant:

Yeah.

Gary:

Everything that is times a godzillion, will you destroy and uncreate it all? Right and Wrong, Good and Bad, POD and POC, All Nine, Shorts, Boys, and Beyonds.

Class Participant:

I got to a place where my body wasn't willing to have me do that. I broke out in hives.

Gary:

Was your body really not willing to have you do it? Or did you know that your body would have to change if you were willing to do it? And did your body know that if you were willing to choose it, it would have to change?

Class Participant:

Yes.

Gary:

Everything that is times a godzillion, will you destroy and uncreate it all? Right and Wrong, Good and Bad, POD and POC, All Nine, Shorts, Boys, and Beyonds.

Gary:

It was telling you, "Okay, this is a warning shot. If you continue down this path, you're going to change way more."

Class Participant:

That's interesting, because hives have always shown up when I was about to choose something else. Then I would make myself wrong. I'd go into "What am I doing wrong? I must be doing something wrong."

Gary:

So do you like to make yourself wrong?

Class Participant:

Well, I'm good at it.

Gary:

If you're doing it, the answer is yes. And you are obviously destroying your life.

Class Participant:

Yeah. I know it. Every time I go into that place of wrongness, it's definitely not creating anything.

Gary:

That's because you really wouldn't want to create anything, right?

Class Participant:

It was interesting for me to be at home, on my own, while my partner was away for a couple of weeks. I recognized the energy of destruction when it came up.

The Energy of Limitation

Gary:

Is it really the energy of destruction or is it the energy of limitation?

Class Participant:
Right. That one.

Gary:

Why is limitation more important to you than possibility?

Class Participant:
Well...

Gary:

Would you have to go beyond the limits of what you have decided is the reality you're willing to have?

Class Participant:

Yeah.

Gary:

Are you willing to do that?

Class Participant:

I get *no*.

Gary:

Why would you not be willing to go beyond the limitations of what you're willing to have? Are you willing to live within the limitations you're currently familiar with? Or are you willing to go beyond what that energy can live with?

Class Participant:

I'm willing to go beyond.

Gary:

This is a demand you have to make of yourself: Okay, no matter what it takes, I'm going beyond every limitation here. I'm not going to live my life from this limited point of view. It doesn't work for me. And no matter who it works for, it doesn't work for me.

Class Participant:

Yep.

Gary:

What if it was never about what works for somebody else? What if it was always about what worked for *you*?

Class Participant:

Yeah. I like that.

Gary:

How much of your life have you done what works for a woman because that's easier than what works for you?

Class Participant:

All of it.

Gary:

That's where you've gone into being a man instead of being a gentleman.

Class Participant:

Exactly.

Class Participant:

Gary, what are your thoughts on the following clearing I've created? Can it be improved in any way? In your awareness, is it effective?

What energy, space, and consciousness can my body and I be to receive the sexual, nurturing, female energies that are vibrationally compatible for me?

Gary:

Well, I'd say there is only one limitation in it.

What energy, space, and consciousness can my body and I be to receive the sexual, nurturing energy that is vibrationally compatible for me and my body in totality?

It may not be just female energies that are sexually nurturing to you. What if there are also male energies that contribute to you in dynamic ways? Would you be willing to receive that? There are some men, who by being your friend, can give you more than females can. If you make it about female energy, you've defined the limitations of what you're willing to have as a reality. And is there actually *female* energy? Or is there the energy of people who have chosen a female body? That's the only difference I would make in the clearing.

Class Participant:

Thanks for these calls, Gary. They're awesome.

Class Participant:

Thank you, thank you, thank you.

Gary:

Thank you, gentlemen, for being on these calls. I hope that they might change the future in some way so there's more freedom for men and women.

Class Participant:

Thank you Gary. You're wonderful.

Gary:

Thanks for being the amazing men you are.

9

WHAT DO YOU ACTUALLY WANT IN A RELATIONSHIP?

If you have a relationship,
it should be something that adds to your life
and makes it greater and better and more fun.
If a relationship doesn't do that, why be in one?

Gary:

Hello, gentlemen. Let's begin with a question.

The Perfection of Women

Class Participant:

On the last call, you said that a gentleman is willing to recognize what a woman needs and requires and he is willing to deliver that. I've been asking myself, "What's the value of that?" It doesn't seem to do any good for the man. My ex-girlfriend used that gentleman thing against me. She would say things like, "You should do this—or you are not a gentleman," and from her point of view, not being a gentleman was a wrongness.

Gary:

No. From your point of view, it was a wrongness, which is why you were willing to have her say, "You need to do this" and you did it. Women will use you to get what they want.

If a woman says, "If you're a gentleman, you'll do this," it means she wants to control you. Are you willing to be controlled? Yes, to a certain extent, but not totally. We recently came up with a new process that is damn good. I'm going to run that on all of you:

What bastardization of the perfection of women are you using to create the judgments, the limitations, and the invitations to the demons, the sirens, and the sylphs of anti-consciousness and unconsciousness are you choosing? Everything that is times a godzillion, will you destroy and uncreate it all? Right and Wrong, Good and Bad, POD and POC, All Nine, Shorts, Boys, and Beyonds.

There is a perfection to women, but it's not about the things we think make them perfect. What makes a woman better than a man is the fact that she doesn't have to come to conclusion. She doesn't have to fix anything. She gets to choose more than a man does. Part of the perfection of women is that she can change her mind—and men have to take it. You have to be able to see this or else you make yourself miserable.

When you create women as perfect, you invite the demons, the sirens, and the sylphs. The *sirens* are women who will call a man to his death. The *sylphs* are wraith-like beings that wisp in and out of life but don't actually become part of it. We lock ourselves out of being aware of what a woman is going to require and desire of us, and then we try to control the desires and requirements she says she has. The desires and requirements *she says she has* and the ones she *actually has* are two different things.

What bastardization of the perfection of women are you using to create the judgments, the limitations, and the invitations to the demons, the sirens, and the sylphs of anti-consciousness and unconsciousness are you choosing? Everything that is times a godzillion, will you destroy and uncreate it all? Right and Wrong, Good and Bad, POD and POC, All Nine, Shorts, Boys, and Beyonds.

Okay, let's go on to the next question.

Class Participant:

As a gentleman, how do you deal with over-demanding bitches?

Gary:

You call them over-demanding bitches! A woman who is truly a woman will fight for creation of a future that has not existed on planet earth. That's what a real woman will do. She will not try to get you to fulfill all of her desires, all of her hopes, and all of her requirements. You have bought into too many of the romantic comedies, the chick flicks you've had to watch. As a gentleman how do you deal with over-demanding bitches? You call them over-demanding bitches.

Pornography

Class Participant:

Can you do some clearings about pornography? Even though I know it's not real and that whatever they are doing is not nurturing to bodies, I find the turn-on of porn more exciting than the real world.

Gary:

Yes, and that would be a surprise based on what? If you are functioning from the illusions of pornography, you don't have to include anybody else in your world. You don't have to have a real person in your life.

Class Participant:

Generally, I find that the girls in porn are prettier and there is more variety. I would like to clear that and be more present with the girls in the real world.

Gary:

Well, you don't need to have that if you'd rather not. If you'd rather have women in your life who are more like women in pornography, you have to be willing to settle for that kind of woman. It sounds like you've been trying to get nice girls to be not nice, and you choose girls who are cute but not too cute, so they won't leave you. At the same time, you're not willing to have the sluts and whores that will give you everything you want sexually.

Everything that brought up times a godzillion, will you destroy and uncreate it all? Right and Wrong, Good and Bad, POD and POC, All Nine, Shorts, Boys, and Beyonds.

The Spells We Create

Dain and I did a radio show tonight where we talked about the spells we create. The way we create spells in our life is by repeating something over and over again as though it's true. You cast your own spell on things. "I want a girl like this," is a spell you're casting. You can't have a girl that's like a porn star unless you go to the place where they make porn flicks and find a girl who's a porn star. And you assume things about her that have nothing to do with reality.

How many spells are you using to create the necessity and love of porn you are choosing? Everything that is times a godzillion, will you destroy and uncreate it all? Right and Wrong, Good and Bad, POD and POC, All Nine, Shorts, Boys, and Beyonds.

Every time you say, "My penis is too small," you cast a spell, so it can never be seen as any bigger. And you can't ever make it bigger.

Class Participant:

And the perfection of woman would also be a spell, right?

Gary:

Yes, you've tried to see women as perfect your whole life. You've seen them as greater than you, or providing more than you, or some other thing.

A spell occurs when you take a fixed point of view that creates a holding pattern in the body. On top of the fixed point of view you have of the body, there is also a place where you say certain things repeatedly. You create a spell whenever you say, "I can't" or "I won't" or "My life sucks" or "You're wrong" or any of that kind of stuff.

How many times have you been told you were wrong by a woman? She was casting a spell on you.

All of the spells that have been cast on you by women to show you that you're wrong, that you're not doing it right, and that you need to be different for them, will you destroy and uncreate all of that? Right and Wrong, Good and Bad, POD and POC, All Nine, Shorts, Boys, and Beyonds.

You don't need to be different for a woman. You need to be what works for you.

Class Participant:

Is that what I've been doing? Trying to see myself through a woman's eyes?

Gary:

Yes. Have you had a spell cast on you so that you can only be seen through a woman's eyes?

Class Participant:

Yes.

Gary:

Everything you've done to make you viewable only through a woman's eyes, and of course, how often does a woman let you step into her life and see you through her eyes? Never. Everything that is times a godzillion, will you destroy and uncreate it all? Right and Wrong, Good and Bad, POD and POC, All Nine, Shorts, Boys, and Beyonds.

Class Participant:

I was at the class where you first used that process, and I perceived how the energy changed in the whole group, for both men and women, after this process. It sounds like it's a process for men, but it seemed like it lightened up the universe for women almost even more than men. Can you talk about that?

Gary:

If you're projecting at women that they're perfect, that is the spell you are casting on them, so they have to be in judgment of themselves to try and make themselves perfect.

Class Participant:

Thank you.

Gary:

You're welcome. When you're trying to make women perfect or you're trying to be perfect for women, you don't have the freedom to choose.

What bastardization of the perfection of women are you using to create the judgments, the limitations, and the invitations to the demons, the sirens, and the sylphs of anti-consciousness and unconsciousness are you choosing? Everything that is times a godzillion, will you destroy and uncreate it all? Right and Wrong, Good and Bad, POD and POC, All Nine, Shorts, Boys, and Beyonds.

If you are always projecting, "This woman is going to be perfect for me," you're casting a spell on her to be perfect for you. Projections are the way spells get cast. Does that give her freedom to be her? Does that give you freedom to be you?

How many spells are you using to create the trap you are choosing? Everything that is times a godzillion, will you destroy and uncreate it all? Right and Wrong, Good and Bad, POD and POC, All Nine, Shorts, Boys, and Beyonds.

"I Can't Stop Thinking about Her"

Class Participant:

I recently met a woman, and I feel like there's a spell on me. I can't stop thinking about her. What's going on with that?

Gary:

Well, how many spells do you have to keep you entranced with women? Everything that is times a godzillion, will you destroy and uncreate it all? Right and Wrong, Good and Bad, POD and POC, All Nine, Shorts, Boys, and Beyonds.

And you have no awareness, so you never know when she's thinking about you, right?

Class Participant:

Exactly, which is weird, because she has cut off all communication, yet the pull is still there.

Gary:

Why did she cut off communication?

Class Participant:

I have mindfucked with that so much. I haven't got an answer for you.

Gary:

Yes, you do. What is it you don't want to know about what she chose that if you knew it would set you free?

Class Participant:

She said she didn't want to get hurt.

Gary:

Yeah, which means she wants to hurt you.

Class Participant:

Yeah. She is doing that right now.

Gary:

Everything that is times a godzillion, will you destroy and uncreate it all? Right and Wrong, Good and Bad, POD and POC, All Nine, Shorts, Boys, and Beyonds.

Class Participant:

What is it when people say they don't want to go into a relationship because they're afraid of being hurt? Is that an attempt to control?

Gary:

It's just manipulation. Women try to control men. Why? Because you are supposedly the guy who is going to go away and do something to them. Do they have any projections and expectations on you?

Class Participant:

Yes.

Gary:

How many of those projections and expectations are creating the wrongness of you?

Class Participant:

Most of them.

Gary:

Everything that is times a godzillion, will you destroy and uncreate it all? Right and Wrong, Good and Bad, POD and POC, All Nine, Shorts, Boys, and Beyonds.

Class Participant:

How can I use that sort of stuff to my advantage? How can I change that? Or can I change it?

Gary:

Do you want to be with somebody who would willingly cut you to bits like that?

Class Participant:

That's a good question. I want to say no, but then, really, it's a yes. But for what reason do I want to be with her?

Gary:

I don't know. Maybe because you're just damn stupid.

Class Participant:

Yeah, I get that. Totally, yes.

Gary:

What stupidity are you using to create the women you are choosing? Everything that is times a godzillion, will you destroy and uncreate it all? Right and Wrong, Good and Bad, POD and POC, All Nine, Shorts, Boys, and Beyonds.

"I've Been Asking for That"

Class Participant:

What I'm stuck on is every time my body is with her, it's like wow. It's nurturing and I feel cared for. I've been asking for that.

Gary:

What stupidity are you using with the women you are choosing? Everything that is times a godzillion, will you destroy and uncreate it all? Right and Wrong, Good and Bad, POD and POC, All Nine, Shorts, Boys, and Beyonds.

What stupidity are you using to create the hurting women you are choosing, where you hurt them or they hurt you? Everything that is times a godzillion, will you destroy and uncreate it all? Right and Wrong, Good and Bad, POD and POC, All Nine, Shorts, Boys, and Beyonds.

So the sex was nurturing and caring?

Class Participant:

Yeah, totally.

Gary:

And you have been asking for that?

Class Participant:

Yes, I have.

Gary:

What was she asking for that she didn't tell you?

Class Participant:

I just went blank.

Gary:

Yes, I know. That's what you do so you don't have to know.

How much energy are you using to create the blankness you are choosing? Everything that is times a godzillion, will you destroy and uncreate it all? Right and Wrong, Good and Bad, POD and POC, All Nine, Shorts, Boys, and Beyonds.

What was she asking of you that she didn't tell you? What was it that you knew she wanted?

Class Participant:

She wants a guy to take care of her and her kid.

Do You Have Enough Money for Her?

Gary:

Yep. Do you have enough money for her?

Class Participant:

Not in this ten seconds, no.

Gary:

No wonder she got rid of you.

Everything that is times a godzillion, will you destroy and uncreate it all? Right and Wrong, Good and Bad, POD and POC, All Nine, Shorts, Boys, and Beyonds.

Gentlemen, you want to get to the point where you have enough money, because when you have the money, you have the power. A woman will always respect that you have the money. It would be highly recommended that you give up the spell and curses you have that keep you from having money.

All of the spells and curses you have that keep you from having money, will you now revoke, recant, rescind, reclaim, renounce, denounce, destroy and uncreate, and return them all to sender? Right and Wrong, Good and Bad, POD and POC, All Nine, Shorts, Boys, and Beyonds.

Class Participant:

Wow. That is opening up a totally new universe.

Gary:

How much money would you have to get for it to go the way you want it to go? Over a million or less than a million?

Class Participant:

Probably over a million.

Gary:

How much energy have you used to never have over a million so you can't have what you would really like to have?

Class Participant:

Fucking tons.

Gary:

Everything that is times a godzillion, will you destroy and uncreate it all? Right and Wrong, Good and Bad, POD and POC, All Nine, Shorts, Boys, and Beyonds.

Class Participant:

This conversation isn't going the way I want it to go.

Gary:

Welcome to being a man. It never goes to the place you want it to go.

Class Participant:

Yeah, I'm frustrated, upset, and angry. I want it to go the way I want it to go. What is that frustration when something's not going your way? Is it just blind stupidity?

Gary:

You're a petulant little boy. When you pitched a fit with your mom when you were a kid, did you get what you wanted?

Class Participant:

Yes.

Gary

Yeah, well, this is not a relationship with your mum.

Class Participant:

So what can I do?

The Loving Sex You'd Like to Have

Gary:

It's not about getting what you want from a female. It's about what you have to be, do, have, create, and generate to have what you'd like.

What would you have to be, do, have, create, or generate to get the loving, nurturing sex you'd like to have? Everything that doesn't allow that to show up times a godzillion, will you destroy and uncreate it all? Right and Wrong, Good and Bad, POD and POC, All Nine, Shorts, Boys, and Beyonds.

Class Participant:

I've never heard you say, "loving sex" before. What's that?

Gary:

I haven't said it before, because for most of you, that idea would be so fucking foreign, you'd die rather than choose it. To have that, you would have to be willing to receive totally.

Class Participant:

When you ran that process, I had a lot of space. It was "Okay, who would I have to be?" It's just me. I can create and choose whatever I like in order to get what I desire, and I can actually receive what I would like to have.

Gary:

You could have it again. You're assuming you couldn't. You're also assuming you're only going to get it from her. How many women create that as a reality—that you're never going to get it from anybody else?

Class Participant:

Holy fuck, yeah.

Gary:

Everything that is times a godzillion, will you destroy and uncreate it all? Right and Wrong, Good and Bad, POD and POC, All Nine, Shorts, Boys, and Beyonds.

Class Participant:

Is that like a love potion or love spell they create or that I buy into?

Gary:

It's one you create on yourself. It's the spell of "I'll never get it again. It was so good this once, I can't possibly get it again." You've completely wrapped yourself up with "There's not going to be anybody else."

How many of you guys have decided that there won't be another one as good as the one you just had? Everything that is times a godzillion, will you destroy and uncreate it all? Right and Wrong, Good and Bad, POD and POC, All Nine, Shorts, Boys, and Beyonds.

Class Participant:

When I go into that vulnerability, it feels so sad. I've been avoiding this space for so long. When I step into, it's *bleh*.

Gary:

Really? Why is it sad? You just stepped into something that you've always wanted, and now you're sad? Did she have to choose what she chose?

Class Participant:

No.

Gary:

Why did she choose that? Could it be that she was getting too close to you and that was scary as hell for her?

Class Participant:

Yes.

Why Women Want to Run Away

Gary:

When you're really vulnerable and you're really present and you're really enjoying sex, it is usually so intimidating to women that they want to run away.

Class Participant:

Oh my God.

Gary:

If you're that vulnerable with women, it scares the shit out of them. They don't have control over you.

Everything that is times a godzillion, will you destroy and uncreate it all? Right and Wrong, Good and Bad, POD and POC, All Nine, Shorts, Boys, and Beyonds.

I once went out with a woman, and we had the best sex I'd ever had in my life. It was just wonderful. She was not a beautiful woman. She was smart, she was fun, she was light, she was airy, she loved the sex, and she was really good at it.

I asked, "Can we go out again?"

She said, "No."

I said, "What? Why not?"

She said, "You're too good looking. You will hurt me. You will leave me." So she had to leave.

Class Participant:

I had a massage from a woman the other day and I was totally willing to receive the massage from her. The next day she said, "It was so cool that you were willing to receive. That's what all women want—for men to receive." Is that actually true?

Gary:

To a certain extent, but not totally. When they get a man to receive like that, they tend to run away.

So you need to be happy with the 1-2-3 system. First time's for fun. Second time you're in relationship. Third time you're getting married. You have to get what's really going to happen, not try to create it the way you think it *ought* to happen.

What stupidity are you using to create the illusions and delusions about women you are choosing? Everything that is times a godzillion, will you destroy and uncreate it all? Right and Wrong, Good and Bad, POD and POC, All Nine, Shorts, Boys, and Beyonds.

"I Shouldn't Leave Her"

Class Participant:

I stayed in my last relationship for at least a year longer than I should have. In the last year of the relationship, it wasn't any fun at all. I wanted to quit, but I didn't know how. I pretended everything was okay when I was with her. Being in a relationship seems to be so hard.

Gary:

It's "This doesn't work for me. See you later." That's how hard it really is.

Class Participant:

I kept having the thought, "She isn't doing anything wrong. I shouldn't leave her," as if the only way I can quit a relationship is if my partner is doing something wrong or something bad.

Gary:

That's where most of us go. It's part of the illusion and delusion of all of this stuff.

Class Participant:

Every time I thought I had to leave, I'd think, "If I leave her just like that, she will feel hurt, and I will be the one with all of the wrongness." I didn't want to be judged that way. Because of that, I've been unwilling to get into another relationship. I'm afraid that something similar will happen again, and I won't know how to handle it. It would be the same old story with a different girl. I see my friends having the same problem. They stay in unhappy relationships and don't have the courage to end them.

Gary:

It's called "Get the balls, dude." You have to go after it and end it. If it doesn't work, it doesn't work. It's not that the relationship is wrong or the person is doing something wrong. You have to recognize what's actually occurring at the time and recognize whether it works for you. I stayed in the relationship with my ex-wife for a long time because I'd tell myself, "There's nothing really wrong here."

One day I asked, "What would have to change for this relationship to work for me?" I sat down and wrote down the eight things that would have to change for it to work for me. Once I got to number eight and looked back at the list, I realized that six of the things I wrote down would require the leopard to change her spots—and you cannot make a leopard change its spots.

Six out of the eight meant this was not a relationship that could expand my reality or my life, and if you don't have a relationship that is about expanding your life, it's of little to no use. I know that the majority of you think that if your penis expands, then everything's right, because all of the blood has left your head and you no longer have awareness.

Class Participant:

That is so true.

Gary:

What stupidity are you using to create the illusions and delusions about women you are choosing? Everything that is times a godzillion, will you destroy and uncreate it all? Right and Wrong, Good and Bad, POD and POC, All Nine, Shorts, Boys, and Beyonds.

Who knows what women really require and desire? Do they truly desire that much vulnerability and intimacy in a relationship? No, it induces fear. Does a man desire that much intimacy in relationship? No, it induces fear. So guess why relationships suck? Ninety percent of them function from fear. They have nothing to do with expanding your life or making anything better.

Class Participant:

Gary, you've often asked me if I desire a relationship, and I've given the Access answer, "no," when I've actually found that it is something I would like to have, but not in that sucky way.

Gary:

So why don't you just say what is true? "Yeah, but I don't want a normal relationship." You guys have to come away from the point of view that I have a fixed viewpoint about relationship. I don't. The only fixed point of view I have is "Why be in a crap one?"

Sometimes people say to me, "You don't like relationships." No. It's that I don't like bad relationships. I see no reason for there to ever be a bad relationship. If you have a relationship, it should be something that adds to your life and makes it greater and better and more fun. If a relationship doesn't do that, why be in one?

If you want a relationship, get clear about what you want as a relationship and what you want in the relationship. If what you want is caring, loving, nurturing sex and a relationship that expands your life, then ask for that to come into your life.

Class Participant:

Gary, just to acknowledge you, I would never be in the relationship I am in now if it weren't for you.

Gary:

Is it more fun for you than any other relationship you've had?

Class Participant:

Yeah, and it looks like nothing I ever thought it would look like.

Gary:

And how much of you do you have to give up in order to have it?

Class Participant:

None.

Giving Up You

Gary:

That's what you've got to ask for, guys—a relationship where you have to give up no part of you, and you get to have all of you no matter what the situation is. Women think they have to require you to give yourself up, but if you give yourself up, they want to get rid of you.

Everything that is times a godzillion, will you destroy and uncreate it all? Right and Wrong, Good and Bad, POD and POC, All Nine, Shorts, Boys, and Beyonds.

Class Participant:

I'm starting to give up giving up me.

Gary:

Now we're getting somewhere! Do you notice there are more women who find you attractive?

Class Participant:

Oh, yeah.

Gary:

Does your partner want you more now than she did before?

Class Participant:

Yes. For so many years, I had somebody else to run my universe when it came to who was allowed to be in my universe and who was not allowed to be in my universe.

Gary:

So you gave up your choice in order to be in relationship?

Class Participant:

Yeah.

Gary:

How many of you have given up your choice of who you could have in your life based on your relationship? Everything that is times a godzillion, will you destroy and uncreate it all? Right and Wrong, Good and Bad, POD and POC, All Nine, Shorts, Boys, and Beyonds.

I was talking to Dain one day and I asked, "How come you stopped running and doing all of the things you like?"

He said, "Because you don't like to do those things."

I asked, "So when did we go into relationship?" I didn't know we were in relationship, because relationship should not be that. I did that when I was married; there were people I wasn't allowed to invite to my house. Dain and I allow whoever the other person wants to come to the house. If we don't want to be around that person, we go to another room, and give them the space to have whatever they want. Stop giving yourself up, because what a woman truly wants, requires, and desires of a man is that he not give himself up. She wants a man who is willing to be everything he is rather than just some of the things he is.

Everything that is times a godzillion, will you destroy and uncreate it all? Right and Wrong, Good and Bad, POD and POC, All Nine, Shorts, Boys, and Beyonds.

What Would Make You Thrilled with Your Life?

In the next month, I would like all of you to look at whether you would actually like to have a relationship. Do you really want a relationship? Would you rather have great sex occasionally? What would you like to have? What would make you thrilled with your life? That's the most important thing you can choose. If you choose that, women will want you like crazy. If you don't choose that, you'll be giving you up all the time as though that's what's valuable.

What bastardization of the perfection of women are you using to create the judgments, the limitations, and the invitations to the demons, the sirens, and the sylphs of anti-consciousness and unconsciousness are you choosing? Everything that is times a godzillion, will you destroy and uncreate it all? Right and Wrong, Good and Bad, POD and POC, All Nine, Shorts, Boys, and Beyonds.

If you truly want to have a relationship, let's get you a good one, damn it. You've got "bad one" down to a fine science. You need to look at whether it's going to work for you and whether it's going to work for the person you want to have relationship with.

About a year ago, I realized there was a woman I could have a relationship with and it would really work for me, but I saw that what she wanted was something I couldn't give her. The relationship wasn't going to work for her. So I gave up the potential of the relationship in favor of her getting what she wanted.

Class Participant:

Are you saying that even if it would have worked for you, since it wouldn't have worked for her, the problems would have just ended up in your lap again?

Gary:

Yes. You have to look at all those things and be aware of them. You have to look at this stuff from a different place.

You Need to Do Deal and Deliver

Class Participant:

I have a woman around me at the moment who is pissed at me a lot. What am I doing to create that?

Gary:

Are you talking about your partner?

Class Participant:

Yes.

Gary:

Why is she pissed at you?

Class Participant:

That's a big part of my question. I don't get it totally.

Gary:

No, you don't want to get it.

Class Participant:

That might be true. Yeah, that is true.

Gary:

You don't want to make her happy. You would rather make her unhappy.

Class Participant:

Is that true?

Gary:

Watch the way you're doing things.

Class Participant:

Can you give me some more information on that? I thought I was trying to make her happy.

I'm ready to hang this up because it's not fun enough at the moment. What question can I ask here?

Gary:

What is it you're not being or doing that you could be or do that would totally change the relationship? You guys have to be willing to totally change the relationship.

Currently you have a woman who is not willing to communicate with you. If you really want her, you have to say, "I want to make a commitment to you. What's it going to take for that to occur, and how's that going to work for you?" You need to do Deal and Deliver. Ask:

- Exactly what would you like this relationship to look like?
- Exactly what do you expect of me?
- Exactly what do you want of me?
- Exactly what can I do to make you happy?

Class Participant:

That makes it so much easier, doesn't it?

Commitment

Gary:

It does. Every woman wants a man who declares himself first. They want you to commit to them. If you commit to them, they know everything's going to turn out fine. That's more important to them than almost anything else.

Class Participant:

What is that energy of commitment, then? What's so powerful about that?

Gary:

It's powerful because you think it actually means something. But for most of you, being committed is a straightjacket in which you have no choice.

Class Participant:

Can you say some more about this?

Gary:

Were you committed to your former wife?

Class Participant:

Yes.

Gary:

Were you able to end the commitment with ease? And how many years was that after you decided to quit?

Class Participant:

Two hundred million.

Gary:

Just thought I'd ask. So *commitment* obviously means to you that you're in a straightjacket and your choices cease to exist.

Class Participant:

If I make a commitment to a woman with regards to Deal and Deliver, is that allowing me to have an exit from the straightjacket? Or doesn't it require the straightjacket?

Gary:

If you make a commitment from Deal and Deliver, you know exactly what's expected of you. Currently you have the idea that if you make a commitment, it means you have to give up everything, including you and everything you are, which doesn't give you much in the way of choice.

Most of us men don't want to know what we know, and you, especially, don't want to know that you could do your life without a woman. You want to believe that without a woman, you're a loser and that having a woman in your life makes you a winner.

Everywhere you've created that curse and that spell, will you destroy and uncreate all of that? Right and Wrong, Good and Bad, POD and POC, All Nine, Shorts, Boys, and Beyonds.

I just got an email called "Men Advice #78." It said, "When a woman says, 'Just do what you want,' do not under any circumstances do what you want." Does that give you any information about men and women?

Class Participant:

Yeah. That's good to hear.

Gary:

So what do you always choose? For you or for the woman?

Class Participant:

I always choose what she wants.

Gary:

Why do you always choose what she wants?

Class Participant:

Because that's hitting me harder in the head than the lightness of the awareness I had just before that.

Gary:

Yes, and if you had actually chosen for you, would you be willing to give up you for anything?

Class Participant:

No.

Gary:

Everything you've done to give you up for somebody else, will you destroy and uncreate all of that? Right and Wrong, Good and Bad, POD and POC, All Nine, Shorts, Boys, and Beyonds.

I've tried to get you to look at this before.

Class Participant:

Yep.

Gary:

Did you want it?

Class Participant:

No, I didn't.

Gary:

Why not?

Class Participant:

It's something about the control of women.

Gary:

Do you like being controlled by women or do you like to control women?

Class Participant:

I'm trying to pretend that I like to control women.

Gary:

Are you pretending you're controlling women or are you actually capable of controlling women and refuse to do it in order to make sure nobody knows what a complete asshole you actually are?

Class Participant:

I'm capable of doing it, but I refuse to do it.

Gary:

How much energy are all of you using to try to hide the fact that you're a fucking asshole by women's standards? Everything that is times a godzillion, will you destroy and uncreate it all? Right and Wrong, Good and Bad, POD and POC, All Nine, Shorts, Boys, and Beyonds.

Class Participant:

Is that the same energy when I'm not willing to make my partner pissed at me?

Gary:

You do exactly what will make her pissed at you so she looks like the idiot.

Class Participant:

Do I really do that? I like that. Yeah. I'm not saying I don't. I was not aware I do that.

Gary:

It wasn't that you weren't aware of it. You just weren't willing to acknowledge it, because if you did, you would not be able to think as many good thoughts about you to counteract what you have decided is the wrongness of you.

Class Participant:

Exactly.

What Can I Be or
Do Different That Will Change All of This?

Class Participant:

So what can I do and be different instead?

Gary:

Now we're getting to a good question! Ask: What can I be or do different that will change all of this?

Class Participant:

It's like I'm on the brink of choosing something different and I have no clue what it is.

Gary:

Is it that you have no clue of what it is—or is it that if you were willing to choose it, it would change too much for you too rapidly?

Class Participant:

Yeah, that too.

Gary:

Everything that is times a godzillion, will you destroy and uncreate it all? Right and Wrong, Good and Bad, POD and POC, All Nine, Shorts, Boys, and Beyonds.

Trying to Override Your Body

Class Participant:

I recently slept with a woman, and then we had lunch. In the evening, up in the hotel room, I realized, "This isn't working. This isn't fun. I can't override my body," so I chose to leave.

Gary:

Why did you try to override your body?

Class Participant:

Because I go into one of those "deliver" moods. Even if I didn't want to, I'd have to perform and deliver. A woman's expectations of me.

Gary:

What stupidity are you using to create you as the eternal delivery boy are you choosing? Everything that is times a godzillion, will you destroy and uncreate it all? Right and Wrong, Good and Bad, POD and POC, All Nine, Shorts, Boys, and Beyonds.

So what do you love about being a delivery boy?

Class Participant:

Nothing anymore.

Gary:

How many lifetimes have you been a concubine? Are you still trying to live up to your reputation? Are you still trying to live up to your commitment to being that? Or are you still trying to live up to delivering—when you promised you would never be delivered to?

Class Participant:

I think it was everything you just said and more.

Gary:

All of the commitments you have to being a universal sperm donor, will you now give all that up, please? Right and Wrong, Good and Bad, POD and POC, All Nine, Shorts, Boys, and Beyonds.

What stupidity are you using to create you as the concubine of all women are you choosing? Everything that is times a godzillion, will you destroy and uncreate it all? Right and Wrong, Good and Bad, POD and POC, All Nine, Shorts, Boys, and Beyonds.

What bastardization of the perfection of men are you using to create you as the concubine, sperm donor, and source for the creation of the bodies of reality are you choosing? Everything that is times a godzillion, will you destroy and uncreate it all? Right and Wrong, Good and Bad, POD and POC, All Nine, Shorts, Boys, and Beyonds.

Class Participant:

With regard to the creation of future bodies, is that in other lifetimes or is that like tomorrow and the next day?

Gary:

Well, it's the next day and forever. That's the value of men. This is why you always think you have to get together with a woman and why you never want to get together with a woman.

Class Participant:

Yes. Universal sperm donor.

Gary:

You have a commitment to not making more children. That's the reason you have not been interested in having sex with some women— because they're capable of getting pregnant at that moment.

If you're committed to not having children and you're with somebody who's ready to have children, and she has decided she's going to trap you into marriage or a relationship by having a child with you, your body will say, "Nope! We're not going there," which is why you're not interested and you go home. Thank your body for saving your ass.

All right, gentlemen. I'd like you to decide to look at your life and ask:

- Would I truly like to have a relationship?

- If I were to have a relationship that was going to expand my life, what would that look like?

- What would I like the person to have as her basic personality?

Do you want her to dress well? Do you want her to spend a lot of money? Where do you want her to be? You also have to put down all of the things you would like her not to be, because the only way you're going to get what you really want is by knowing what you want as well as what you don't want.

Please look at this and see if you'd actually like to have a relationship. You are humanoid men who would prefer to have an extremely comfortable place to nest. That's not a wrongness, but you have a tendency to pick the wrong women for that. I want to get you on the track of being able to choose the kind of women you really want.

All right, my friends, great to have you on the call.

Class Participant:

Thanks Gary, you're awesome.

Class Participants:

Thank you.

10

THE AGGRESSIVE PRESENCE OF SEXUALNESS

The more you have question, the more presence you are.
The more presence you are, the more control you have.

Aggressive Presence

Gary:

Hello, gentlemen. I'd like to talk about aggressive presence. Aggressive presence means you don't give yourself up for anybody and you always have a question. When you're an aggressive presence, you do not adjust yourself to other people's realities. People tend to adjust their reality to yours.

Class Participant:

Recently there was someone I didn't want to be around because I didn't like the way he had treated my son. I was stuck on that rather than asking, "What would it look like if I could just be me around anyone?" I realized how much of me I cut off in order to avoid him. What's it going to take to have aggressive presence?

Gary:

What if you had been willing to say, "Hey, be kind to my son, mister. He's important to me"?

Class Participant:

Is that aggressive presence?

Gary:

It's also an unwillingness to eat shit. If you're aggressively present, you don't take shit from anybody.

Class Participant:

And you become aware of things when they show up?

Gary:

Yeah. You become aware: "Oh, this guy is being forceful with my son. He is not being aggressively present with him." You've got to be kinder. You've got to be aggressively kind.

Class Participant:

When I've seen you do that, Gary, you don't make things into a fight. I seem to go into a place of fight.

Gary:

That's what you've been taught. You think that makes you a man. It makes you a man's man.

Class Participant:

Can you say more about what a man's man is?

Gary:

The idea is that when you're a man's man, you will always be liked by men and not necessarily by women. A man's man is somebody that all men think is sexy and good too. Sean Connery would be considered a man's man, but Roger Moore, who also played 007, wouldn't. He'd be considered too pretty.

Class Participant:

So a man's man is considered a man through a man's eyes?

Gary:

Yes.

What can you be or do as a man that if you would be or do it would give you everything you desire in life? Everything that is times a godzillion, will you destroy and uncreate it all? Right and Wrong, Good and Bad, POD and POC, All Nine, Shorts, Boys, and Beyonds.

Choosing for You

This is where you have to determine what you want to have as your life. If you were to have your own life, what would you choose?

Class Participant:

That question is such a great tool for me. It's my number one question at the moment: If I was choosing my reality, what would I choose? The awareness I had on that was how little I was actually choosing for me.

Gary:

It's interesting, isn't it, when you realize how little you choose for you?

Class Participant:

I also ask, "If I was choosing my reality, who would I be?"

Gary:

Yeah.

If you were choosing your reality sexually, who would you choose not to get fucked by? Everything that is times a godzillion, will you destroy and uncreate it all? Right and Wrong, Good and Bad, POD and POC, All Nine, Shorts, Boys, and Beyonds.

How many of you tend to let women and friends fuck you over?

Class Participant:

Yeah. And family.

Gary:

Yeah, and family. It's much better with family.

Class Participant:

And ourselves.

Gary:

Yeah.

If you were choosing who to have sex with, who would you not allow to fuck you over? Everything that is times a godzillion, will you destroy and uncreate it all? Right and Wrong, Good and Bad, POD and POC, All Nine, Shorts, Boys, and Beyonds.

Being Sexually Aggressive

I am aggressive sexually, because I will not cut my sexual energy off for a male, or a female, or any one person, or any two people—or anybody. I'm always that no matter what. When you are aggressively sexual, people are more likely to adjust their reality to yours. How many of you are always trying to adjust your reality to a woman's reality?

Class Participant:

That would be a *yes*.

Gary:

That's a yes for everybody.

What bastardization of total sexualness are you using to create the elimination and eradication of the aggressive presence of sexualness you could be choosing are you choosing? Everything that is times a godzillion, will you destroy and uncreate it all? Right and Wrong, Good and Bad, POD and POC, All Nine, Shorts, Boys, and Beyonds.

As men, we tend to be aggressive in the sense of using force to get a woman to go to bed with us. It has nothing to do with kindness and caring. You say, "Hey, baby, you ready?" How's that going to work? It's not! How many women are going to go for that? Not very many!

We're taught how to be sexual from porn flicks—none of which have kindness or caring as part of their reference material. It's about how you can twist her nipple six times this direction and six times in the other direction and it turns her on so much she's got to have you. Those images are not real or true. That is not your best choice.

You want to be so aggressively sexual that women want to go to bed with you just because you are so aggressively present. How do you do that? You get there by going to question:

- Will it be easy?
- Will it be fun?
- Will I learn something?

Functioning from Presence

The more you have question, the more presence you are. The more presence you are, the more control you have.

You keep trying to create conclusion as a source of control. Let's say you wanted to sleep with somebody. What question is that? It's not a question! It's a conclusion. When you come to conclusion, you think you're going to have more control over the situation and that people will do what you want them to do. But it ain't so.

What makes conclusion greater than question? Everything that is times a godzillion, will you destroy and uncreate it all? Right and Wrong, Good and Bad, POD and POC, All Nine, Shorts, Boys, and Beyonds.

Have you misidentified control with conclusion? Everywhere you've come to the conclusion that conclusion is creation, or conclusion is what's necessary for you to have control, will you destroy and uncreate all of that? Right and Wrong, Good and Bad, POD and POC, All Nine, Shorts, Boys, and Beyonds.

If you function from question at all, women look at you and think, "Oh. He might be the man for me." That's because if you're doing question, you're asking, "Is this woman the right person for me?" and they pick it up from your head. When you come to conclusion, their point of view is you don't care about them.

The more you function from questions, the more you'll realize that what you want is more fun sex. And the kind of sex you want doesn't exist much. Is that at all real to you? So it reduces the number of people you can choose to have sex with, but it expands your willingness to receive.

The Woman Who Doesn't *Need* You

Gary:

There's another part of this. When you function from aggressive presence, the person doesn't need you.

How many of you function from the point of view that you want a woman who needs you? Everything that is times a godzillion, will you destroy and uncreate it all? Right and Wrong, Good and Bad, POD and POC, All Nine, Shorts, Boys, and Beyonds.

What you want is a woman who has no need for you. This is the place you should be functioning from. You're asking: "Okay, what would be fun for me?" Not: "What do I have to do right? What do I have to do wrong? What is necessary?" but "What would I like to create and generate here?"

How many of you have spent your life trying to be needed by a woman? How many of you were taught by your mothers that every woman wants a man who needs her? Everything that is times a godzillion, will you destroy and uncreate it all? Right and Wrong, Good and Bad, POD and POC, All Nine, Shorts, Boys, and Beyonds.

Class Participant:

I just realized I'm being something for my woman and not for me.

Gary:

Yeah, that would be trying to make yourself a needed item.

Class Participant:

Yeah.

Class Participant:

Is that what we define as love when we're kids?

Gary:

Yeah, and that's what you also define as what will give you sex.

Class Participant:

Right. I watch it with my son. He goes to his mom and she needs him. She needs him and then he comes to me and I don't need him at all. Does he have confusion with that?

Gary:

No. He's being taught by his mother to have a woman who will need him.

Class Participant:

Right.

Gary:

How many of you were taught to be the man you were supposed to be, to be needed by your mother? Everything that is times a godzillion, will you destroy and uncreate it all? Right and Wrong, Good and Bad, POD and POC, All Nine, Shorts, Boys, and Beyonds.

Class Participant:

When I'm with my father, it's so simple. When I go to see my mother, she needs me. It has always been that way. What is that? Are women entrained to that?

Gary:

Women are entrained to believe that's the way it's supposed to be. Your father wanted you to grow up to be a man's man. Your mother wanted you to grow up to be needed by a woman. Nowhere were you involved in the computation. No one asked you, "What do you want? What do you want to be? What's important to you?"

Class Participant:

That feels like abuse to me. Is it?

Gary:

Nope. It's neglect.

Class Participant:

Can you talk more about the difference between neglect and abuse?

Gary:

You think it's abuse to not be acknowledged as you. But it seldom has anything to do with abuse. It has to do with neglect, because most parents don't know what is actually happening. They don't know how to deal with anything, so they go into a neglectful state. And most of you choose women who go into neglect of you after a while, too, because your tendency is to find somebody who's like one or both of your parents. Being neglected seems more real to you than anything else.

Class Participant:

The woman I'm seeing right now has no need of me whatsoever.

Gary:

Does that make you incredibly needy of her?

Class Participant:

No, it's something else.

Gary:

Do you feel neglected by her?

Class Participant:

That's it. Yeah. It's like I've misidentified that non-need as neglect. What is it that I'm unwilling to look at here?

Gary:

So are you willing to be totally needless of a woman?

Class Participant::

Not in this ten seconds, no.

Gary:

What stupidity are you using to create the needfulness of women you are choosing? Everything that is times a godzillion, will you destroy and uncreate it all? Right and Wrong, Good and Bad, POD and POC, All Nine, Shorts, Boys, and Beyonds.

Aggressive Needlessness

Class Participant:

What would aggressive needlessness with women look like?

Gary:

It would be the place where, instead of looking for how you can get laid, you're asking:

- What do I really want from this person?
- Can she provide it?

You seldom go into what somebody can provide for you. Have you ever noticed that?

Class Participant:

No, I'm always looking for what I can provide for them.

Gary:

Yeah. You're looking to be a contribution. And they're looking for you to contribute even more. You think that you never deliver enough. They're always right, and you're wrong. How's that working?

Class Participant:

Is that instead of saying, "If you can't give me what I want, piss off"?

Gary:

Yeah, and most women have that point of view, "You can't provide me with what I want? Fuck off and go away."

Aggressive Sexualness

Aggressive sexualness is the place where you're not willing to go out of question. In this reality, aggression is seen as anything that creates a question. Have you ever had someone say, "Stop asking all of those questions! Why are you asking all those questions? What do you want from me? How can you be like that?" Asking a question is considered wrong. It's considered aggression unless you say in advance, "Hey, can I ask you a question, please?"

If you ask, "Can I ask you a question?" nobody takes offense. But if you present a question without first asking, the other person will go to offense. They go to offense and then they go to defense. Those are places you get into trouble with women.

When a Woman Can't Have an Orgasm

Class Participant:

What is it when a woman has difficulty having an orgasm or can't have an orgasm?

Gary:

Usually the reason a woman can't have an orgasm is because she's not actually in her body. When you're having sex, keep the lights on. Lift your body off of hers; do not lay down on her so she can hide her eyes. And every time you see her close her eyes, say, "Come back, please. Come back. Open your eyes. Please look at me. I want to feel the connection to you. I want to feel the connection to you and I want to feel the connection to your body. Let me feel all of you." That's how you start bringing her back to her body and back to what's possible.

You just have to do that one thing of getting her to stay with her body. Most women who are non-orgasmic or non-multiple orgasmic tend to be disconnected from their body. Some of them like to watch from the ceiling. When you feel them go away or you feel them step out of their body, ask, "Where are you? Where'd you just go? What happened?" When you ask those questions, she'll start to question. You've got to get her back into question because question creates presence.

Class Participant:

What questions can I ask of me that would allow me to be aware when my wife is doing that?

Gary:

Have the lights on—or at least have candle light. Ask her to put her legs over your shoulders so you can see one another. Be with her and say, "I'm so glad to be able to look into your eyes. Looking into your eyes is the most amazing thing. Stay with me, honey. I really need this. I really need this."

And then you have to ask, "Can you cum or should I?"

Class Participant:

My wife and I have been together now for about eight years and it's only in the last three months that she's starting to have an orgasm with me during sex. She's quite capable of doing it on her own, but with me in the picture, it seems to be a lot harder for her. I will start going down the track that you've suggested.

Does She Like to Have Sex *with* Her Body— or *as* Her Body?

Gary:

Some people, especially women, try to stay out of their bodies during sex. They don't actually like to have a connection to their body. If you really want to have fun with sex, you have to ask, "Does this person like to have sex with her body or as her body?" A lot of women stand outside the body and look at it. Does the being have sex—or does the body have sex?

Class Participant:

The body has sex.

Gary:

So you need to connect with the being and the body. You want both. If you've got both, you have the capacity for greater stimulation.

Class Participant:

What would that look like? Or what questions could I ask to be even more connected in the body and the being during sex?

Gary:

You have to have the willingness to see what the other person is willing to have.

How much of your energy are you using to blind yourself to what other people are capable of? A lot, a little, or megatons? Everything that is times a godzillion, will you destroy and uncreate it all? Right and Wrong, Good and Bad, POD and POC, All Nine, Shorts, Boys, and Beyonds.

Class Participant:

And then you ask, "Where to touch her? When to touch her? How much to touch her?"

Gary:

All you have to do is ask the body. It will tell you where to touch.

"There's an Energy with My Penis"

Class Participant:

I've been having lots of really great sex, and I'm finding that there's an energy with my penis that is much more dynamic. What tips would you have for when I have my penis in the woman's vagina? What energies could I be with that that would give me more awareness?

Gary:

When you have your penis in a woman's vagina, instead of doing the in-and-out thing, try holding still and flexing your penis while putting energy into it, so it's as though you're going in and out without moving.

Class Participant:

I can do that.

Gary:

And put energy through your whole hip structure as well. There's a good chance that the woman will have an orgasm just by you doing that.

Class Participant:

Thank you.

Class Participant:

I've noticed that when I'm inside the woman, there seems to be a lot more space in the vagina than I've been used to.

Gary:

Are you trying to fill up that space or are you creating the space?

Class Participant:

I've been trying to fill that space rather than creating it.

Gary:

What if you created the space as something that contributed to the orgasmic quality of what you're doing?

Class Participant:

Wow! I see that I bought the idea that it should be a tight fit.

Gary:

Well, how many pieces of crap told you that was the way it was supposed to be?

Class Participant:

Lots.

Gary:

Everything that is times a godzillion, will you destroy and uncreate it all? Right and Wrong, Good and Bad, POD and POC, All Nine, Shorts, Boys, and Beyonds.

Could you ask your penis to be the *energy* that filled the space instead of the *organ* that fills the space?

Class Participant:

Will do.

Gary:

Cool.

Class Participant:

Thank you so much. Wow.

"Why Can't I Have Multiple Orgasms, Too?"

Class Participant:

I'm getting a bit jealous of women. Why can't I have multiple orgasms, too?

Gary:

You can have multiple orgasms. You don't have to ejaculate to have an orgasm. If I lie on my back, I can have six or eight orgasms without ever ejaculating.

Class Participant:

How do you do that?

Gary:

I trained myself so that when I was on my back I wouldn't cum too quickly; I wanted the woman to get more aroused.

Class Participant:

How did you train yourself?

Gary:

I just asked my body to show me a different way.

Class Participant:

That question thing…

Class Participants:

(Laughter)

Gary:

I read about men being multiple orgasmic and I asked, "How can I have that?" I got "Get on your back," so I said, "Okay." I got on my back and I let her sit on top of me and grind till her heart's content, and I would use my fingers with her and do all of that kind of stuff. I'd do everything I could to make things better for her, and eventually I started having orgasms when I was on my back. I would start to have orgasms that wouldn't necessarily be ejaculations.

It's a matter of asking your body, "Body, what would it take for us to have an orgasm without ejaculation?" When you start looking at what you can create, a different possibility starts to show up. But you have to look from that place, not from the other places you go.

With multiple orgasms, it feels like you don't need or desire to ejaculate, but you don't lose your erection. You have a sense that if you go again you might have an ejaculation, but you manage to not have an ejaculation and things just get better. You feel like you came, but you didn't cum. It feels like an inner orgasm instead of an ejaculation.

Pleasing Yourself

Gary:

Aggressive sexualness is not about waiting for a woman to want to have sex with you. It's about your willingness to have sex for you. We tend to give up masturbation, especially when we get into relationships. When you give up masturbation, you give up pleasing yourself, and you give up the idea that you're going to have sex whether anybody else likes it or not.

A man who is aggressive sexually will have sex and then he'll get in the shower and masturbate.

Class Participant:

How does that work in a marriage?

Gary:

You beat off when you choose. You do whatever you choose. You can say, "Honey, I'm sorry. I really just have to go beat off." If she doesn't like it, she'll say, "Why don't you let me help you?" or you could say to her, "You could come and help if you want."

Class Participant:

Yeah, I've done that a few times. That's been fun.

Gary:

There's a different place to function from. Try asking: If I was being all of the sexualness I am, how would I function in life?

If you were being all of the sexualness you really are, how would you function in life? Everything that brought up times a godzillion, will you destroy and uncreate it all? Right and Wrong, Good and Bad, POD and POC, All Nine, Shorts, Boys, and Beyonds.

Run these processes:

If I was functioning as I truly am, how would I function sexually? Everything that is times a godzillion, will you destroy and uncreate it all? Right and Wrong, Good and Bad, POD and POC, All Nine, Shorts, Boys, and Beyonds.

If I was functioning sexually as me, how would I function in life? Everything that is times a godzillion, will you destroy and uncreate it all? Right and Wrong, Good and Bad, POD and POC, All Nine, Shorts, Boys, and Beyonds.

There was a time when four women a day were what I considered functioning. Unfortunately, I didn't get much of anything else done.

Class Participant:

So Gary, what would that look like?

"What Would It Be Like to Have Sex with This Man?"

Gary:

It would be looking at a man and asking, "What would it be like to have sex with this man?" It doesn't mean you have to have sex with him. When you're willing to look at what it would be like to have sex with somebody, especially someone of the same sex where that's not your usual preference, you begin to see the sexual energy of women in a different way, because you stop trying to put sexual energy into "man" or "woman."

So start asking, "What would it be like to have sex with this person?" When you start to have that kind of aggressiveness sexually, you begin to see what works and what doesn't work. And if you're willing to see what works and what doesn't work, you're willing to do what you do in a different way.

Class Participant:

I love that question, "What would it be like to have sex with this man?" That opens up a totally different possibility of receiving. I received a totally different energy from asking that about a man.

Gary:

Yeah, when you're willing to ask that about a man, you're willing to see more about what women will choose.

Class Participant:

Yeah.

Gary:

And when you are a man and you're straight, and you look at a man from the point of view "What would he be like to have sex with?" you have to look at the being and the body and see whether that would be fun, which is what you don't do with women. You say, "Oh she's beautiful. I want her," which is what question? It's not! With men, you'll maintain question.

With women you tend not to. If you were willing to maintain the question, would you have something greater? Yeah, and that's the important part of it. When you get to the place where you can look at a man and ask the question, "Would he be fun to have sex with?" you can begin to look at women and ask the same question, "Would she be fun to have sex with?" You'll say, "Wow! I had no idea I had so much awareness."

Class Participant:

Oh, that's great! Practice choosing what's lighter.

Gary:

That's how you learn to choose better people to have sex with.

Class Participant:

I have done that and it works.

Gary:

It does. It's great.

Class Participant:

Wow. Awesome. I'm grateful.

Gary:

Okay, gentlemen, we're through.

Class Participant:

Thank you, Mr. Douglas. You're wonderful.

Class Participant:

You are.

Class Participant:

It's always a good one.

Gary:

And remember, try being on your back and getting multiple orgasms. That's home play until next time. The first person who gets to six orgasms before he ejaculates wins a prize. Thank you. I will talk to you next time. Bye-bye.

11
CHOOSING COMMITMENT

When you do commitment from choice,
you have to realize what is actually possible.
It's asking: What is possible here that I haven't considered?

Gary:

Hello, gentlemen. Let's go to some questions.

Manliness and Masculinity

Class Participant:

Can you talk about manliness, masculinity, and how to look and sound more manly and masculine? I don't have a deep voice like other men. Do you have any suggestions for ways to develop a deeper, more manly voice? And what about the beard? I don't have a lot of beard, either. Is this genetic—or is it changeable?

Gary:

It is genetic—and it can be changeable. You need to ask: What energy, space, and consciousness can my body and I be to grow massive amounts of hair with total ease? The only problem with that is you're liable to also grow hair on your chest, your back, and your testicles. Try it.

Class Participant:

Does that also work in the reverse? For less body hair?

Gary:

Try: What energy, space, and consciousness can I be to have less hair with total ease?

But the problem with that is you might also go bald.

So you've got a choice. You can be bald with a lot of body hair, and then she'll spend all of her time working on your body, or you can have thick, wavy hair on your head, and she'll spend all of her time with her hand in your hair. Where do you want her to put her hands?

Class Participant:

Everywhere.

Gary:

Exactly. That's why you grow hair everywhere. Stop judging it. Where did you get the judgment about hair? There are lots of women who don't like hairy men, but if they don't like hairy men, they won't want you, and you won't want them. Choose the ones who like lots of hair. And if you have a lot of hair on your chest, take your shirt off at every opportunity to show that you have a hairy chest. Some women will like that. And if you don't have hair on your chest, then take the opportunity to take your shirt off so they know what your equipment is like. Being masculine only means you are willing to be something that is not valuable on this planet.

For deepening your voice, try this:

What energy, space, and consciousness can my body and I be that would allow our voice to drop two octaves with total ease? Everything that is times a godzillion, will you destroy and uncreate it all? Right and Wrong, Good and Bad, POD and POC, All Nine, Shorts, Boys, and Beyonds.

A Slipstream of Energy

Class Participant:

What is it when you feel like you're in a slipstream of energy that propels you forward to be with another person and it feels so light and easy? I had an experience after the last Access Consciousness seven-day event, where for one week I vividly dreamed I was having sex with a particular lady, and the next week, it was actually happening. We were in bed enacting the dream.

Leading up to this enjoyable time, I was following a wave of energy toward her and it felt so easy and energetically pleasing. It felt like the energy of crazy possible. It was very nice, I must say. However, now I'm not sure about what to do next.

Gary:

This is a place you have to stop going, folks. You have a tendency to go into "Oh, now what do I do?" Duh. Keep going is what you do. If you have a slipstream happening, slip it in, slip it out, slip it in, slip it out, and enjoy the hell out of yourself.

Everything that is times a godzillion, will you destroy and uncreate it all? Right and Wrong, Good and Bad, POD and POC, All Nine, Shorts, Boys, and Beyonds.

Class Participant:

I am trying not to be too keen in case I scare her off. How do I change it to get more ease around where to go or what to do next after having sex? I'd like to take this possibility further.

Gary:

You're going into head tripping, my friend.

Everything you've done to make yourself into a head tripper, will you destroy and uncreate all of that? Right and Wrong, Good and Bad, POD and POC, All Nine, Shorts, Boys, and Beyonds.

What bastardization of infinite sexualness are you using to create the head tripper, heart tripper, and crotch tripper you are choosing? Everything that is times a godzillion, will you destroy and uncreate it all? Right and Wrong, Good and Bad, POD and POC, All Nine, Shorts, Boys, and Beyonds.

Class Participant:

Could you explain what you meant when you said he was going into head tripping? Why is that head tripping?

Gary:

Number one, "I'm trying not to be too keen." That's head tripping. It's about what you have to try to be or do. Number two, "How do I change it to get more ease around where to go or what to do next?" Head tripping.

Class Participant:

Is that like trying to work out what's going to happen in the future rather than asking a question?

Gary:

It's what you create when you have judgments about what you're supposed to have as a relationship or how you're supposed to be. When you make a choice and judge that choice, you create a solidity that requires the judgment to extend forward and create your future. You create a solid future based on those judgments. Is that really what you would like to choose?

"No judgment" equals a future without judgment. "Judgment," even a positive judgment, equals a future with judgment.

How Many Futures Have You Created That Are Blocking Your Ability to Create?

Every time you choose, you create. Every choice creates, whether it is a choice for you or against you. If you put a judgment in there with that choice, you create a future that is starting to happen, which will create the judgment as future. Let's say you're thirteen years old. You find a girl and she has sex with you. You say, "Oh my God, I have to love her forever. I have to stick with her. I have to have children with her. I have to have all of that stuff." Those are potential futures you start to create based on your judgments about what you did and what you should do.

Class Participant:

Yeah.

Gary:

All of those become something that lock in as a potential future, and every time you come close to somebody who matches something like that, you add that energy to that future to create a future you decided should come true. None of them are real.

How many futures with women have you created that are currently blocking your ability to create? I'm going to count to four. The "one, two, three" clears the past and the present. When "four" is added, it changes the future you are creating based on the decisions, choices, and judgments you are making. On four, we're going to destroy and uncreate them all. One... two... three... four. Thank you.

All the stuff you've created about the future with women, and how you can't have a future with a woman, and how you have to have a future with a woman, and without a future with a woman, you're not a real man, and all of the places in which you can't be without having a woman, all of those futures, will you destroy and uncreate all of those on four: One... two... three... four. Thank you.

What bastardization of infinite commitment of being are you using to create the necessity of sex, relationship, copulation, and sexuality are you choosing? Everything that is times a godzillion, will you destroy and uncreate it all? Right and Wrong, Good and Bad, POD and POC, All Nine, Shorts, Boys, and Beyonds.

How many of you have the point of view that without a woman, you can't be? Everything that is times a godzillion, will you destroy and uncreate it all? Right and Wrong, Good and Bad, POD and POC, All Nine, Shorts, Boys, and Beyonds.

Have any of you ever had the feeling that you were driven by your need for sex or copulation or relationship?

Class Participant:

Yes.

Class Participant:

Yeah.

Gary:

That's what this is about. It's the place where you think you have no choice. You think you have to do it. Where's your choice?

Getting to a Place Where There Is a Real Choice

The whole idea of this series has been to get you to the point where you can have choice instead of thinking that you somehow have no choice and you have to do sex. If you can get to a place where there is real choice, you don't have to give up any part of you to create a relationship or sex, and in so doing, you can have more presence and more fun. What would it be like if sex was totally fun for you?

Class Participant:

Yes, please.

Gary:

All the time. Every time.

What bastardization of infinite commitment of being are you using to create the necessity of sex, relationship, copulation, and sexuality are you choosing?

Everything that is times a godzillion, will you destroy and uncreate it all? Right and Wrong, Good and Bad, POD and POC, All Nine, Shorts, Boys, and Beyonds.

Now, why do I say sexuality? Because you get to a place where you figure you have to have sex with a woman in order to prove you're a man. What does that have to do with choice?

Class Participant:

Nothing.

Gary:

That means you only get to have sex with half the population. The only time you realize that it doesn't really matter is when you get put in prison and you have nobody else but a man to have sex with.

Everything that is times a godzillion, will you destroy and uncreate it all? Right and Wrong, Good and Bad, POD and POC, All Nine, Shorts, Boys, and Beyonds.

That was supposed to be funny. Where is your sense of humor? Is it too late for you to have a sense of humor?

Class Participant:

I think you have to do a POD and POC about your humor so we can laugh at your jokes.

Gary:

Everything that doesn't allow you to recognize my humor and how brilliant it is, and everything that doesn't allow you to have a sense of humor about sex, copulation, relationship, and sexuality, and everything that doesn't allow you to play with every form of sex, relationship, copulation, sexuality you could possibly have, will you destroy and uncreate all of that? Right and Wrong, Good and Bad, POD and POC, All Nine, Shorts, Boys, and Beyonds.

Commitment as a Decision/Commitment as a Choice

Class Participant:

Gary, can you talk about commitment and choice? Are we creating commitment as a decision instead of having it as a choice?

Gary:

Yes.

Class Participant:

Is that this reality's take on what commitment means?

Gary:

Yes.

All the futures you've created based on that, will you destroy and uncreate them all: One... two... three... four. Thank you.

You guys have to get that you make decisions about a commitment and then you try to validate the commitment in order to make it real and right.

Commitment as a Ten-Second Choice

Class Participant:

You talk about choosing in ten-second increments, and you've said that commitment is a ten-second choice. I'm confused about that. How does that work?

Gary:

When you are choosing in ten-second increments, in one ten-second increment, you can say, "I love her." In the next ten seconds, you can say, "I don't love her." You can say, "I love my business," and ten seconds later, you can say, "I don't love my business." When you choose in ten-second increments, there exists the possibility of constant creation.

You guys have somehow come to the weird point of view that commitment is permanent. You think that once you make a commitment, no other choice is possible.

When you do commitment from choice, you have to realize what is actually possible. It's asking: What is possible here that I haven't considered? What if you looked at what was possible instead of what you think it ought to be? That's different from trying to commit to the commitment you already committed to.

Class Participant:

That would be just too damn easy.

Gary:

Yeah, and that's why you won't have ease in your life. You keep trying to look for the hard parts and the bad parts instead of what would make something easy. What if you were doing whatever it was from what was easy instead of what was hard?

Class Participant:

That's so brilliantly simple.

Gary:

It is simple. We keep looking at how we can make something work that seems not to work, rather than asking the questions:

- What works about this?
- What doesn't work about this?

For example, let's say you make a commitment to get married. Does that mean you have to follow through? If you get married to a woman, are you married to her forever?

Class Participant:

No.

Gary:

You keep trying to come to a place you think you can function from. You think that's going to create something greater than actually being present. You keep trying to figure out what it's going to be before you've even chosen it. How many possible futures are you creating and how many possible futures have you created in order to create what doesn't work in your life? On four: One... two... three... four. Thank you.

You've got to choose from a sense of peace. What kind of peace and possibility are available here that you haven't considered? The only reason to be in a relationship is to have a sense of peace, which is the sense of joy and possibility and the sense that there is somebody who has your back all the time, somebody you can have fun with sexually.

Class Participant:

And not just sexually.

Gary:

Yeah, and there should be a sense of peace with the sex. If you have sex, you shouldn't have the point of view, "I wish I hadn't done this." It should be "What could I choose that I haven't chosen?" What would it be like if you chose something that was greater?

Creating a Relationship with Your Partner's Kid

Class Participant:

Gary, I have a question about a relationship I'm choosing with a four-year-old girl. She is doing...I'm not sure what to call it...protection or defense or competition with me. Can I talk to her in a way that will allow her to get that I'm not stealing Mommy? That's the thing that's coming up.

Gary:

Yes, you can say, "I like hanging out with your mom. You like hanging out with your mom. What kind of relationship do you want to have with me?"

Class Participant:

Cool. That's really light.

Gary:

"What do you want me to be for you? Do you want me to be your extra dad? Do you want me to be your mother's friend? Do you want me to be your friend? What do you want?"

Class Participant:

Yeah, and that will give her choice. Awesome.

Gary:

Yep. She needs to have the choice. When I got together with my ex-wife, she had a son, Adam, who was sixteen and out of control, and a daughter, Shannon, who was six and out of control. I asked Adam, "What do you want me to be in your life? How do you want me to be in your life? Do you want me to be your mother's husband? Do you want me to be your stepdad? Do you want me to be your wicked step dad? What do you want me to be?" He chose for me to be his dad and I said, "Okay, from now on I am your dad."

Class Participant:

And then you be that energy of whatever the dad is?

Gary:

Yep. Exactly.

Class Participant:

So that might be the lawmaker or whatever it is.

What's a Dad to You?

Gary:

You have to ask, "What is a dad to you?" Find out what their definition is of being a dad or a brother or whatever.

Class Participant:

Yeah.

Gary:

Let them define the relationship and you do everything you can to be that.

Class Participant:

That makes it a lot easier.

Gary:

Yeah. You can adjust. They cannot.

Class Participant:

Yeah. I get that.

Gary:

Everybody expects a kid to adjust, and it's the wrong thing to do. At one point in my relationship with my ex, Shannon was treating me like shit. I asked her, "How come you treat me like shit?"

She said, "Because you're not my real family."

I said, "If you're going to treat me like shit, I'm going to treat you exactly the same way you treat me, only worse."

When she would treat me like shit, I would treat her like shit. I'd give her exactly the same shit she gave me, and within three weeks, it all changed.

Class Participant:

Three weeks. That's a long time!

Gary:

Yeah, it was a long time, but I got through it. You've got to be the more conscious one.

Class Participant:

Why can't kids adjust?

Gary:

Because their whole life is about having to change to everybody else's point of view. They feel like they have no control over anything.

Class Participant:

So they can adjust, but we shouldn't expect them to?

Gary:

Well, everybody expects them to adjust. You expect your kid to adjust to your reality all the time. So the kid's point of view is "I have no control." And if a kid has no control, where does he or she go to gain control? Anger, rage, fury, and hate.

Class Participant:

Exactly.

Class Participant:

Is that what I'm doing with my son? Creating my life and expecting that he will want to come along?

Don't Create a Conflict or a Separation in Your Kids

Gary:

The other day you told him, "You've got a choice. Do you want to go home to your mom and school?" Saying "Do you want to go back to school?" is one thing, but using going home to his mom as a punishment was not a good thing, because his loyalty to his mom comes in conflict with his desire to be with you. Don't create that in your kids.

Class Participant:

What could I have said?

Gary:

"Hey son, if you want to go home, I can try to find somebody to take you home."

Class Participant:

Yup.

Gary:

Then he has choice.

Class Participant:

That's so interesting! I never looked at that till now. That would be treating him the way I would like to have been treated.

Gary:

Yeah. If you're in a relationship with someone and you treat your kid like that, the kid has to create anger against the person you're in relationship with.

Class Participant:

Oh, all right.

Gary:

And that gives them little to no choice in life.

Class Participant:

I am looking at how unkind it was to ask my son, "Do you want to go home to your mom and school?" Do you have any more information you can give me about how I was creating a separation with…

Gary:

Let's say that you told him that because you consider it a punishment to send him to his mother. Does he consider it a punishment?

Class Participant:

No.

Gary:

If you do that, he has to choose between his mother—and you and your partner. Who is he going to take it out on?

Class Participant:

My partner.

Gary:

Yeah, because she's the problem.

Class Participant:

Why would I do that? It's so clear now that it was unkind.

Gary:

It was just a moment of thoughtlessness. You weren't trying to do anything intentionally. You were not functioning from the awareness of the result that was going to occur by the choices you made.

Class Participant:

Yeah. Thanks.

Gary:

You haven't done permanent damage.

Class Participant:

No, and his mom tells him, "I'll send you to live with your father! You're just like your father!" All of that is such an unkindness. I hated her for doing that, and I didn't even notice I was doing it with him too, until you said it.

Gary:

That's because I'm willing to say things no one else is willing to say.

Class Participant:

Can you tell me where else I'm doing that?

Where Are You Trying to Get Him to Prefer You over Her?

Gary:

You have to look at where you're trying to get him to prefer you over her.

Class Participant:

Yeah.

Gary:

The easier way to get him to prefer you over her is to let him go stay with her and just be you when he comes back.

Class Participant:

Yeah.

Gary:

My son's mother was always trying to prove that she was better than I was. Today he wants her to go away and he wants me to be around all the time. Shannon's mother never wanted me to be anywhere near Shannon and never wanted me to touch her. And today Shannon wants to be around me. She doesn't want to be around her mother.

This is the way it works. The parent who tries to prove he or she is better, the parent who tries to control the kid, loses the kid. If you're not living with your child's mother, know that the kid is always going to prefer you over your mate. You have to make your kid number one over your mate, and let your mate know that you're only doing it to keep the kid happy. Who is your number one priority? Your kid or your partner?

Class Participant:

My kid.

Gary:

So if he's your number one priority, what is your partner? She's number one, as well. You have to take time for each one of them. Each one has their own special time with you. Each one knows that they are number one in your book.

Class Participant:

Right, rather than trying to combine them.

Gary:

Yeah, because the kid will begin to feel like he's losing his position and he will resent your partner. You have to put in a certain amount of time with the kid until the kid feels like he no longer needs you. It's like pushing massive amounts of energy at him until he's had enough.

If you push massive amounts of energy at a person, they either fill up or they want to go away. Either way, they don't feel they've been left out.

Class Participant:

Whereas I've tried to give him everything his mom can't so...

Gary:

So that he'll like you better.

Class Participant:

Yeah.

Gary:

That's only creating a place where he has to choose *against* instead of *for*.

Class Participant:

That helps a lot. Thank you.

Gary:

The great thing for you is that your partner likes your kid and she's willing to do things for him and give him things that make him happy. That's the thing that makes it workable. When a kid lives with his mother and his father, both parents will dote on the kid. When there's a stepparent, the stepparent often begins to feel resentful of the fact that the kid takes so much energy and time. You must never allow resentment to run your relationship, which is why you must be in question and ask: What can I create here that I haven't even considered?

"I've Tried to Be the Cool Dad"

Class Participant:

I'm so grateful for the stuff we brought up. I'm looking at all of the places where I've tried to be the cool dad or the rich dad or the dad who has no point of view, rather than somebody who could just be around his kid. I've created all of these places where I was trying to *do* something.

Gary:

Yeah. And what did your mom teach you? Did she teach you to try to be better than your father?

Class Participant:

She tried to teach me to not be my father, so I had to become him in order to figure out how to not be him.

Gary:

Yeah, and at the same time, you're still trying to do what she did, which was to prove that your father wasn't as good as she was.

Class Participant:

Yeah, so how much of my future is still created by that?

Gary:

A lot. So can we destroy and uncreate all of that?

Class Participant:

Yeah.

Gary:

One... two... three... four! Thank you.

A fair few others of you have mothers and fathers who do the same thing.

Class Participant:

I want to say how grateful I am for this conversation. I'm not a stepdad and I don't have a stepmom or anything like that. I don't even have kids, but the awareness that is brought up by this conversation is applicable to life in general. It's brilliant.

Gary:

If you see people making choices that are going to create things they're not looking for, then you at least know what to help them with or how to help them.

Class Participant:

Yeah.

Class Participant:

Can I ask one more thing about that? Can we destroy and uncreate all of the places where I've created it as my son's future?

Gary:

Everything you've done to create this kind of future. All of the projections and expectations you've had about others that you've created as futures that are locked in their universe and all of the projections and expectations: One... two... three... four! Thank you.

This happens with women too, when women project that you should be in their future. They look at you and say, "Oh, he's the man for me." They start trying to solidify into your reality a future that should be, based on you being with them. How many of you guys still have those kinds of futures being created?

Class Participant:

Oh, Jesus Christ!

Gary:

Yeah. Can we destroy and uncreate all of those: One... two... three... four! Thank you.

Class Participant:

That one is a huge one. Thank you so much for bringing that up.

Class Participant:

And this applies with money, too. When I met you, how many projections did I have with money?

Gary:

Yep. Apparently the process about having projections taken off of you for your futures is giving you guys more freedom than anything I've done tonight.

Class Participant:

You've told me that I'm inappropriately generous, yet sometimes my wife still accuses me of being selfish. She thinks I don't take her into account enough. What is that?

Learn to Be Manipulative

Gary:

She's a woman. If she's not the number one priority in your life and the number one person you listen to and talk to, her point of view is you're not paying enough attention to her. There are all kinds of ways you can change this.

For example, make sure you bring her a present at least once a week. It doesn't have to be big, just something that shows you're thinking about her. It can be a single flower. Find a beautiful flower and say, "Honey, I wanted to give this to you, because it reminded me of you. It's so close to perfect, and I couldn't imagine anything more beautiful." That's good for three days, and you're likely to get a blow job with it, as well. Guys, you have to learn to be more manipulative.

Class Participant:

Just little tokens of "I'm thinking of you?" Can you go over a few more of these things that would make life with a woman even more fun and easy?

Gary:

Ask her, "What is it you would like from me?" and be willing to hear the answer she doesn't tell you. Women do something that I call subtext. You'll ask a question like that and they'll say, "Oh, nothing," but it doesn't mean "nothing." It means "I want you to know what I want without my saying anything."

If your woman does this, go shopping with her and ask, "What do you like in this window? What's really exciting to you?" until you begin to get an idea of what her taste might be. Then you have a choice.

Every time you're with her, express gratitude for her being in your life. "I'm so grateful you're in my life. I'm so grateful for the gift of you."

Class Participant:

I once said that to my partner, and she almost cut my nuts off.

Gary:

Yes, because she thought it was a manipulation. You should have said, "Darling, I was serious. I really meant it."

Class Participant:

I see him tell her how beautiful she is all the time. Is that expressing gratitude, as well?

Gary:

Yes, that's the one way she can receive it.

Class Participant:

Yes, she can.

Gary:

She can receive "You're so beautiful. How did I get so lucky to have you in my life?" You have to find out what the person can receive. Give her what she can receive. Don't use the lines I give you here. You've already got it worked out. I've watched your partner get prettier and prettier every year, and I've watched the two of you get more in sync and more connected to each other all of the time.

Class Participant:

You once told me to give my partner things nobody has ever given her. That was fucking "Wow."

Gary:

Dain and I once gave a woman who works for us a necklace that was the most expensive thing she'd ever received, and it just cracked her universe. As a result, we've made even more money. When you're willing to acknowledge the fact that women deserve that kind of stuff, they'll say, "Oh my God. This guy is really here for me. I've got his back. I'm going for him."

And as Dain says, it's not done from the place of "Oh, this is going to be a manipulation." It's done from the gratitude and joy that are actually there, because there's a gratitude for everyone who is in your universe and for everything they gift and provide.

All right, gentlemen, it has been a pleasure. I think you are some of the coolest guys on the planet and the only ones with courage enough to become men.

Class Participant:

You're awesome, Gary!

Class Participant:

Thanks Gary.

12

DECODING WOMEN'S SUBTEXT

Subtext is the way women function.
There's "This is what she says" and there's
"This is what she's thinking.*"*
What she's thinking is what you're supposed to do.

Gary:

Hello, gentlemen. Is anybody happy?

Class Participant:

Yeah. We're really happy.

Class Participant:

We're happy! Happy!

Gary:

All right, let's go. Let me see what I can create here. Let me see how miserable I can make you. Who has a question?

Cultural Entrainment

Class Participant:

I find myself more attracted to women who are the same race and ethnicity as me and who have the same skin color. Is having sex with people of the same race and ethnicity an implant or some programming in the body?

Gary:

No, it's an entrainment you learned from your culture. We tend to be most excited by people of the same "ethnicity" because we've been trained to believe they're the most attractive. It's not programming; it's entrainment.

A lot of guys look at a woman and say, "Oh! She's hot!" Is that really looking at her? No, you're objectifying her and turning her into a "what" in your world instead of being with her as a being.

How many entrainments do you have to determine who or what you will sleep with and who you won't sleep with are you choosing? Everything that is times a godzillion, will you destroy and uncreate it all? Right and Wrong, Good and Bad, POD and POC, All Nine, Shorts, Boys, and Beyonds.

"I Frequently Attract Gay Men"

Class Participant:

It seems to me that I frequently attract gay men. They like to flirt with me, and it always makes me uncomfortable because I'm not sure how to respond. How do I create this?

Gary:

Well. I don't know. It could be that you're actually sexy! The thing about gay men is that they like men who are sexy. If you're sexy, gay men are going to go after you. It doesn't mean you're gay, although it would make it much easier if you were. It means you're good look-ing. Too bad you're a fool. You think you're not good looking because women don't go after you the way the men do. Dope, dope, dope.

Class Participant:

Am I sending the wrong signal to gay guys?

Gary:

No.

Class Participant:

How can I change this?

Gary:

Enjoy it. Recognize that it is just an acknowledgment of what you've done and what's working for you.

Where Do You Need to Put Your Energy?

Class Participant:

I'm starting a conscious relationship with a woman, and I have found that I have been moving more into my own business and less into Access Consciousness and supporting other facilitators. Am I excluding Access to create my relationship and my own business?

Gary:

No. You have to be willing to see where you need to put your energy each day. That's the most important part of all of this. It's not about giving up Access. You have to go with: What's going to be the priority that's going to create the best result for me?

Class Participant:

What can I be or do different to have them all as a priority?

Gary:

You can't have them all as a priority. You could recognize that there are times when one thing is a priority and there are times when another thing is. And if you're with a woman, she's always the priority.

Class Participant:

What can I be that will allow me to receive more from Access Consciousness and from you?

Gary:

What you can be is you. And if you're doing your business, if you're doing all of the things you're talking about here, everything should get better.

A Relationship with a Kid Attached

Class Participant:

The relationship I have now has a kid attached. I have found that talking to my enjoyable other about how we facilitate her daughter has created a great connection between us. Is this a contribution to the child, me, and the woman—or will this backfire?

Gary:

No, it's is a contribution. You have to get that's where you're going here. This is what can be contributed and what's really possible.

Class Participant:

After the last call, I asked my stepdaughter what would she like me to be in her life, and she said, "Happy." After we talked about it some more, she said, "A friend." We talked about that, too, and her point of view is that a friend is a playmate. How can I use that?

Gary:

Be a playmate.

Class Participant:

She has also been playing with changing her name to my name and she called me *Dad* once.

Gary:

That would mean she's trying to make you into a dad. You have to see whether you're willing to be that, because even if you end up not staying with this woman, you've got to be willing to be the dad for the kid or the woman will hate you.

Class Participant:

My stepdaughter likes making videos about entities and things like that with me, and I asked her mom and her if I can use them to promote my business. They are both happy with that. What will this create?

Gary:

This will create their being involved in your business, which should create more profit for you.

Class Participant:

Should this be done as a Deal and Deliver?

Gary:

Yes. Everything should be done as a Deal and Deliver.

An Undefined Life

Class Participant:

First, I want to say thank you so much for these calls. They have been life changing for me in so many ways. I have gotten more clarity about how I function with women, with relationship, and what I can do different to make things work. I'm not going to the wrongness of me so much anymore and I have more peace within. Right now I feel like there's nothing to hold onto in any area of my life. I've been asking for an undefined life, which to me means being free from the definitions and limitations other people impose on me. I don't have any idea how to function with this, though, besides asking questions.

Gary:

If you function from question in your relationships and with everything you do, you start moving toward having an undefined life. If everything is a question, you open the door for a relationship that has not yet existed. Ask:

> What energy, space, and consciousness can my body and I be that would allow us to have a relationship beyond this reality with total ease? Everything that doesn't allow that to show up times a godzillion, will you destroy and uncreate it all? Right and Wrong, Good and Bad, POD and POC, All Nine, Shorts, Boys, and Beyonds.

You might want to put that on a loop and run it nonstop for at least thirty days until you start to get that there's a different place from which you can deal with everything.

Dealing with a Woman's Anger

Class Participant:

When my woman delivers anger or projects it at me, I still go into a beyond and dismiss me. Sometimes I go into the wrongness of me. I've run clearings with the beyonds and the SHICUUUU implants, but there's still resistance to receiving the energy of her anger.

Gary:

Anger is never anything except a way to control you. What if you could have a different choice? Would you be willing to have that?

Class Participant:

Should I run: What energy, space, and consciousness can my body and I be that will allow me to be the pathetic pile of shit, wrongness, and weakness I truly be?

Gary:

That's not a good one. You want to run:

What bastardization of infinite capacity am I using to create the wrongness, the pathetic pile of shit, and the weak, lily-livered coward I am trying to be, I am pretending to be am I choosing? Everything that is times a godzillion, will you destroy and uncreate it all? Right and Wrong, Good and Bad, POD and POC, All Nine, Shorts, Boys, and Beyonds.

Class Participant:

I've also tried using energy pulls, lowering my barriers, doing interesting point of view, and POC and POD, and they all work sometimes. But when I go into a beyond, all of those tools are gone. Is there any other way to be free here and let go of that?

Gary:

Sometimes you have to be willing to get angry. You can do anger without judgment and without force. Doing anger without judgment and without force is the generative element of anger. You have to be willing to do that. Be willing to go to anger when you need to. Most of us think that not being angry is the target. What if that wasn't it? What if there was a different choice we haven't chosen yet?

Class Participant:

Can anger without judgment be used with kids, as well?

Gary:

Yeah. With kids you can say, "Stop. That's all there is."

Class Participant:

Is anger without judgment the same as killing energy?

Gary:

No, anger without force or judgment is "You know what? Do that again and you and I are done." People tend to have the point of view that anger is always a wrongness, but it's not. It's just that you're a man, so you're a wrongness in general.

Everything you've done not to perceive, know, be, and receive the other options you have, will you destroy and uncreate all of that? Right and Wrong, Good and Bad, POD and POC, All Nine, Shorts, Boys, and Beyonds.

Aggressive Presence in Relationship

Class Participant:

Can you talk more about aggressive presence in relationship and what that could look like?

Gary:

Aggressive presence is the willingness to be you and to be present in a relationship regardless of the outcome. It's about having no point of view. Everything is just an interesting point of view, nothing more. When you are willing to function without the sense that you have to do anything other than just be present, you start to create a reality in which nothing becomes a wrongness, and everything becomes a possibility.

How to Approach a Woman

Class Participant:

Can you talk about how to approach women?

Gary:

It depends on what you're looking for. You've got to ask:

- What do I really want to create here?

- What do I want to do?
- How's this going to work for me?
- What do I want to get from this woman?

If you really wish to create something with a woman, you've got to ask the question, "What do I really want to create here?" A lot of you try to create something based on a lie.

How many lies are you using to create the relationships you are choosing? Everything that is times a godzillion, will you destroy and uncreate it all? Right and Wrong, Good and Bad, POD and POC, All Nine, Shorts, Boys, and Beyonds.

"The Word *Commitment* Is Still Sticking Me"

Class Participant:

The word *commitment* is still sticking me. For example, the idea of committing to relationship makes me feel like I have to exclude all other women I would like to have sex with or be close with. Or committing to a business deal or a job means I have to exclude all other business possibilities.

Gary:

How many of you are buying the crap that you're only capable of, or willing to, or would like to have only one person or one business as the sum total of your reality? Everything that is times a godzillion, will you destroy and uncreate it all? Right and Wrong, Good and Bad, POD and POC, All Nine, Shorts, Boys, and Beyonds.

Class Participant:

The other person's expectations make me want to run in the other direction.

Gary:

What if you were just aware—instead of an idiot?

Class Participant:

(Laughter)

Gary:

Recognize that you are aware. You are way more aware than ninety percent of the guys on the planet. So what does that mean? It means you have more possibilities with more women than other guys do.

Use your awareness and ask:

- What does this person want to hear?
- What does this person want to create?
- What is this going to look like?

Start to reach into that universe, and you'll be able to talk to anyone without the sense that you can't choose to be with her. You'll be able to create your empowerment channel as greater than what you've currently been doing.

Class Participant:

I'm scared that if I commit to someone or something that I'll lose me to that person or thing again.

Gary:

Is that really yours? I hate to tell you, my friend, but you're way more aware than you want to know. Ninety percent of what you guys think is messing you up is not even yours. How weird is that?

You Can Be You without a Woman

Class Participant:

I met a woman who is twelve years younger than I am. She lives about sixty kilometers away from me, and her life is very different from mine. She works in the arts, and I work in business.

Gary:

Why do you think she's interested in you? Her basic point of view is that you must be successful. She wants to learn how to be successful.

Class Participant:

Everything was really easy with us and neither one of us was looking for a serious relationship, so we were just going along. I really liked her, and she developed feelings that she didn't want, and pushed them away. It's as if she has the point of view that she doesn't want to be in a relationship, so nothing else can happen. Even if she moves on with her life in whatever way she chooses, I would like to have some more clarity about what's going on.

Gary:

What bastardization of the infinite freedom from women are you using to create the unconscious relationships with women you are choosing? Everything that is times a godzillion, will you destroy and uncreate it all? Right and Wrong, Good and Bad, POD and POC, All Nine, Shorts, Boys, and Beyonds.

Class Participant:

Whoa! That's the energy I've been feeling.

Gary:

What bastardization of the infinite freedom from women are you using to create the unconscious relationships with women you are choosing? Everything that is times a godzillion, will you

destroy and uncreate it all? Right and Wrong, Good and Bad, POD and POC, All Nine, Shorts, Boys, and Beyonds.

You guys have the weird point of view that you can't be you without a woman. That's fucking strange, because you can be you without a woman. In fact it's a lot easier, but for some reason, you have decided that without a woman, you can't be you.

Everything that is times a godzillion, will you destroy and uncreate it all? Right and Wrong, Good and Bad, POD and POC, All Nine, Shorts, Boys, and Beyonds.

What bastardization of the infinite freedom from women are you using to create the unconscious relationships with women you are choosing? Everything that is times a godzillion, will you destroy and uncreate it all? Right and Wrong, Good and Bad, POD and POC, All Nine, Shorts, Boys, and Beyonds.

Class Participant:

Run it again, please.

Gary:

What bastardization of the infinite freedom from women are you using to create the unconscious relationships with women you are choosing? Everything that is times a godzillion, will you destroy and uncreate it all? Right and Wrong, Good and Bad, POD and POC, All Nine, Shorts, Boys, and Beyonds.

And all of the futures unactualized and unrealized that you have about your future as always with a woman and the only way you're going to have a future is with a woman, can we have those destroyed, please: One... two... three.... four. Thank you.

You're Always Going to Go to Relationship Because That's What the Woman Wants

Class Participant:

I don't really desire relationship; still, I met an awesome woman who I really enjoy spending time with, and even though everything is easy, it ends up creating a relationship.

Gary:

You're a man. You're an idiot. I love you, but are you kidding me? You're always going to go to relationship because that's what the woman wants. You will give yourself up for the woman every time, guys. It's just damn stupid. You have a penis. Your IQ is only as large as your penis.

Class Participant:

Can't things just be enjoyable without all of this other stuff?

Gary:

No, I'm sorry. You are cute as hell, but you're dumber than dirt. There's no such thing as a friendship with benefits. Every woman always assumes that if you're friendly and you're easy, and on top of that, you're cute, it means that eventually you're going to get into a relationship, and the only reason you want to hang out with her is because you really want relationship. Sorry guys. You have one brain that works, and it's the one that hangs between your legs. The rest of your brain power is useless.

Class Participant:

Is there any way around this shit?

Gary:

Is there any way around it? Yeah. Get smart. Look at it. After doing the sex and relationship class, I got a text message from a lady that said,

"What do I have to do to have you? Can I send you a picture of my clit? Do I have to do aggressive withdrawal? What do I have to do to get you?" Did she ask me my point of view? No. Did she ask me if I was interested? No! Why? Because she's a woman and her basic point of view is "If you're a man, you have no point of view other than the one I want you to have." You have to get this, guys, because if you don't, you'll spend your entire life trying to make the woman right and trying to figure out how you can make it work for her. Not for you, for her.

The Woman Is Not the Source of Your Sexual Reality

Class Participant:

I have stopped making the woman the source of my sexual reality. This has given me great freedom.

Gary:

Yeah. The woman is not the source of your sexual reality. How many of you have made women the source of your sexual reality? You make sex the source of how you live. You decide you can't live without sex. The truth is you can live without sex—but it's way more fun to have it. But you guys don't do sex for the fun of it. You do it to make sure you can continue to live.

You think sex is serious. I have a different point of view. I have the point of view that sex is something you get to do for the fun of it. Why not do it just because it's fun?

What stupidity are you using to create the serious sex you are choosing? Everything that is times a godzillion, will you destroy and uncreate it all? Right and Wrong, Good and Bad, POD and POC, All Nine, Shorts, Boys, and Beyonds.

When you get to the point where sex doesn't matter, where it's okay for you one way or the other, you're creating a place where you can actually have choice, and the sex you do have will be much greater.

Women make all kinds of weird, forceful invitations to me, and I have no desire to have sex with them. I like somebody who's fun, not somebody who's forceful. There has to be a sense of fun in it for me personally. When you get to the point where you have no need of it, you begin to choose who to have sex with—and when. It's an easier place to function from, and when you get there, you'll end up with better sex. I can guarantee you that.

How Many Jobs Have You Been Given?

Class Participant:

I see that I've been trying to be a peacemaker in sex and relationship. I've been running the clearing "What stupidity am I using to create the peacemaker I'm choosing," and it seems like things are shifting.

Gary:

Did you take on the job of being a peacemaker—or were you given the job? Were you given that job in utero?

Class Participant:

Given feels lighter.

Gary:

So you were given the job of being the peacemaker in your family. Does that give you choice or does that make them the choosers for you?

Class Participant:

It makes them the choosers.

Gary:

If they're the choosers, what choices do you have? Do you have a lot of choices or do you have a little choice?

Class Participant:

Little choice.

Gary:

The reality is that what you really want to create is a greater possibility, not a lesser possibility. What would it be like if you could have the greatest possibility you've ever had? What would that be like?

Notice you have no answer, because no answer is the place you were never given a choice. You were given a job and that was the job you were supposed to have. No other job works.

Everything you aligned and agreed with or resisted and reacted to that allowed that job to be given to you, will you destroy and uncreate all of that? Right and Wrong, Good and Bad, POD and POC, All Nine, Shorts, Boys, and Beyonds.

How many jobs have you been given this lifetime by women who require you to not choose for you, to not be you, and to do what they want you to do? All of those, will you destroy and uncreate it all? Right and Wrong, Good and Bad, POD and POC, All Nine, Shorts, Boys, and Beyonds.

All of the futures that have been created based on those jobs, can we destroy and uncreate all of those, please: One... two... three... four. One more time: One... two... three... four. One more time: One... two... three... four. Okay, do you feel more free to choose?

Class Participants:

Yeah.

Gary:

You keep thinking that because the woman has given you the job, whether your job is to take out the trash or to be the trash, that you've been given the job. A lot of you were given the job of being the man of the family, especially if you had divorced mothers. You were given the job of being the man of the family, but you were never told what that meant and you definitely didn't get any of the benefits of it. Usually they told you that your father was so terrible, awful, and vicious that you decided you didn't want to turn out like that, so you didn't get to be you at all. The way you know what you are as a man is by the father you had, even if you only had him for the thirty seconds it took for him to cum.

Everything that is times a godzillion, will you destroy and uncreate it all? Right and Wrong, Good and Bad, POD and POC, All Nine, Shorts, Boys, and Beyonds.

The Job of Judging Yourself

If you had a mother who judged your father in any way, shape, or form, the only choice you had was the job of judging yourself.

How many of you have been given the job of judging you nonstop right the fuck out of existence? Everything that is times a godzillion, will you destroy and uncreate it all? Right and Wrong, Good and Bad, POD and POC, All Nine, Shorts, Boys, and Beyonds.

Class Participant:

How does that work? If your mother's judging your father then you're....

Gary:

You are the offspring. In the Bible, it says, "The sins of the father shall be visited upon the child." That's it. That's the entrainment to assuming that you're as bad as your father. And if you spend your life not wanting to be like your father, the end result is you've already become that in order to not be it, which means you're stuck. In actual fact, you're better than your father. Have any of you ever noticed? Were you ever acknowledged for being way better than your father?

Class Participant:

No. My mom used to tell me, "You look like your father," and people would say, "You look like your father" and one day I realized, "Wow, my body's turning into my father's."

Gary:

Yeah. All of those points of view were delivered at you. How many of you have the point of view that you look like your father, or you look like your mother, or you look like your uncle or your grandpa? The truth is none of you look like anybody except you.

Everything you've done to make you agreeable to looking like somebody else's body, will you destroy and uncreate all of that? Right and Wrong, Good and Bad, POD and POC, All Nine, Shorts, Boys, and Beyonds.

What's the Subtext Here That I'm Not Acknowledging?

Class Participant:

When I ask my woman what she would like, what something would look like, or what I could do for her, I rarely get any information. She doesn't want to answer, so we can never get to Deal and Deliver. I heard you say that women never tell what's true for them so they can control the man. What questions can I ask or what energies can I be here? Can you talk more about that? Am I looking for the answer, not the awareness?

Gary:

Yes, you're looking for the answer, not the awareness. What would you like to create? What would you like to create with a woman?

Everything that does not allow you to perceive, know, be, and receive that, will you destroy and uncreate it all? Right and Wrong, Good and Bad, POD and POC, All Nine, Shorts, Boys, and Beyonds.

Class Participant:

I have a problem with this, too. Can we talk a bit more about it? Whenever I've tried to do a Deal and Deliver, the woman keeps asking me the question I asked her, so we go around and around.

Gary:

Why does somebody ask you a question that you've just asked them? Because a) They don't want to answer it, and b) They want to find out what your answer is before they answer.

If you ask a woman, "Do you like this color?" she will reply, "What color do you like?" Her point of view is "If you don't like the color I like, I'm not going to like you. If I don't like the color you like, we're not going to get along." This is the subtext of every conversation. You have to ask the question: What's the subtext here that I'm not acknowledging?

Class Participant:

I've run into a couple of women. We like the same things, we like to do the same stuff, and we have a lot of things in common with each other....

Gary:

Every woman is going to tell you that you have things in common, whether it's true or not. In common means "We're destined to be together." That's the subtext of that comment. When a woman says, "We have a lot in common," it means "We're getting married."

Class Participant:

That's what I was leading up to. When a woman says, "We've got a lot of stuff in common," I say, "Yeah, and what does that have to do with anything?"

Gary:

Every woman is going to look for what you have in common so she can decide you're the man she wants. It has nothing to do with your point of view. They don't care about your point of view.

Class Participant:

True, true, true.

Gary:

When are you going to get that there is a subtext to every female conversation? "You're so interesting" means "Oh, I can have sex with you." "Wow, this was really fun" means "What are you going to do next?" and "When do I schedule the church?"

Class Participant:

I get it.

Gary:

You guys have the point of view that women hear what you say. No, no. They don't hear what you say. They've already concocted what's going to happen.

How much of your ability to comprehend is overridden by a woman's concoction of what she wants to hear? Everything that is times a godzillion, will you destroy and uncreate it all? Right and Wrong, Good and Bad, POD and POC, All Nine, Shorts, Boys, and Beyonds.

What Part of "Women Have Subtext" Are You Not Getting?

Women communicate in a circuitous way, thinking they're going to get what they want by changing the way they ask for it, so you eventually get out of the way and do what they say. Women always expect men to do what they want. Why do you not get that? What part of "Women have subtext" are you not getting?

A woman's point of view is that if you say what she says, you're telling the truth. If you tell her what she wants to hear, you're telling the truth. Everything else is a lie.

You've got to get this, guys. Women function from subtext. Ask: What's the subtext I'm not listening to here? Subtext is the way they function. There's "This is what she says" and there's "This is what she's thinking." What she's thinking is what you're supposed to do. She's saying, "Oh, it's not a problem. Do whatever you want." That means "You do that and I'll kill you."

Someone said we should have a subtext app to decode what women say. Wouldn't that be great? She says, "x, y, z" and it comes up "That means blah, blah, blah." In a class we did this week, I told the women what subtext was and they all said, "Yes, but..."

I would say, "The subtext of that is 'blah, blah, blah.'"

They'd say, "What do you mean? I wasn't doing subtext!"

I'd say, "Yeah you were! You just did it! It's not wrong; it's just what you do. If you want to be honest about what you're saying, you have to see when you're doing it. It's just one of the ways in which women are different from men."

There is a great YouTube video called "It's Not about the Nail."

A lady says to a man, "I need you to listen. I have this pain in my head."

The man says, "Well, what about the nail that's in your head?"

The woman says, "No, that's not the problem! I want you to listen. Why do you never listen? Stop trying to fix me!"

You know, the thing is, guys. You're men.

Class Participant:

Do you have any clearings for more ease in decoding subtext?

Gary:

Women always have ulterior motives. They always have a subtext. Nothing is ever straight. It's never direct.

What stupidity are you using to create never perceiving and receiving the subtext are you choosing? Everything that is times a godzillion, will you destroy and uncreate it all? Right and Wrong, Good and Bad, POD and POC, All Nine, Shorts, Boys, and Beyonds.

"We Have a Relationship Now"

Class Participant:

Is there anything I haven't looked at with my relationship that if I'd look at it, could create more space and possibility?

Gary:

You're always doing that anyway, so I don't think you have to worry about it. Both you and your partner are trying to create your relationship. You're not trying to live in it. And that's essential. The biggest mistake people make is when they say, "We have a relationship now." That's the end? No, it's not the end. It's just the beginning of what else is possible. You're in a constant state of creation of your relationship when you function from:

- What else is possible?
- What other choices do we have?
- What else can we create?
- How would we like this to be?
- Can we destroy and uncreate everything it was yesterday?

Asking these questions keeps you in the present moment and opens the door to levels of possibility nobody else could ever have.

Thank you so much. You guys have been an amazing gift. This series has been a huge contribution to a greater possibility. You guys are about the bravest guys I've ever met, because you're willing to talk about being something different from what other people are willing to be.

Class Participant:

Awesome. I want to say thank you for a great series.

Class Participant:

Thank you so much, Gary.

Gary:

Thank you all for being on this call. I'm so grateful that you guys are in the world. You guys take care—and go out and get laid! But remember, you only want to get laid once. If you go to two, you're going to be in relationship, and if you go to three, you're getting married. And if the girl says, "We have so much in common," her point of view is you're going to get married soon. So you'd better be ready for the aftermath if you don't show up the way you're supposed to.

Love you guys. Take care!

THE ACCESS CONSCIOUSNESS CLEARING STATEMENT®

*You are the only one who can unlock the points of view
that have you trapped.
What I am offering here with the clearing process is a tool you can use
to change the energy of the points of view that have you locked
into unchanging situations.*

Throughout this book, I ask a lot of questions, and some of those questions might twist your head around a little bit. That's my intention. The questions I ask are designed to get your mind out of the picture so you can get to the energy of a situation.

Once the question has twisted your head around and brought up the energy of a situation, I ask if you are willing to destroy and uncreate that energy, because stuck energy is the source of barriers and limitations. Destroying and uncreating that energy will open the door to new possibilities for you. This is your opportunity to say, "Yes, I'm willing to let go of whatever is holding that limitation in place."

That will be followed by some weird-speak we call the clearing statement:

Right and Wrong, Good and Bad, POD and POC, All 9, Shorts, Boys, and Beyonds®

With the clearing statement, we're going back to the energy of the limitations and barriers that have been created. We're looking at the energies that keep us from moving forward and expanding into all of the spaces we would like to go. The clearing statement is simply short-speak that addresses the energies that are creating the limitations and contractions in our life.

The more you run the clearing statement, the deeper it goes and the more layers and levels it can unlock for you. If a lot of energy comes up for you in response to a question, you may wish to repeat the process numerous times until the subject being addressed is no longer an issue for you.

You don't have to understand the words of the clearing statement for it to work because it's about the energy. However, if you're interested in knowing what the words mean, there are some brief definitions given below.

Right and Wrong, Good and Bad is shorthand for: What's right, good, perfect, and correct about this? What's wrong, mean, vicious, terrible, bad, and awful about this? The short version of these questions is: What's right and wrong, good and bad? It is the things that we consider right, good, perfect, and/or correct that stick us the most. We do not wish to let go of them since we decided that we have them right.

POD stands for the **p**oint of **d**estruction, all the ways you have been destroying yourself in order to keep whatever you're clearing in existence.

POC stands for the **p**oint of **c**reation of the thoughts, feelings, and emotions immediately preceding your decision to lock the energy in place.

Sometimes people say, "POD and POC it," which is simply shorthand for the longer statement. When you "POD and POC" something, it is like pulling the bottom card out of a house of cards. The whole thing falls down.

All 9 stands for the nine different ways you have created this item as a limitation in your life. They are the layers of thoughts, feelings, emotions, and points of view that create the limitation as solid and real.

Shorts is the short version of a much longer series of questions that include: What's meaningful about this? What's meaningless about this? What's the punishment for this? What's the reward for this?

Boys stands for energetic structures called nucleated spheres. Basically these have to do with those areas of our life where we've tried to handle something continuously with no effect. There are at least thirteen different kinds of these spheres, which are collectively called "the boys." A nucleated sphere looks like the bubbles created when you blow in one of those kids' bubble pipes that has multiple chambers. It creates a huge mass of bubbles, and when you pop one bubble, the other bubbles fill in the space.

Have you ever tried to peel the layers of an onion when you were trying to get to the core of an issue, but you could never get there? That's because it wasn't an onion; it was a nucleated sphere.

Beyonds are feelings or sensations you get that stop your heart, stop your breath, or stop your willingness to look at possibilities. Beyonds are what occur when you are in shock. We have lots of areas in our life where we freeze up. Anytime you freeze up, that's a beyond holding you captive. That's the difficulty with a beyond: it stops you from being present. The beyonds include everything that is beyond belief, reality, imagination, conception, perception, rationalization, forgiveness, as well as all the other beyonds. They are usually feelings and sensations, rarely emotions, and never thoughts.

Glossary

Allowance

You can align and agree with a point of view, or you can resist and react to a point of view. That's the polarity of this reality. Or you can be in allowance. If you are in allowance, you are the rock in the middle of the stream. Thoughts, beliefs, attitudes, and considerations come at you and they go around you, because to you, they're just an interesting point of view. If, on the other hand, you go into alignment and agreement or resistance and reaction to that point of view, you get caught up in the stream of insanity and you go along for a ride. That's not the stream you want to be in. You want to be in allowance. Total allowance is: Everything is just an interesting point of view.

Bars

The Bars® are a hands-on Access process that involves a light touch upon the head to contact points that correspond to different aspects of one's life. There are points for joy, sadness, body and sexuality, awareness, kindness, gratitude, peace and calm. There is even a money bar. These points are called bars because they run from one side of the head to the other.

Be

In this book, the word *be* is sometimes used rather than *are* to refer to *you,* the infinite being you truly *be,* as opposed to a contrived point of view about who you think you *are.*

Being and Beingness

Being is you, the infinite being you are.

Beingness is something you do to prove that you're being.

Energetic Synthesis of Being (ESB)

ESB is a class that Dr. Dain Heer teaches. It's about how you, as a being, bring things together to change everything around you.

Energetic Synthesis of Communion (ESC)

This is a process that Dain does. Basically, the energetic synthesis of communion puts you in connection with all the molecular structures of the universe in a different way. You can find out more about this on Dain's website (www.drdainheer.com). He offers free "tasters" so you can get a sense of what it's like.

Head Tripping, Heart Tripping, Crotch Tripping

When you are head tripping, you think about *it* (whatever *it* is) all the time. "What's next? What are we going to do next? What's the next step?" A head tripper is always going into "next, next, next."

A heart tripper is always going into "Why didn't you call me? Don't you love me anymore? What's the matter with you? What's the matter with me?"

Crotch trippers are always trying to prove how sexual they are rather than actually *being* sexual. It's a *proof* of sexualness—not *being* sexual. Women who dress provocatively but who don't have an ounce of sexual energy are crotch trippers. They look like they ought to be sexual—but they're in the image, not the reality.

Holding Patterns

These are patterns we hold in our bodies. They can be unlocked by a hands-on Access Consciousness process.

Humans and Humanoids

There are two different species of two-legged beings on this planet. We call them humans and humanoids. They look alike, they walk alike, they talk alike, and they often eat alike, but the reality is they're different.

Humans will always tell you how you're wrong, how they're right, and how you shouldn't change anything. They say things like, "We don't do things that way, so don't even bother." They are the ones who ask, "Why are you changing that? It's fine the way it is."

Humanoids take a different approach. They are always looking at things and asking, "How can we change that? What will make this better? How can we outdo this?" They're the people who have created all the great art, all the great literature, and all the great progress on the planet.

Implants

Implants are things that have been done to us in one lifetime or another that have an action on the body and the mind. An implant creates a particular kind of vibration within us; it becomes something that impacts us and holds us. We've found that it's possible to remove or undo these implants using a process from Access Consciousness.

Interesting Point of View

Interesting point of view is an Access Consciousness tool. It is a great way to neutralize judgment by reminding yourself that whatever the judgment is, it's just a point of view that you or someone else has at this moment in time. It's not right or wrong or good or bad.

Any time a judgment comes up, just say, "Interesting point of view." It helps to distance you from the judgment. You don't align and agree with it—and you don't resist and react to it. You just allow it to be what it is, which is no more than an interesting point of view. When you can do this, you are in allowance.

Is This Mine?

"Is this mine?" is a question you ask to find out if the thoughts, feelings, and emotions you're having actually belong to you—because 98% of thoughts, feelings, and emotions we have do not belong to us. We continuously pick up everybody else's stuff and assume it's ours, especially if it's bad. And we assume the good stuff belongs to someone else.

Killing Energy

Killing energy is the energy it would take for you to kill something if you were willing to do it without any judgment. It takes energy to kill a cow or a deer or anything you're going to eat. That energy, delivered at somebody the way you would deliver it if you were actually slaughtering an animal, is the energy that will change things for people.

Lighter/Heavier

That which is light is always true, and you sense the lightness of it. That which is a lie is always heavy, and you sense that heaviness.

The Place

A novel by Gary Douglas about what you've always been looking for and how and where it might be possible.

POD and POCing

POD and POCing is a short way of saying that you are going back in time to the point where you destroyed yourself with something or to the point of creation of something that locks you up.

Pulling Energy, Energy Pulls

Most men push energy at the women they are attracted to. Women get lots of that and their response is pretty much, "No thank you!" Instead of pushing energy at someone you're attracted to, try pulling energy from him or her. That's the way to attract them. They'll suddenly feel drawn to you. Energy flows are the way you create connections with people. You just ask the energy to pull. It's that easy.

Put (Something) on a Loop

This is something you can do on your computer, which allows you to listen to something over and over again.

Receiving

In this reality, people believe the only ways to receive are through sex, copulation, or money.

True receiving is being able to receive all the information there is. It has to do with the awareness of everything that's possible. It's the capacity to perceive all awareness without a point of view.

Sex and No Sex

In Access Consciousness, when we say *sex* and *no sex*, we're not referring to copulation. We're talking about receiving. We chose these words as they bring up the energy of receiving and not receiving better than anything else we've found.

People use their points of view about sex and no sex as a way of limiting their receiving. Sex and no sex are exclusionary universes—either/or universes—where you either make your presence known (sex) to the exclusion of everyone else, or you hide your presence (no sex) so that you cannot be seen. In either case, given the focus on yourself, you don't allow yourself to receive from anyone or anything.

SHICUUUU Implants

These are implants that are secret, hidden, invisible, covert, unseen, unsaid, unacknowledged, and undisclosed.

Signs, Seals, Emblems, and Significances

These are the badges you wear all the time that have nothing to do with who you are.

What stupidity are you choosing?

Infinite beings, in order to be unaware, have to create themselves as stupid. Questions that contain the phrase "What stupidity are you choosing....?" are not meant to suggest that you are stupid. Rather, they seek to bring up the energy of times you have chosen a lack of knowing—a stupidity—in order to create yourself as unaware.

WHAT IS ACCESS CONSCIOUSNESS®?

What if you were willing to nurture and care for you?
What if you would open the doors to being everything
you have decided it is not possible to be?
What would it take for you to realize how crucial you are to the
possibilities of the world?

Access Consciousness is a simple set of tools, techniques, and philosophies that allow you to create dynamic change in every area of your life. Access provides step-by-step building blocks that allow you to become totally aware and begin functioning as the conscious being you truly are. These tools can be used to change whatever isn't working in your life so that you can have a different life and a different reality.

You can access these tools via a variety of classes, books, tele-calls, and other products, or with an Access Consciousness Certified Facilitator or an Access Consciousness Bars Facilitator.

The goal of Access is to create a world of consciousness and one-ness. Consciousness is the ability to be present in your life in every moment without judgment of yourself or anyone else. Consciousness includes everything and judges nothing. It's the ability to receive everything, reject nothing, and create everything you desire in life, greater than you currently have and more than you can ever imagine.

For more information about Access Consciousness, or to locate an Access Consciousness Facilitator, please visit:

www.accessconsciousness.com

www.garymdouglas.com

THE GENTLEMEN'S CLUB INDEX OF CHAPTER TITLES AND HEADINGS

Chapter 1: Stepping Up to Something Different **9**

Trusting Yourself as a Man/Trusting Other Men 9

Creating Partnership with Men 11

Cutting Off Your Sense of Beauty 15

"We've Got Each Other's Back" 17

The Kindness Men Have 20

Creating Separation 23

Sexual Energy and Receiving 26

Choosing Something Different 28

Change vs. Different 30

What Can I Do Different? 34

Possibility, Choice, Question, and Contribution 39

Have You Ever Been Encouraged to Be a Man? 41

**Chapter 2: Creating Sex and Relationship from
an Awareness of What Is**.. **43**

Creation vs. Invention..43

The Way It Looks vs. The Way It Is............................44

The Rule of Dick..46

If You're a Man, You're Wrong...................................48

The Invention of Contraception 51

What If Success Is Just a Choice? 53

You Can Create—or You Can Invent.........................55

Creating Something That Is Different........................57

Are You Making Yourself Less Sexual? 59

Are You Trying to Heal Those Who Are Dying from a
Lack of Sexual Energy? 60

Sexual Attraction...63

Focus on the Creation...65

Going on Vacation 66

What Would It Be Like to Create Sex and Relationship
from a Totally Different Reality? 68

Chapter 3: You Are the Valuable Product................. **71**

The Demons of Necessity 71

Permeating Consciousness into a Demon's World 76

Are You Making Someone Righteous?........................77

Deal and Deliver...80

Will This Expand My Agenda? 81

When You're the Leader, You Become the Valuable Product.........83

The Wrongness around Desiring Sex 86

Total Presence in Sex and Copulation 87

Cultural Entrainment..88

Being the Sexual Energy You Are 90

What Would I Like to Create for Me? 92

Orgasm by Contraction/Orgasm by Expansion 93

Integrity with Self 98

Chapter 4: Become the King of Possibilities........................ 103

The Eternal Season of Discontent...103

A Twisted Discontent that Creates Separation between Men......106

What If There Was No Sense of Need in Your Life?....................108

Being Undefended 111

Will She Make Me a Valuable Product? 112

The Avoidance of the Joy of Sex and Copulation.......................113

The Turn-On You Are..115

The Ultimate Arousal...119

Sex Is a Life Force 123

Seeing You as Valuable 125

What Will It Take for This Relationship to Work?......................126

The Subtlety of Awareness You Actually Have.............................127

The Hard-On You Could Be Choosing..128

Step into the Role of the King 133

What If You Were Willing to Be the King of Possibilities? 135

**Chapter 5: The Phenomenal Sex, Copulation,
      and Relationship You Could Be Choosing..................... 139**

Creating Demon-Augmented Occurrences....................................139

It Didn't "Just Happen"..143

"I Want Him to Give Up His Life for Me" 146

Romance 148

"I Seem to Attract Married Women" 150

Are You Giving Up You? 153

Inculcation of Realities 155

Be Honest about Where You Are in Your Life 159

How Can I Use Being a Sleaze Ball to My Advantage? 160

Using Your Sexual Energy 162

What Are You Creating with Your Sexual Energy? 166

Great Sex 167

Don't Make Other People's Judgments True 168

Chapter 6: What Do You Really Desire? 173

What If Everyone Was Willing to be a Slut? 173

What Do You Want to Have in Your Life? 174

Choosing Awareness 176

You Have to Desire It 178

Are You Making Yourself Wrong for the Truth of You? 179

An Ideal Relationship with a Woman 180

Spending Time Together 181

What's the Most Important Thing to Me? 184

Make a List: "What I Would Like in a Partner?" 185

You Also Need an "I Don't Want to Have" List 186

What Stupidity Are You Using to Create the Women
　　You Are Choosing? 187

Becoming Needless of a Woman 188

"I've Stopped Creating" 190

Abdicating Your Voice 191

Chapter 7: Being Good in Bed **195**

Create a Galvanic Response in Her Body.................................195

Go Slow 196

Learn about the Parts of a Woman's Body 196

What Kind of Touch Would She Like?......................................196

Decreased Libido...197

Stimulating Her Body 200

Masturbation...201

Receiving...203

Creating a Molecular Vibration between You and the Woman...204

Talk to Her 206

People Connect as Bodies..207

 "You're Mine"...207

What Does This Person Want?/What Do I Want? 209

Nagging 211

Chapter 8: What Is a Gentleman? **217**

Being a Gentleman..217

A Gentleman Chooses Possibility over Judgment 221

Ask Her to Step Up to a Greater Possibility 222

You Have to Create from Your Reality 226

What Do You Want to Create?..228

Why Is Lust Considered a Wrongness?....................................228

Being Mean to Other Men...233

Trying to Steal Other Men's Women 235

Taxation 237

A Sexual Reality beyond This Reality 238

It's All a Judgment of Receiving 239

What Kind of Future Is She Trying to Create? 243

Stepping Out of Being Stoppable..247

The Energy of Limitation 254

Chapter 9: What Do You Actually Want in a Relationship? ...259

The Perfection of Women 259

Pornography..261

The Spells We Create 262

"I Can't Stop Thinking about Her" 265

"I've Been Asking for That"..268

Do You Have Enough Money for Her? 269

The Loving Sex You'd Like to Have 271

Why Women Want to Run Away..273

"I Shouldn't Leave Her" 275

Giving Up You 278

What Would Make You Thrilled with Your Life? 279

You Need to Do Deal and Deliver 281

Commitment 282

What Can I Be or Do Different That Will Change
    All of This? 287

Trying to Override Your Body..288

Chapter 10: The Aggressive Presence of Sexualness 291

Aggressive Presence 291

Choosing for You 293

Being Sexually Aggressive..294

Functioning from Presence..295

The Woman Who Doesn't Need You 296

Aggressive Needlessness...300

Aggressive Sexualness 300

When a Woman Can't Have an Orgasm 301

Does She Like to Have Sex *with* Her Body—or *as* Her Body? ...302

"There Is an Energy with My Penis" 303

"Why Can't I Have Multiple Orgasms, Too?" 305

Pleasing Yourself...307

What Would It Be Like to Have Sex with This Man? ...308

Chapter 11: Choosing Commitment 311

Manliness and Masculinity..311

A Slipstream of Energy..313

How Many Futures Have You Created That Are
    Blocking Your Ability to Create?.............................314

Getting to a Place Where There Is Real Choice............316

Commitment as a Decision/Commitment as a Choice 318

Commitment as a Ten-Second Choice 318

Creating a Relationship with Your Partner's Kid..........320

What's a Dad to You?...322

Don't Create a Conflict or a Separation in Your Kids................324

Where Are You Trying to Get Him to Prefer You over Her?.......326

"I've Tried to Be the Cool Dad" 329

Learn to Be Manipulative..331

Chapter 12: Decoding Women's Subtext............................ **335**

Cultural Entrainment..335

"I Frequently Attract Gay Men" 336

Where Do You Need to Put Your Energy?.............................337

A Relationship with a Kid Attached 338

An Undefined Life 339

Dealing with a Woman's Anger 340

Aggressive Presence in Relationship.....................................342

How to Approach a Woman 342

The Word *Commitment* Is Still Sticking Me...........................343

You Can Be You without a Woman..345

You're Always Going to Go to Relationship
  Because That's What the Women Wants...............................347

The Woman Is Not the Source of Your Sexual Reality 348

How Many Jobs Have You Been Given? 349

The Job of Judging Yourself 351

What's the Subtext Here That I'm Not Acknowledging? 352

What Part of "Women Have Subtext" Are you Not Getting?.....354

"We Have a Relationship Now" 356

OTHER ACCESS CONSCIOUSNESS® BOOKS

Salon des Femmes
By Gary M. Douglas

Salon des Femmes is based on a series of teleclasses Gary Douglas held with a group of women. They discuss men, sex, relationships, men's and women's roles, and creating amazing, harmonious relationships. It blends the ground-breaking Access Consciousness® tools and processes, insightful revelations and heart-warming inspiration.

Beyond the Utopian Ideal
By Gary M. Douglas

Most people operate from a fixed idea or concept of how things are supposed to be, rather than functioning in the moment, where they can change anything as needed to accomplish and create more. These things are not actually real; they are conceptual realities that have been dropped into our existence. This book is about becoming aware of the ideal concepts and constructs that create limitations and barriers to what is possible for you. The constructs have to come off so you can create a world that works for you.

Leading from the Edge of Possibility: No More Business as Usual
By Chutisa and Steven Bowman

Just imagine what your business and your life would be like if you stopped functioning on autopilot and began to generate your business with strategic awareness and prosperity consciousness. This is truly possible, except you have to be willing to change. Recognizing a different possibility requires a different mindset and almost always demands a kind of awareness that is not part of prior experience. With this book you'll get the awareness you need to lead your business in any environment!

Divorceless Relationships
By Gary M. Douglas

A Divorceless Relationship is one where you don't have to divorce any part of you in order to be in a relationship with someone else. It is a place where everyone and everything you are in a relationship with can become greater as a result of the relationship.

Sex Is Not a Four Letter Word but Relationship Often Times Is
By Gary M Douglas & Dr. Dain Heer

Funny, frank, and delightfully irreverent, this book offers readers an entirely fresh view of how to create great intimacy and exceptional sex. What if you could stop guessing—and find out what REALLY works?

Scan for more information

For more Access Consciousness® Books go to
www.accessconsciousnesspublishing.com

ABOUT THE AUTHOR

Gary Douglas

Best-selling author, international speaker and a sought-after facilitator, Gary Douglas is known for his intensity of awareness and his incredible capacity to facilitate people to *know what they know.* He chooses to embody consciousness in everything that he does, which inspires others to choose to become more conscious as a result.

Gary came with an exceptional level of awareness into the Midwest middle class "white bread" family and lived the *Leave It to Beaver* childhood. He has a very different view on life and realized that he was very different from most of the people he knew when he was only six years old. He became aware of this difference by watching people create their lives and seeing that none of it was about the joy and the possibilities—it was always about the wrongness of everything. Gary knew there had to be more than this reality was offering, since there was nothing about it that was magical, joyful or expansive. So, he began seeking deeper awareness to life's mysteries at an early age. Along the way, he uncovered a new way forward—one that would create change in the world and in people's lives. He discovered that magic is all around us; it's something we create—it's consciousness. He recognized that the capacity to be more aware and more conscious was every person's gift if they were willing to choose it.

Over time what he recognised as the gift he was, was his intensity of awareness and his capacity to invite people to consciousness and to recognise that everything is possible and nothing is impossible. His gift is his ability to look at life, the universe and the consciousness that we all are, as well as the possibilities that are an intrinsic part of it from a space that no one else has ever chosen.

Empowering People to See Different Possibilities

Gary has become an internationally recognized thought leader in transforming lives and creating different choices—willing to empower people to see different possibilities and to recognize what is truly possible for them. Gary is acknowledged worldwide for his unique perspectives on personal transformation that is unlike anything else in the world. He is not aligned with any particular religion or tradition. Through his writing and workshops, he gifts processes and tools that bring within reach the ease, joy, and glory of life, and the magic of happiness that expands into more awareness, joy, and abundance. His simple, yet profound, teachings have already facilitated countless people throughout the world to *know what they know* and to realize what they can choose that they never realised they could choose.

At the Core of His Teachings Lies the Transformation of Consciousness

After recognising that greater consciousness in people can change the direction of their lives and the future of the planet, the creation and expansion of Access Consciousness by Gary has been primarily driven by a single question, "What can I do to help the world?"

He continues to inspire others, inviting the awareness of a different possibility across the world and making an immense contribution to the planet. He facilitates people to know that they are the source for creating the change they desire and creating a life that goes beyond the limitations of what the rest of the world thinks is important. He sees this as an essential aspect to creating a future that has greater possibilities in it for everyone, as well as the planet. This is a priority not only for personal happiness but also for the ending of violent conflict endemic on our planet and creating a different world. If enough people choose to be more aware and more conscious, they will start to see the possibilities of what they have available to them and change what is occurring here on planet earth.

Author

Gary Douglas is the author of the best-selling novel *The Place,* about people knowing that all things are possible and choice is the source of creation. Gary is also the co-author of a variety of books on the subjects of money, relationships, magic, and animals, with internationally renowned Energy Transformation virtuoso Dr. Dain Heer.

Inspiring People Worldwide

Gary pioneered a set of transformational life-changing tools and processes known as Access Consciousness˚ over twenty years ago. These leading edge tools have transformed the lives of thousands of people all over the world. His work has spread to forty-seven countries, with 2,000 trained facilitators worldwide. Simple, but so effective, the tools facilitate people of all ages and backgrounds to help remove limitations holding them back from a full life.

Lightning Source UK Ltd.
Milton Keynes UK
UKHW022156200220
359047UK00015BA/1174